THE ENIGMATIC LINCOLN CENTS OF 1922

WITH D • WORN D • FAINT D • NO D

Tom DeLorey

THE ENIGMATIC LINCOLN CENTS OF 1922

©2025 Whitman®
4001 Helton Dr., Florence, AL 35630
whitman.com

PROFESSIONAL SERIES is a trademark of Whitman-CDN Publishing, LLC.

All rights reserved, including duplication of any kind and storage in electronic or visual retrieval systems. Permission is granted for writers to use a reasonable number of brief excerpts and quotations in printed reviews and articles, provided credit is given to the title of the work and the author. Written permission from the publisher is required for other uses of text, illustrations, and other content, including in books and electronic or other media.

Correspondence concerning this book may be directed to the publisher,
Attn: *The Enigmatic Lincoln Cents of 1922*, at the address above.
ISBN: 978-0794854201 / ZT1956 09/25 / Ebook ISBN: 978-0794855215
Printed in China

No part of this book may be reproduced or copied in any form without written permission from the publisher.

For a complete catalog of numismatic reference books, supplies, and storage products, visit Whitman online at Whitman.com.

If you enjoy United States coins, visit Greysheet.com for up-to-date news, pricing, and research.

CONTENTS

INTRODUCTION

For just over a century now, collectors of United States coins have been bemused, amused or just plain confused by the Lincoln cents struck at the Denver Mint in 1922. Some are perfectly normal coins with a crisp portrait of Abraham Lincoln, a strong 1922 date, and a bold D for Denver mint mark. No problems there.

However, some 1922 cents resemble hardened blobs of metallic goo. They may show a weak, mushy portrait of Lincoln and/or nearly smooth wheat stalks on the reverse with hardly any detail in them even on Uncirculated specimens. They might have indistinct or illegible obverse and/or reverse lettering, a date that is soft and blurry in various of its digits, and a mint mark that can range from slightly worn to well worn to faint to very faint to completely missing.

Some of these coins are so defective that they have become highly prized collectibles. Other coins fall somewhere between the two extremes, and are generally (but not always) of lesser interest.

Normal 1922-D date and mint mark, early die state. Photo by the author.

1922-D Worn D, Mushy. Photo by the author.

1922-D Faint D, DP #5, LDS/LDS. Date and mint mark area. Courtesy Mark Sokoloff.

1922 No D, Strong Reverse, DP #2, MDS/EDS. Date and mint mark area. Coin property of J.P. Martin. Photo by the author.

The causes for these deficiencies are multiple and varied. There was never intended to be any coinage of cents in 1922, when for a variety of very good reasons the Nation's Mints were expected to strike nothing but gold Double Eagles for the nation's bullion reserves, to be used as backing for Gold Certificates (GCs), and/or Standard Silver Dollars to be used as backing for Silver Certificates (SCs).

However, a botched change to the standard silver dollar design in the very last days of 1921, from the anachronistic Morgan design of 1878 (discontinued in 1904 but hastily resurrected in 1921) to the Peace design celebrating the official end of World War One (so far as the United States of America was concerned) in December of 1921, left the Denver Mint with unexpected down time on its hands as 1922 began.

Unable to strike gold coinage because its refinery was in the middle of a complete overhaul that lasted from February of 1920 to April of 1923 (its silver refining needs were being met by a private refinery in Leadville, Colorado), the Mint could only have struck fractional silver coins or minor coinage to keep from having to lay off its work staff. There apparently having been a quantity of coinage-ready bronze cent planchets on hand sufficient to produce over seven million cents, the logical snap decision was made to strike 1922-D Lincoln cents until revised versions of the new Peace Silver Dollar dies were available.

That many cent planchets could reasonably have been expected to require approximately 50 obverse dies and 50 reverse dies to maintain good striking quality. Forty of each would probably have worked out okay, with just a little bit of overuse on each. On Monday, Jan. 2, 1922, when it was closed because the New Year's Day holiday had fallen on the Sunday before, the Denver Mint had 30 undated reverse dies left over in its die vault from previous years, and zero obverse dies, with 10 of them coming by train from Philadelphia.

Those dies arrived some time on January 3rd, allowing coinage to begin immediately once the dies were unpackaged and logged into inventory, and more obverse dies were quickly requisitioned on the 5th. Because of this unanticipated but severe shortage of dies, the Mint was forced to practice from day one the drastic overuse of the dies that it did have, since it did not know when, or even if, it might be receiving additional obverse dies. This is probably just one of the factors involved in the often poor striking quality found on 1922-D cents.

Poor striking quality was not confined to the 1922-D issue. According to the late Lincoln Cent expert David W. Lange, poor die quality was not uncommon on the minor coins struck at the Denver and San Francisco Mints in the years 1917 through 1927, and nobody is completely sure why. However, it is generally agreed that the worst of the lot was struck in 1922 at Denver.

The Philadelphia Mint coins of this time period are generally well made, so it is a mystery as to why the branch mint coins often show die problems. Some writers have speculated that the Philadelphia Mint's die shop may have received a bad batch of die steel from a supplier, and then deliberately diverted the dies made from that batch to the Denver and San Francisco Mints, keeping the best dies for itself.

(Note: the official term "Branch Mint," as in "The Branch Mint at San Francisco," was retired by the Coinage Act of 1873, but common usage still calls any U.S. Mint other than Philadelphia a lower-case "branch mint.")

This is highly unlikely, but not impossible as something similar occurred in the 19th Century, when dies with engraving blunders seemed to be more likely to end up at the southern mints before the Civil War, or the western mints afterwards. I doubt that it is a coincidence that the coins struck from such problem dies would thus be less likely to be seen by the "Powers That Be" in the East.

1844-O Half Dollar, Doubled Date, Closeup. Courtesy CoinFacts.

1865-S $10, 1865 over inverted 186. Closeup of date. Courtesy of CoinFacts.

Another long-held popular theory was that the branch mints received otherwise finished but unhardened dies from Philadelphia, a practice speculated to have been normal starting in 1838 to minimize the usefulness of a die to a counterfeiter should the die be stolen during shipping. This theory presumed that the dies were then not hardened properly at the branch mints, a plausible explanation for mushy dies of any Mint or era.

However, modern research by the renowned author Roger W. Burdette has suggested that this practice was gradually phased out around the time that the Morgan Dollar design was introduced, and that soon thereafter unhardened dies were only shipped to the San Francisco and Carson City Mints up until about 1890, because both Mints were using a variety of coin presses that required dies of different lengths. By receiving un-hardened dies they were able to trim them to the required lengths and then harden them for use.

My occasional numismatic co-author, Dan Owens, has provided me with a copy of correspondence from the San Francisco Mint complaining about the quality of the hardening of a batch of Morgan Dollar obverse dies it had received in early 1904, which were flattening out in use. Then there is the odd-looking 1907-O Barber half dollar with the "Mumps Variety" die deterioration at the top of the neck, which could only have resulted from an improperly hardened obverse die.

This shows that Philadelphia was capable of sending out dies that had not been hardened properly. It is certainly a plausible explanation for the poor die quality seen on many 1921-D&S Morgan Dollars and many 1922 and 1923-D&S Peace Dollars that the U.S. Mint *wanted* to strike, so it is not that hard to accept that Philadelphia could have sent out poorly hardened 1922-D Cent Dies *that were never intended to be used!* More on this later.

I agree with Burdette that by the 1920s all branch mint dies were shipped from Philadelphia pre-hardened, whether or not they were properly hardened. I would take this one step further and assume that when the Philadelphia Mint's die shop made dated dies without mint marks specifically for its own use, such as "Contingency Dies" that will be explained later, it would immediately harden those dies and transfer them to the Coining Department, to be ready for use without delay if needed.

Burdette has published books on the minting process, and he has noted that undated reverse dies that might need a mint mark were stockpiled, unhardened, in a vault and then mintmarked (or not), hardened, and shipped (or not) as the various Mints needed more dies. Of course this did not apply to the St. Gaudens $20, the Lincoln Cent, the Standing Liberty Quarter, and 1916 and some 1917 Walking Liberty Half Dollar dies, which were mintmarked on their obverses.

One possible contributing factor which I have not seen previously suggested elsewhere in regards to the poor quality of the 1922 cent coinage is the fact that the Philadelphia Mint's die shop was overwhelmed during this time period. The 1920 Mint Report talks about how busy the Engraving Department had been during the Fiscal Year ended June 30, 1920.

In addition to 4,340 dies made just for cents and nickels and 2,665 dies for fractional silver coins, it made thousands of other dies and hubs for World

War One military decorations, foreign coins, and even embossed stamp envelopes. This heavy demand may not apply to the entire 1917-1927 period mentioned above, but it is a fact that the often-mushy cent reverse dies used in Denver in 1922 were all made in late 1920. In 1921 and 1922 there was a heavy demand for Silver Dollar and Double Eagle dies.

We must also consider the mundane possibility that during part of this 1917-1927 time period the Denver and San Francisco Mints were simply but deliberately overusing their dies to keep from being charged approximately $25 each by the Philadelphia Mint for more new ones. The Mints paid for many miscellaneous expenses, such as the shipping of bags of coins, out of the seigniorage profits made on minor coins, and with the production of Cents and Nickels way down in 1921-1923 this profit was also way down.

The Mint was and still is a vast bureaucracy, and yet not one sparrow fell but that some accountant did not reckon it. Cost accounting can be a terrible thing.

Finally, I have a brand new and somewhat radical theory that some of the Denver Mint's cent die problems in 1922 were caused by the Philadelphia Mint's die shop sending Denver ten 1922-D cent dies that had previously been made and hardened without mint marks for use in Philadelphia, but into which it subsequently punched D mint marks in a very non-standard manner. More on this below.

What makes the 1922 "No D" cents highly prized is the fact that the Philadelphia Mint itself never needed to strike any cents in 1922, for reasons that will also be explained below. That makes the 1922 cents without mint marks appear to be something that should not exist, and in many people's eyes something rare and wonderful! In this work we shall explore why cents were only struck at Denver in 1922, and why some of those cents were issued with worn, faint or completely missing mint marks.

(Note: Be advised that both the causes and the effects of the many 1922 Lincoln Cent anomalies can be very technical in nature. I will attempt to explain them as best I can as I go along, but be warned that the explanations will sometimes be very technical as well. I have been a professional Numismatist since 1973, and I have been told that I explain numismatic anomalies very well, so good luck and be prepared to be challenged!)

CHAPTER ONE

A Little Background History

For background, know that all three U.S. Mints struck large numbers of coins in the denominations of one cent through 50 cents during the 1916-1920 period, partly because of the new silver designs of 1916 and the high novelty demand for them, but mainly because of the booming World War One economy. More people working in defense-related jobs meant more coins going into cash pay envelopes at the end of each pay period. Paychecks are a modern invention.

There were also many temporary sales taxes put into effect for the duration of the War, increasing the need for all coins but especially cents to make change for odd amounts. For an interesting and somewhat humorous commentary upon these wartime taxes and other needs for cents, see the March 1921 issue of *The Numismatist*, P. 123.

The same economic factors that increased the demand for coinage likewise resulted in a huge increase in the demand for small denomination notes to stuff into those pay envelopes as well. In 1916 the supply of $1 and $2 notes consisted almost exclusively of Silver Certificates. The SCs were common because the Bland-Allison Act of 1878 had caused hundreds of millions of unwanted silver dollars to be struck between 1878 and 1904. Though the dollar coins were not popular in circulation because of their weight, people seemed to like the SCs because they *could* be redeemed in precious metal coins if a person felt like doing so. That redeemability of paper for precious metal had not been the case for most of the 1860's and much of the 1870's, and some people remembered that.

Other types of $1 and $2 bills had been issued over the years, but the National Bank Notes of these two denominations had last been issued in the very early 1880's, while the Treasury Notes of 1890 and 1891 had been a disaster in all denominations. When any came back into the Treasury system, they were replaced with other notes and destroyed.

The last $1 and $2 United States Notes (USNs) had come off the printing presses in the late 1890's. The USNs (also called Legal Tender Notes) had been authorized during the Civil War to help pay for the costs of the War, and a fixed total face value of them (precisely $346,681,016 of all denominations according to the Act of May 31, 1878) was theoretically still in circulation.

However, many of them were in fact held by National Banks as part of their reserves of Legal Tender currency, as required to be held as backing for their National Bank Notes. As the nation's currency supply had stabilized towards the end of the 19th Century, the Treasury Dept. had let the mix of USN's drift towards the higher denominations, knowing that they were just going to be held by banks as part of their reserves. That made life simpler for the Bureau of Engraving and Printing (BEP), by reducing the numbers of different types of notes that it had to print on a regular basis.

A column by Peter Huntoon & Lee Lofthus entitled "1917-1924 A Burst of New Type Notes" in the Sept./Oct. 2020 issue of *Paper Money* shows how the total number of $1 bills in circulation had doubled from roughly 200 million in 1915 to 400 million in 1918. Since the number of SC's that could be issued was limited by the number of actual silver dollars physically on hand in the Treasury's vaults, much of the increase was met by printing two new Series of 1917 USNs in the $1 and $2 denominations.

$1 1917 Legal Tender Note, front. Courtesy Frederick J. Bart, Executive Currency, Roseville, MI.

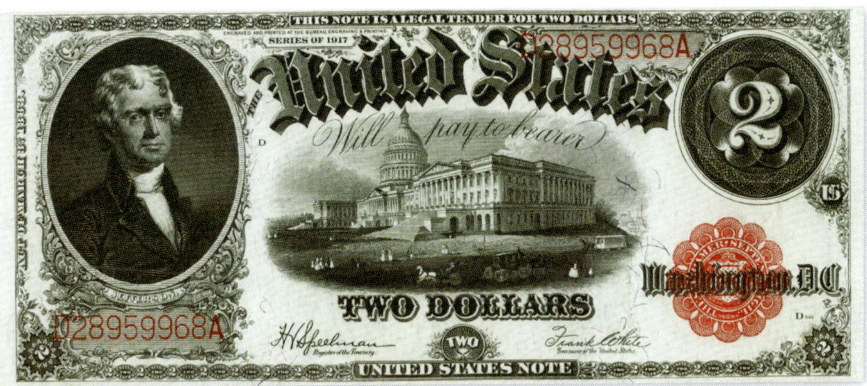

$2 1917 Legal Tender Note, front. Courtesy Frederick J. Bart, Executive Currency, Roseville, MI.

This temporarily helped the problem at the bottom end of the money supply, but since the total face value of all USNs was limited it required that many of those higher denomination USNs being held in cash reserves be replaced with other notes, such as GCs. However, the striking of gold coins had been suspended in 1916, as the U.S. Treasury adopted a policy of aggressively discouraging the issuance of both gold coins and Gold Certificates for the duration of World War One. The early days of the War had seen much U.S. gold flow out of the U.S. towards Europe as U.S. securities were dumped into the U.S. markets and the proceeds converted into gold, and the Treasury began hoarding all the gold it could.

No more gold coins were struck through the end of 1919, and the printing of Gold Certificates was suspended for the Fiscal Years of 1919 through 1921. To create an alternative to the higher denomination Gold Certificates, the Federal Reserve Act of 1913 was amended to authorize the Series of 1918

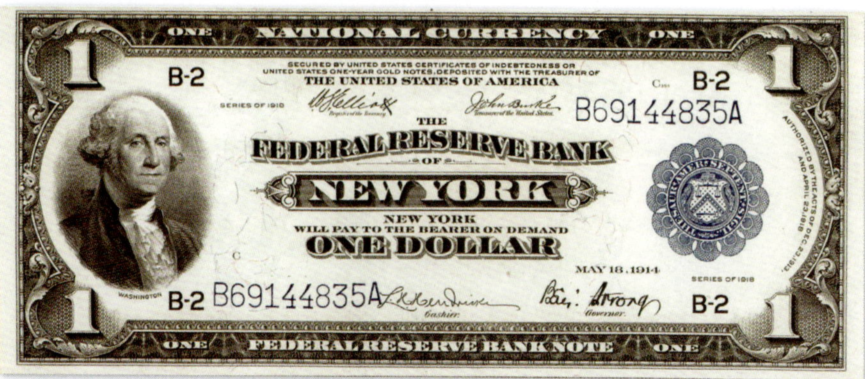

$1 1918 Federal Reserve Bank Note, front. Courtesy Frederick J. Bart, Executive Currency, Roseville, MI.

$2 1918 Federal Reserve Bank Note, front. Courtesy Frederick J. Bart, Executive Currency, Roseville, MI.

$2 1918 Federal Reserve Bank Note, back. The famous Battleship Note. Courtesy Frederick J. Bart, Executive Currency, Roseville, MI.

$500, $1,000, $5,000 and $10,000 Federal Reserve Notes (FRNs) to replace them. For an excellent history of this period, see "The Impact of WW I on Gold Certificates and the origin of the Series of 1922" by Peter Huntoon in the May/June, 2021 issue of *Paper Money*. Those 1922 GC's played a part in the creation of the 1922-D cents.

While all of this was going on, the Pittman Act of April 22, 1918 completely gob smacked both the coin and currency supply. Between April of 1918 and the end of 1919 the U.S. either melted down or simply rolled flat and shipped in bulk approximately 260 million silver dollars, and then loaned the silver so generated (roughly 200 million troy ounces net) to Great Britain. This bullion was shipped to India to be coined into rupees, which would then back the paper currency used there to pay workers in munitions plants and other war-related industries. The ultimate purpose was to allow Great Britain to avoid having to curtail its War efforts just as our United States troops were starting to fight "over there" in France on a serious basis.

Another 10 million silver dollars were to be melted down in late 1919 and early 1920 for conversion into fractional silver coins. This combined destruction of roughly 270 million silver dollars forced a reduction by the same face value in the circulating supply of Silver Certificates, mostly lower denominations, which were 100% backed by those silver dollars.

Because of the statutory cap on the total face value of USNs, the U.S. Treasury was forced to issue an obscure type of currency called Federal Reserve Bank Notes (FRBN's) to replace some Silver Certificates in the money supply. These were originally authorized in 1915 in the $5 to $50 denominations to help some of the 12 Federal Reserve Banks (which were individually responsible for redeeming them, rather than the Federal Reserve System as a whole) maintain their local circulating paper money supply during the introduction of Series of 1914 FRNs. Almost 200 million FRBN $1 bills were issued, plus decreasingly smaller numbers of $2s, $5s, $10s, $20s and $50s.These had the advantage of there being no limits on the total face value of them issued, but they came at a price.

Unlike Gold Certificates (backed 100% by physical gold, though not necessarily in the form of U.S. gold coins); Silver Certificates (backed 100% by Standard Silver Dollar coins, but not fractional silver coins); and Federal Reserve Notes (backed 40% by gold and the rest by high quality commercial paper); these FRBN's were only secured by U.S. Certificates of Indebtedness that paid 2% interest to their bearers. To save that several million dollars' worth of annual interest costs (yes, the U.S. government used to care about such trivial sums), the Treasury began a huge coinage of silver dollars on

$1 1899 Silver Certificate, front. Courtesy Frederick J. Bart, Executive Currency, Roseville, MI.

$2 1899 Silver Certificate, front. Courtesy Frederick J. Bart, Executive Currency, Roseville, MI.

February 19th of 1921 to replace the coins destroyed in 1918 through 1920. As these dollars were struck over the next few years or so, new Silver Certificates were issued and immediate used to retire the FRBN's.

Getting back to coins, though the economy slowed down quite a bit after the war ended, aggravated by the lingering effects of the ongoing Spanish Influenza pandemic, the supply of coins with a face value less than one dollar, both old and new, remained high. As late as 1920 the three Mints struck over 405 million cents for circulation, plus over 82 million nickels, 92 million dimes, 37 million quarters and 12 million half dollars, or over 630 million individual coins. The supply of these denominations was good.

As mentioned earlier, U.S. gold coinage had been suspended in 1916. This was partly because of the Treasury policy for holding on to gold, and partly because of a change to the Gold Standard Act of March 14, 1900, which

$1 1923 Silver Certificate, front. Courtesy Frederick J. Bart, Executive Currency, Roseville, MI.

$5 1923 Silver Certificate, front. Courtesy Frederick J. Bart, Executive Currency, Roseville, MI.

placed the U.S. on the Gold Standard. The original Act had required that the gold held in reserve against Gold Certificates be physically held at least two-thirds in the form of minted U.S. gold coins, and no more than one-third in other qualified forms of gold such as bars assayed by the New York Assay Office or reputable coined foreign gold such as British Sovereigns or French 20 Francs or the like.

As WWI slogged into its third bloody year in Europe, the various combatant countries found it necessary to ship so much gold coin to neutral America to buy vital supplies that the one-third non-US coin limit was in danger of being breached. To keep this from happening, the Act of June 12, 1916 reversed the 2/3 vs. 1/3 proportions, so that incoming gold could simply be warehoused and GCs issued against it without it needing to be coined first. As a bonus side effect, this freed up capacity at the U.S. Mints for the striking of fractional silver denominations rather than gold, as well as other demands upon its time.

The U.S. survived the war in much better financial shape than most major countries, and gold continued to flow into the U.S. Treasury for a variety of reasons even after the war ended. (See the book *The Lords of Finance*, by Liaquat Ahamed for a good explanation of this inflow.) According to Roger W. Burdette (private correspondence), by the end of 1919 this new gold inventory threatened to exceed the two-thirds non-US limit on U.S. gold reserves set back in 1916. To stay within these legal limits, gold coinage was resumed in 1920 and subsequent years, almost exclusively in the form of $20 Double Eagles, except for a small coinage of $10 Eagles at San Francisco in 1920.

Much of this new gold coinage (including virtually every 1921 Double Eagle not purchased directly from the Philadelphia Mint by collectors in the 1920s) was simply warehoused in anticipation of a new Series of 1922 Gold Certificates, which mainly differed from pre-War GCs in declaring themselves to be Legal Tender. The new bills also cited the Gold Standard Act of 1900 and the Edge Act of Dec. 24, 1919, which was primarily intended to encourage U.S. investment abroad but also included the Legal Tender clause.

(Curiously, the earlier Gold Certificates were NOT Legal Tender when issued, on the circuitous logic that they were fully redeemable in gold coins which WERE Legal Tender, which made a Legal Tender status for the GCs redundant. The 1919 law made the older GCs Legal Tender as well, which qualified them to be used as backing for National Bank Notes, but the good bureaucrats at Treasury wanted to get it in writing, hence the Series 1922 GCs.)

The production of gold coinage was arguably the U.S. Mint's highest calling, at least in its own eyes, and any problems with the silver and minor coinages would simply not have been allowed to stand in the way of gold coinage if and when it was needed. After Double Eagle mintages under one million in both 1920 and 1921, all of which were held until the Series of 1922 Gold Certificates were almost ready to be issued, over four million Double Eagles were struck at Philadelphia and San Francisco in 1922 alone, almost equal to the production from all three mints in the years 1913 through 1916.

All of this explains why as 1921 dawned the Treasury Dept. needed to concentrate on striking Double Eagles and Standard Silver Dollars. Because the supply of coinage less than a dollar was more than adequate to meet the day-to-day demands of commerce for quite a while, the Mints simply cut back or discontinued production of those denominations after January of 1921, and eliminated them entirely in 1922, except for the unintended cent.

1922 $20 Gold Coin. Courtesy Heritage Auctions (www.HA.com)

$20 Gold Certificate, front. Courtesy Frederick J. Bart, Executive Currency, Roseville, MI.

An article in the October 1921 issue of *The Numismatist* quotes the *Philadelphia Public Ledger* as telling how its hometown Mint had, for a while, been working three shifts a day, six days a week coining silver dollars, all to save paying that dreaded interest on the National Debt. It estimated that it would take approximately two years to complete the silver dollar coinage, after which the Mints "would go back to the coining of the smaller coins."

(Note: the mints struck various commemorative coins in these years in response to Congressional mandate, but they will be ignored in this work.)

No fractional silver coins were struck after January of 1921, and just a few millions each of the cents and nickels through July at Philadelphia and San Francisco. After a three-month hiatus, a paltry 868,000 cents were struck in November and 805,000 nickels in November and December, all at Philadelphia. In the 1922 Mint Report for Fiscal Year 1921-22, these are explained thusly: "Of coins below the dollar but few were executed in the last year, those struck being confined to memorial half dollars and a small number of nickel and bronze coins for cleaning up partially completed lots."

In other words, the Bureau of the Mint simply wanted to finish up some work in progress to get it out of the way, as well as maybe to be able to book

Regarding the actual production of coins for the period covered, the report says:

"The coinage of gold was resumed during the past fiscal year, nearly $53,000,000 in value having been executed. This permits the issue of additional gold certificates, the issue of certificates against bullion being limited by law to two-thirds of such certificates outstanding. Over 92,000,000 silver dollars were coined during the year from bullion purchased under the terms of the Pittman Act, practically all of these dollars going into storage and being represented in circulation by silver certificates issued against them in lieu of Federal Reserve Bank notes retired. Retirement of the Federal Reserve Bank notes permits retirement of certificates of indebtedness held as security against them, thus reducing the public debt and the interest thereon. Of coins below the dollar but few were executed during the past year, those struck being confined to memorial half dollars and a small number of nickel and bronze coins for cleaning up partially completed lots. Approximately 12,000,000 pieces of coin were executed for foreign governments, making the year's aggregate number of pieces

The beginning of a summary of the 1922 Mint Report, from The Numismatist, Mar. 1923. Reprinted with permission of *The Numismatist*, the official publication of the American Numismatic Association (money.org)

the seigniorage profits made on minor coinage. In a letter dated Dec. 29, 1922, the Acting Director of the Mint informed the Assistant Cashier of the Federal Reserve Bank of Cleveland: "Coinage for the calendar year 1922 was confined to a few one cent pieces issued early in the year to complete partial coinage, and $20.00 gold pieces and silver dollars."

In the case of the 1922 Denver cents, this "partial coinage" might have been in the form of numerous bins of raw-cut (Type One) blanks or mechanically upset (Type Two) planchets, either of which might have been made weeks or months earlier during slow times in anticipation of future needs and/or to keep the workers busy when there was nothing more important for them to do. However, a telegram dated Jan. 27th from the Director of the Mint to the Superintendent of the Denver Mint said, among other things including potential layoffs: "New silver dollar dies will not reach you (until) approximately February 15th." … "While not necessary it was my desire Denver clean up nickel and bronze ingots already prepared."

I don't think that any such ingots were actually processed, if indeed any existed. During this time period there was no melting down and recasting of the webbing left over when new blanks are punched from planchet strip. A table in the 1922 Mint Report listing ingot melts for FY 1921-22 shows that the Denver Mint made zero minor coin ingot melts in that period, while striking over seven million cents. That plus the fact that production began on the first day of business, January 3rd, tells me that the planchets had already been made, upset and (presumably) annealed. (Of course, it is also possible that at that time unstruck minor coinage planchets were simply carried on the books as so much raw material, and inventoried along with ingots and coils of unblanked planchet strip under the general heading of "ingots.")

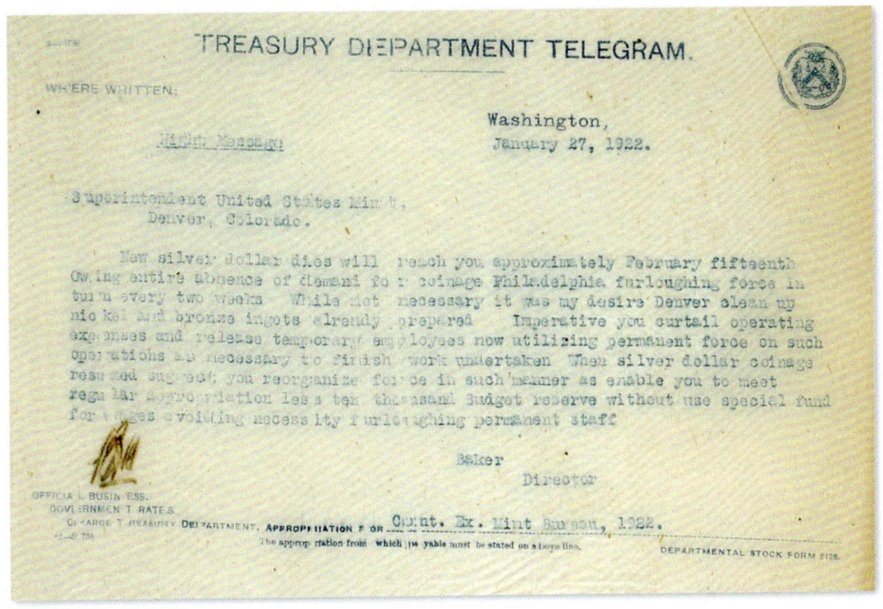
TREASURY DEPARTMENT TELEGRAM.

WHERE WRITTEN:

Night Message

Washington,
January 27, 1922.

Superintendent United States Mint,
Denver, Colorado.

New silver dollar dies will reach you approximately February fifteenth Owing entire absence of demand for coinage Philadelphia furloughing force in turn every two weeks While not necessary it was my desire Denver clean up nickel and bronze ingots already prepared Imperative you curtail operating expenses and release temporary employees now utilizing permanent force on such operations as necessary to finish work undertaken When silver dollar coinage resumed suggest you reorganize force in such manner as enable you to meet regular appropriation less ten thousand Budget reserve without use special fund for wages avoiding necessity furloughing permanent staff

Baker
Director

OFFICIAL BUSINESS.
GOVERNMENT RATES.
CHARGE TREASURY DEPARTMENT, APPROPRIATION FOR Cont. Ex. Mint Bureau, 1922.
The appropriation from which payable must be stated on above line.

DEPARTMENTAL STOCK FORM 2128.

Jan. 27, 1922 Telegram from the Director of the Mint to the Supt. of the Denver Mint regarding the expected arrival date of 1922 Peace Dollar dies (Feb. 15); his desire to use up existing bronze and nickel ingots; and the need to reduce expenses, including via layoffs. From the National Archives, thanks to researcher and author Roger W. Burdette.

Interestingly, the Denver Mint may also have had a supply of copper-nickel five cents planchets on hand, as on Feb. 9, 1922, the Superintendent of the Denver Mint sent a letter to the Director of the Mint requesting that (an additional) “20 obverse five cent nickel (dies) be manufactured for the use of this institution.” There is no indication that these dies were ever made, presumably because the first batch of the long-awaited revised Peace dollar dies was shipped to Denver on February 13th. Had that not happened, the 1922-D Cents could have had a low-mintage Five Cent sibling!

FWIW, Philadelphia made only 24 bronze melts for domestic coinage in FY 1921-22, plus three nickel melts, vs. over 21,000 silver melts for mostly dollar coins. Philadelphia did (up until 1924) sometimes purchase millions of pre-made minor coin planchets from private vendors to free up its furnaces for precious metal melts, but the 1922 Mint Report says that none were purchased in FY 1922.

(Note: The Philadelphia Mint also struck millions of mostly silver coins to fulfill existing orders from various foreign countries in CY 1921, and the S.F. Mint millions more, but those were accounted for separate from the domestic coinage. Most of these pieces were struck in January and February of 1921, before the coinage of dollars got underway, or in November and

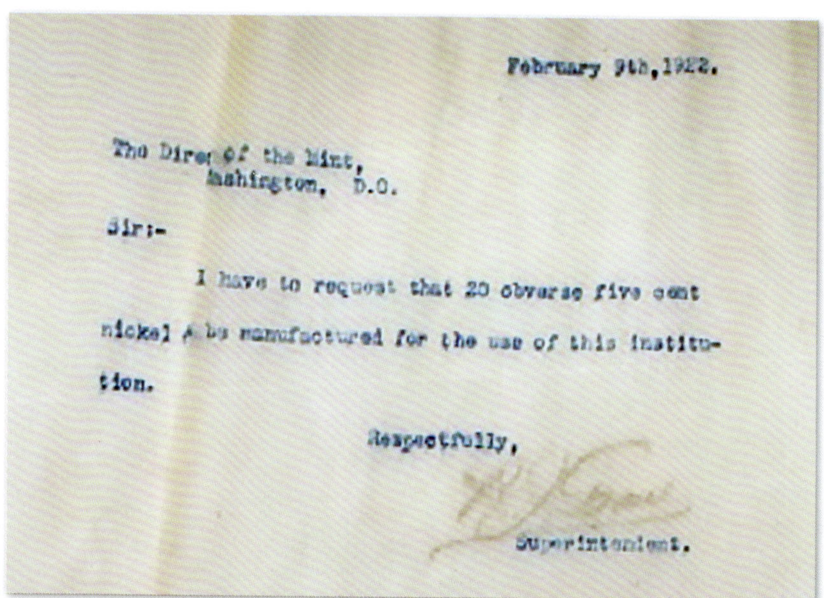

February 9th,1922.

The Director of the Mint,
Washington, D.C.

Sir:-

I have to request that 20 obverse five cent nickel be manufactured for the use of this institution.

Respectfully,

Superintendent.

Feb. 9, 1922 Letter from the Supt. of the Denver Mint to the Director of the Mint requesting 20 1922 obverse dies for nickels. From the National Archives, thanks to researcher and author Roger W. Burdette.

INGOTS OPERATED UPON BY COINING DEPARTMENTS AND PERCENTAGE OF COIN PRODUCED.

FOR DOMESTIC COINAGE.

Mints.	Gold.		Standard silver dollars.		Subsidiary silver.		Nickel.	
	Ingots operated upon.	Percentage good coin produced to ingots operated upon.	Ingots operated upon.	Percentage good coin produced to ingots operated upon.	Ingots operated upon.	Percentage good coin produced to ingots operated upon.	Ingots operated upon.	Percentage good coin produced to ingots operated upon.
	Ounces.	*Per ct.*	*Ounces.*	*Per ct.*	*Ounces.*	*Per ct.*	*Ounces.*	*Per ct.*
Philadelphia	2,608,605.069	32.40	76,218,875.12	51.47	321,038.78	36.06		
San Francisco	3,804,071.004	45.18	31,932,766.45	52.06				
Denver			27,225,740.28	57.74			1,001,929.90	72.38

Table from 1922 U.S. Mint Report showing Ingots Processed for Domestic Coinage during FY 1922, during which the 1922-D cents were struck. There was no column for bronze ingots processed at any Mint. Curiously, Denver did process "Nickel" ingots in FY 1922, even though it struck no Five Cents pieces in 1921-23. Perhaps this was simply a conversion of leftover copper-nickel materials from the Colombia coinage program (last delivered in May of 1921) into ingots and/or planchets prepared during slow periods in anticipation of future Five Cents coinages. Such preparedness is why the Denver Mint had One Cent planchets ready to go on January 3, 1922.

December, when the production of dollars was temporarily suspended at those two mints.)

(The Denver Mint, which seldom struck foreign coins because it was not in a seaport to ship them from, gradually finished striking a large order of copper-nickel one and two centavo coins for Colombia that it had begun in October of 1920, delivering approx. 26.6 million pieces in Jan.-May of 1921. Though its precious metal refinery equipment was being overhauled, it could still do base metal domestic and foreign coins, which was probably why this particular order was assigned to the Denver Mint.)

Once again the ripples sent out by World War One intervened in the 1921 coinage with the belated authorization of the Peace themed silver dollar, eagerly anticipated for most of 1921 but only legally enacted in November, with great determination to get it struck in 1921. (The Senate having refused to confirm the Treaty of Versailles with Germany and other international Treaties with Austria and Hungary, the U.S. was forced to negotiate separate Treaties with the three nations. Those with Germany and Austria were formally exchanged in November of 1921, and that with Hungary in December. Thus the 1921 Peace Dollar was viewed as a timely necessity.)

San Francisco ceased production of the Morgan design dollars on Nov. 14th and Philadelphia reduced its production three days later, thereby enabling those two mints to work on their backlogs of foreign coin orders while they stockpiled Silver Dollar planchets and awaited the new Peace dollar dies.

Philadelphia struck its last Morgan dollars on Dec. 27th. Only Denver, which had no foreign coin orders on hold, continued to strike Morgan dollars through Saturday, Dec. 31, 1921, thereby overlapping the beginning of the Peace dollar coinage in Philadelphia.

Mary M. O'Reilly, the Acting Director of the Mint, sent a telegram to the Superintendent of the Denver Mint on Dec. 27, 1921 concerning the new Peace dollar: "Dies for standard silver dollar new design now being made for you. Cannot reach you until after first of new year. Utilize (work) force best you can while waiting probably two or three days." In other words, find something for the regular workers to do because you have to pay them, but be prepared to stop doing it on a moment's notice. What they did was strike over 7 million 1922-D cents over the next eight weeks. Other communications ordered Denver to lay off many of the temporary workers it had hired to help strike silver dollars in 1921.

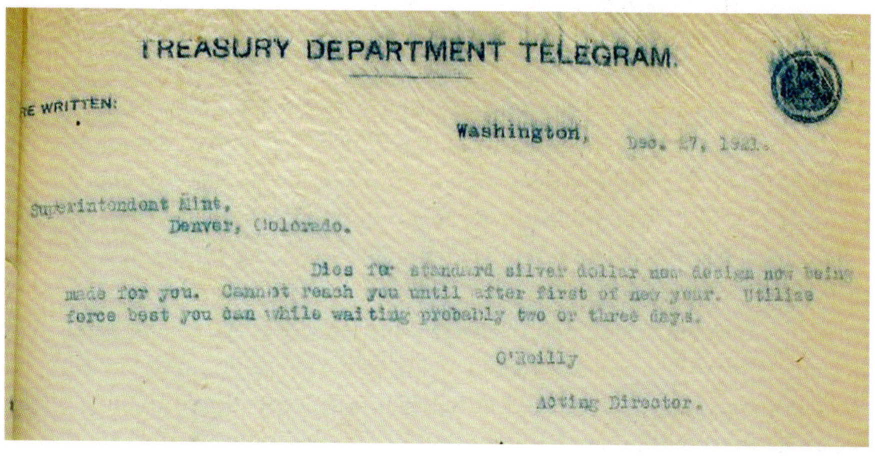

TREASURY DEPARTMENT TELEGRAM.

RE WRITTEN:

Washington, Dec. 27, 1921.

Superintendent Mint,
Denver, Colorado.

Dies for standard silver dollar new design now being made for you. Cannot reach you until after first of new year. Utilize force best you can while waiting probably two or three days.

O'Reilly

Acting Director.

The Birth Certificate for the 1922-D Cents, a Dec. 27, 1921 Telegram from the Acting Director of the Mint to the Supt. of the Denver Mint: "Dies for standard silver dollar new design now being made for you. Cannot reach you until after first of new year. Utilize force best you can while waiting probably two or three days." From the National Archives, RG 104 E-235 VOL 444 Denver Dec. 1921, thanks to Roger W. Burdette.

Unfortunately, the High Relief design of the 1921 Peace dollars, struck only at Philadelphia for just a few days starting Dec. 28th, proved very difficult to adequately strike up, and so work on the first of multiple lower relief versions of it was immediately begun. It took several weeks for the Engraving Department to create a version that satisfied everybody, with various proposed modifications getting struck and then remelted. See Roger W. Burdette's *Renaissance of American Coinage 1916-1921* to see how chaotic those few weeks were.

While the nobs dithered about the new dollar design, which might or might not be ready at any time, the Philadelphia and San Francisco Mints simply kept on striking foreign coins into January and February of 1922 to stay busy. Because Denver had no foreign coin orders pending, some practical soul apparently decided to take advantage of this uncertain window of opportunity to strike some or all of the millions of one cent planchets it had on hand into coins fit for inventory. The results were less than spectacular.

CHAPTER TWO

The Traditional Knowledge About 1922-D Cents

1922-D cents were traditionally collected in four classes. The first of these was, and still is, the large population of "Normal 1922-D" coins, or what an average collector would have used to fill a hole in his album (after albums were first commercially available in 1928, of course.) These may or may not exhibit a routine amount of die wear, but generally nothing extraordinary.

Normal 1922-D Cent, extremely well struck from new Obv. and Rev. dies. The finest *normal* 1922-D Cent I have ever seen. Courtesy of Blaine Neupert.

1922-D Cent. Closeup of a well-formed date and mint mark, as hubbed and punched, with no changes to either due to die erosion. However, there is a tiny bit of die marking at the top end of the first 2 that I am not familiar with otherwise. Note the slight difference in the bases of the two 2's, with the second one turning up a bit at the end. Courtesy of Blaine Neupert.

What LIBERTY should look like on a 1922-D Cent from new dies. Courtesy of Blaine Neupert.

What IN GOD WE TRUST should look like on a 1922-D cent. The slightly irregular height and spacing is actually normal. Courtesy of Blaine Neupert.

Next came the "1922 No D, Strong Reverse" coins, referred to below as Die Pair #2, the most popular of the varieties. It remains the one impregnable rock in a sea of die state chaos.

1922 No D Cent. D.P. #2. Overpolished Obv. and Strong Rev. LDS,EDS. Courtesy PCGS.

Finally we had the "1922 Weak D, Weak Reverse" coins and the "1922-D No D, Weak Reverse" coins, either of which might be referred to below as Die Pair #1 OR Die Pair #3, as both die pairs exhibited similar general characteristics at different times. Since the late 1980s the "1922-D Weak D, Weak Reverse" Class Three has also included Die Pair #4, discovered by ANACS and recognized by it but not, for any good reason that I can see, by the other Third Party Grading Services (TPGs). ANACS was certainly right to add it to the 1922-D Canon, and the other TPGs should recognize it as well in the appropriate die states. I will teach you below how to recognize those appropriate die states.

1922 No D Cent, Weak Rev. D.P. #3. This coin is in a PCGS holder as an MS63BN, with a CAC sticker, described as a Weak D, but I have examined it in hand and there is absolutely no trace of a mint mark. None whatsoever. Courtesy West Coast Coins of Toledo, OR.

Thus, by 1990 a sophisticated variety collector's complete set of 1922-D cents consisted of seven coins, a normal coin, a DP #2 coin, a DP #1 coin with a weak mint mark, a DP #1 coin with no mint mark, a DP #3 coin with a weak mint mark, a DP #3 coin with no mint mark, and a DP #4 coin with a weak mint mark. A few collectors even collected 1922-D cents by die crack varieties, which will be discussed in Chapters 11, 12 and 13, but that was and is a niche collecting field.

1922-D Very Faint D Cent, Weak Rev., DP #1. Author's coin, Photo by Robert Kelley Courtesy of the American Numismatic Assoc.

Unfortunately, because of the difficulties sometimes encountered trying to tell a "Weak D, Weak Reverse" coin from a "No D, Weak Reverse" coin from the same pair of dies (and yes, it can be tough, mainly depending on the condition of the coin), two of the three major TPG's have stopped certifying any "Weak Reverse" coin as a "No D, Weak Reverse" coin, even if it unquestionably IS a "No D, Weak Reverse" coin (and there ARE such coins). The best they will do is call it a "Weak D" coin, perhaps with the qualifier "Weak Reverse," regardless of whether the "Weak D" is present or not. As of this writing only the Numismatic Guaranty Corporation (NGC) will certify a "No D, Weak Reverse" coin. They do not specify the Die Pair number.

Furthermore, the TPGs have tightened up the requirements for what they will call a "Weak D" coin, not that this is necessarily a bad thing. Over the years many coins where the D had lost a noticeable, but not significant, fraction of its height above the field were optimistically labeled by their collector or dealer owners as "Weak D" coins, simply because the price guides and coin books said that "Weak D" coins were worth a premium.

The TPGs tended to be more conservative than that, but they had no proper guidelines to use for determining where a "Weak D" began. Therefore, about the time that two of them stopped recognizing the "No D, Weak Reverse" coins and lumping them in with the "Weak D" coins, they also decided that only coins with a very, very weak D could qualify for this designation (about what I am calling a "Faint D" below.) Many coins that used to be certified as "Weak D" coins no longer were.

I will not say that by making this massive (but not widely publicized) revision to the 1922-D Canon the TPGs in question were entirely wrong. Some reform was necessary. However, I will say that, in my opinion as somebody who has been involved with 1922 cent varieties in some capacity or other since 1974, the elimination of the "No D, Weak Reverse" class was a mistake, AND the revisions have rendered the term "Weak D" completely meaningless. Buy a coin sight unseen slabbed as a "1922 Weak D" cent and you will have absolutely no idea at all what you will be receiving, as many coins slabbed under the old guidelines are still out there.

Everything else of mediocre quality that was not good enough, or should I say bad enough, to qualify as one of those three non-normal classes, i.e., the ones commonly recognized as collectible die varieties, was lumped into the "Normal" category, even though some of it should not have been. Many other coins are known that were struck from broken, cracked, chipped or just plain grossly overused obverse and/or reverse dies, but which have been overshadowed by the "Big Three" classes listed above. I shall list some of them below, in the name of education.

I submit to you that 1922-D cents come in six major classes. The first of these **(Class One)** are, as above, simply the relatively normal die coins with relatively normal to slightly worn D's, which naturally constitute a large percentage of the coinage. They may have routine light die erosion on their obverses and sometimes severe die erosion on their reverses, but they are not given any die variety designations.

Some include relatively insignificant die markers such as die scratches or die gouges which are useful to coin Authenticators (which I used to be one of from 1978 to 1984), because they can prove that a coin with a removed mint mark came from a non-variety pair of dies. A brief section on die markers will follow the varieties listed below in Chapter 14, simply to get them on the record.

Next comes **Class Two**, also as above, the coins with absolutely "No D" below the date on an evenly ground-down but still fairly decent looking obverse, paired with a very normal looking reverse die, the aptly-named "Strong Reverse." This only includes Die Pair #2. These are the most popular and universally certifiable 1922 "No D" coins, sometimes referred to as "The Redbook Variety."

The major Third Party Grading services (TPGs) will certify it as "No D. Strong Reverse." ANACS will usually add "Die Pair 2," though some older paper certificates and slabs might not give the Die Pair number. It is listed in the Sixth Edition of the *Cherrypickers' Guide to Rare Die Varieties of United States Coins* by Bill Fivaz and the late J.T. Stanton as FS-01-1922-401. Please note that some earlier editions of the CPG used a different numbering system.

Then we have the intermingled **Class Three** and **Class Four** coins. The **Class Three** "Weak D, Weak Reverse" Coins have what I call "Faint" to "Very Faint D's" set in worn-out or weak obverse dies, usually paired with worn-out or weak reverse dies. See Die Pairs #1 and #3 below, plus the late to penultimate die states of Die Pair #4B, and the late die states of my newly added Die Pair #ZeroB. (Note: Die Pair #4 is now Die Pairs #4A and #4B, a slight change to the ANACS Canon, because I have recently discovered a new die pairing of the earliest die state of the Die Pair #4 obverse (before it got interesting) with a different, worn reverse die. The obverse of Die Pairs #ZeroA&B likewise comes with two reverse pairings. See the listings.)

The **Class Four** "No D, Weak Reverse" coins have traditionally been limited to Die Pairs #1 & #3, though I am introducing here the discovery specimen of the long-rumored, but never confirmed, Die Pair #4B coin on which the "D" is completely, 100%, cross my heart and hope to die missing. I believe that it is missing due to die wear, unlike Die Pairs #1 & #3 which are due to transitory Mint grease over a longer period of time, but (and this is very important) only on the very last die state of its existence.

Other specimens were known, in lesser grades, but they were awaiting the discovery of a high grade specimen to prove the existence of a true DP #4B "No D" coin. That high grade specimen is now here. I hope that there are others out there. In my professional opinion based on 50+ years in the hobby it is a true "No D, Worn Reverse" coin. Period. I have shown it to three current and former professional Authenticators and Graders, and they agree with me.

These Class Four Die Pair #1, #3 & #4B coins exhibit very similar die wear characteristics as their Class Three cousins in adjacent die states because they were struck from the very same dies. (A qualifying Class Four specimen of Die Pair #Zero remains a possibility, but none seen to date.)

The Class Four coins can be quite tricky because on both Die Pairs #1 and #3 the mint marks faded in and out throughout their late die states, as grease first dripped onto the dies and then gradually wore off the dies by being slowly carried away on just-struck coins. I believe that some of these Class Four pieces can and should be certified as "No D, Weak Reverse" coins

IF, and only IF, the coins are in high enough condition to properly attribute the status of the mint mark area. Such coins do exist for all three die pairs.

As mentioned above, because that proper attribution can be difficult, especially in lower grades, two of the three major TPG's nowadays will only certify Class Four cents as "Weak D" coins, ignoring the reverse die, even if the mint mark is completely missing. ANACS will specify "Die Pair 1," "Die Pair 3" or "Die Pair 4."

Die Pairs #1 & #3 coins, regardless of the presence or the absence of the D, are listed in the *Cherrypickers' Guide* jointly as FS-01-1922-402. Because some Die Pair #ZeroB coins have long been mistaken for Die Pair #1 coins, due to their very similar obverses and the shared "Jogging Die Crack" reverse, I believe that they also qualify for the *Cherrypickers' Guide* designation. That said, I hope that future editions of the *Cherrypickers' Guide* will greatly expand their listings based in part upon this work.

Only ANACS will certify its Die Pair #4 coins (my DP #4B) as having a "Weak D, Die 4," with no mention of the reverse, and only if it has what I am calling an Extremely Late Die State obverse, or later. (See text for details.) This obverse had a very long life, and can actually be traced back to a much earlier, almost normal die state that shows none of the extreme die erosion seen in the lower right quadrant of the obverse. The rarely seen earliest obverse die state (#4A) is paired with a well worn reverse die, which was soon replaced with a new reverse die that shows a long progression from normal to weak status.

ANACS does not recognize my Early, Middle or merely Late Die States of this die pair, with either reverse, as their "Die Pair #4" variety, but simply calls them normal 1922-D cents, which arguably they are. I present the two die combinations and the many different die states listed below merely as an intellectual exercise in how, with infinite time, money and patience, the life cycle of just one obverse die can be traced from youth to old age. Perhaps someday every 1922-D obverse die can be so sequenced.

In its late to penultimate (but not final) die states, Die Pair #4B could conceivably have struck both "Weak D, Weak Reverse" coins and "No D, Weak Reverse" coins in the same manner as Die Pairs #1 & #3, but no such coins are known for the die states where the die erosion lobes (see listings) have not yet touched the rim. Let me know if you find one in a high enough grade to properly attribute. Until such a coin is discovered it will be assumed that no such coin exists.

I wish I had more than one Die Pair #4B "No D" coin in very high grade to prove the "No D" status, but it took me five years of research to find the one. They are very rare in near-Mint State condition, and it is not impossible that this specimen is unique in this grade range. I believe that that is because of the horrible conditions of the dies by the time this piece was struck, which would have caused most collectors of the day to pass over such a coin in favor of a nicer but boringly normal one. See the comments in the next chapter.

Together my Class Three and Class Four coins represent the traditional Third and Fourth classes above, with the additions of Die Pairs #4B and #Zero (in their appropriate later die states) in Class Three, and Die Pair #4B (in its final die state) in Class Four. D.P. #4B (in the appropriate die states) should have been there ever since ANACS first published it, and D.P. #Zero has to be included in Class Three because it is so tightly linked to Die Pair #1. Heck, people have been mistaking late die state D.P. #ZeroB coins for D.P. #1 coins for decades! I know I did, and I am one of the experts on the Cents of 1922. That plus a dime will get me two nickels.

I am now adding a new class of 1922-D cents, **Class Five**, which will include any Die Pair that has a significant "Worn D," "Well Worn D," "Faint D" or "Very Faint D," regardless of the condition of the reverse die, that is not in Class Three. Basically this will include the previously uncatalogued DeLorey Varieties #5 through #9 below (in their appropriate die states), plus certain intermediate die states of Die Pair #4B struck after it had deteriorated to a recognizable die state but prior to it having reached a significant die state that ANACS recognizes. I am also including in Class Five certain late die states of Die Pairs #11B and #13B, which otherwise belong in Class Six. Those coins will belong to both classes.

1922-D Cent, Very Faint D. New DP #5. New Class Five (in this die state and die marriage). Heavily polished Obv. die, well worn Rev. die. This Obv. die was later repolished, completely removing the mint mark, after which it was put back in a coin press with a new Rev. die to become DP #2 in Class Two. Author's coin. Photos courtesy of seller, GN Coins of Lemont, IL, used with permission.

Class Five DeLorey Variety #5 is special because it was struck from the same obverse die that later struck Class Two Die Pair #2 coins, but BEFORE the D was COMPLETELY polished off of the die. In its "Faint D" obverse die state it was paired with a different, weak reverse die, as opposed to the strong reverse die found on Die Pair #2. Let me make this perfectly clear: a DeLorey Die Pair #5 coin is NOT an ANACS Die Pair #2 coin. Period.

Class Six coins generally have nothing to do with the mint mark, but rather include pieces with collectible die cracks and/or other die failures. These include various cracks in the reverse fields and/or slightly less interesting but very real cud die breaks on the obverse rims, plus one whopping cud die break on an obverse. See DeLorey-10 through 14 below. In an attempt to categorize these die cracks and rim cuds, I have assigned them Die Crack Variety Numbers DC-2, 3, 4, 5 and 6 in Chapter Thirteen.

1922-D Cent, Normal D. New DP #12. Class Six. Closeup of die crack at 4 o'clock rev. Author's coin.

1922-D Cent, Worn D. New DP #13B. Class Six. Rim Cuds K-6 to K-4. Part of a progression of rim cuds that eventually encircle almost the entire obverse. Author's coin.

(The reverse die with the jogging Die Crack-1 was shared by Die Pairs #Zero and #1 in Class Three [and sometimes Four] above. Because they are so well documented below, I will not be including those dies in Class Six, but you can collect them that way if you wish. Likewise other coins can legitimately belong to more than one Class in certain die states, such as the latter die states of Die Pair #11B and #13B coins which can be in both Class Five and Class Six. I will try to identify such as I go along.)

(Note: I am listing these various die cracks, and certain other "die marker coins" at the end, for the benefit of future generations of numismatic Authenticators, by identifying dies known to have NOT struck "No D" or "Worn D" or "Faint D" coins. I was an Authenticator for the American

Numismatic Association Certification Service from 1978 to 1984, and Senior Authenticator from 1982 to 1984, and I would have found such a listing of die characteristics useful to be able to prove that this coin or that coin had had its mint mark removed. [You can use them when looking at 1922 cents on a popular online auction site that shall remain nameless here.] If collectors choose to collect these newly-listed die varieties for their own enjoyment they are most welcome to do so, but I do not insist that any collector must do so!)

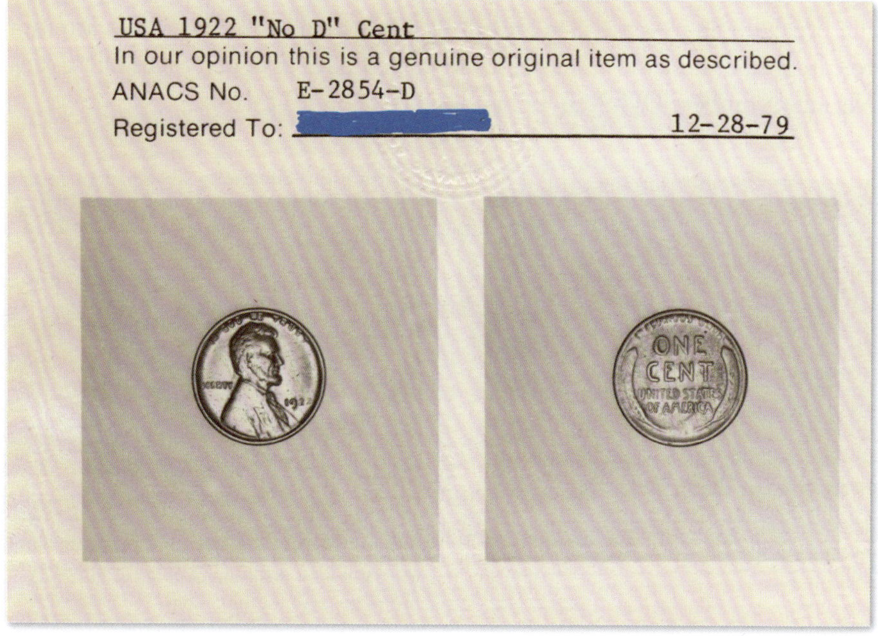

USA 1922 "No D" Cent
In our opinion this is a genuine original item as described.
ANACS No. E-2854-D
Registered To: 12-28-79

An old ANACS certificate showing a 1922 "No D" Cent. The Author was an ANACS Authenticator from November of 1978 to June of 1984. Certificate courtesy ANA Museum Archives.

(Note on jargon: Many online auction listings for what the hobby considers "Normal" 1922-D cents cite the coin being sold as having either a "Strong Reverse" or a "Weak Reverse," perhaps in an attempt to associate themselves with the Second, Third and Fourth Classes just listed. Though I applaud the descriptive effort, you should consider the strength of the reverse die generally irrelevant until you determine which obverse die is involved. The same goes for "Weak Obverse.")

CHAPTER THREE

The Hobby Reacts to the 1922-Dated Cent

Early collectors knew none of the preceding. Part of the problem was that most 1922-dated cents were warehoused at the Denver Mint for a few years, except for 10,000 pieces ($100.00 face) shipped to the Philadelphia Mint in late October of 1922, and made available to visitors at that Mint. (There is a slight possibility that this batch may have included a high percentage of "No D" cents, but more on that later.)

Prior to 1917, collectors could have obtained current year coinage directly from each Mint by the simple expedient of writing to the Superintendent of each Mint and enclosing payment for the coins desired plus a trivial amount for postage. Many years ago I had the opportunity to examine a three-generation collection in upstate New York that had been put together from the early 1880's to the late 1930's, and from about 1895 on the second-generation collector had used this technique to assemble an utterly astounding collection of Barber silver coins and their contemporaries. Included in the instructions left by the second generation collector to his ultimate heir in the early 1910's were the names of the current Superintendents and their mailing addresses. The Superintendents must have taken this task seriously, as the coins that their staffs selected and sent out (to this collector at least) tended to be well struck and relatively mark free.

However, according to Roger W. Burdette, the Secretary of the Treasury decided to relieve the individual Mints of this burden in 1917, and made the Office of the Treasurer of the United States responsible for numismatic sales. Each Mint was supposed to send to the Treasurer's Office a quantity (unknown) of each year's coinage shortly after the first batch of each

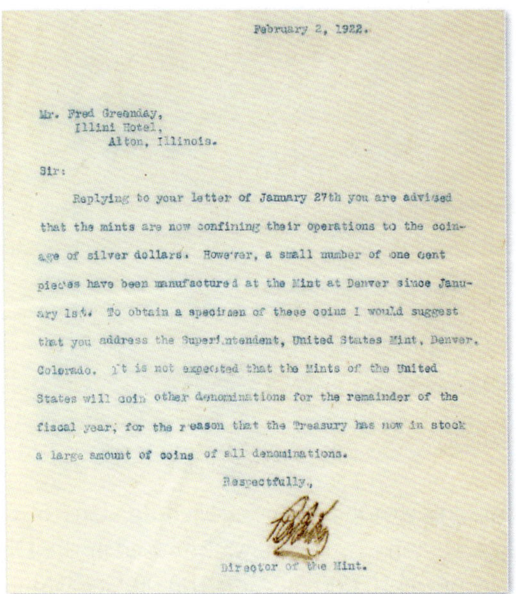

February 2, 1922.

Mr. Fred Greenday,
Illini Hotel,
Alton, Illinois.

Sir:

Replying to your letter of January 27th you are advised that the mints are now confining their operations to the coinage of silver dollars. However, a small number of one cent pieces have been manufactured at the Mint at Denver since January 1st. To obtain a specimen of these coins I would suggest that you address the Superintendent, United States Mint, Denver, Colorado. It is not expected that the Mints of the United States will coin other denominations for the remainder of the fiscal year, for the reason that the Treasury has now in stock a large amount of coins of all denominations.

Respectfully,

Director of the Mint.

Feb. 2, 1922 letter from the Director of the Mint to Fred Greenday of Alton, IL, saying that the Mints were confining their operations to the coining of silver dollars, but that "However, a small number of one cent pieces have been manufactured at the Mint at Denver since January 1st. To obtain a specimen of the coins I would suggest that you address the Superintendent, United States Mint, Denver, Colorado. It is not expected that the Mint of the United States will coin other denominations for the remainder of the fiscal year, for the reason that the Treasury has now in stock a large amount of coins of all denominations." (Note: It is possible that "Fred Greenday" is a typo for the same "Fred Greenclay" mentioned below). From the National Archives, RG 104, E-235, Vol. 446, Misc. Jan-June 1922, thanks to Roger W. Burdette.

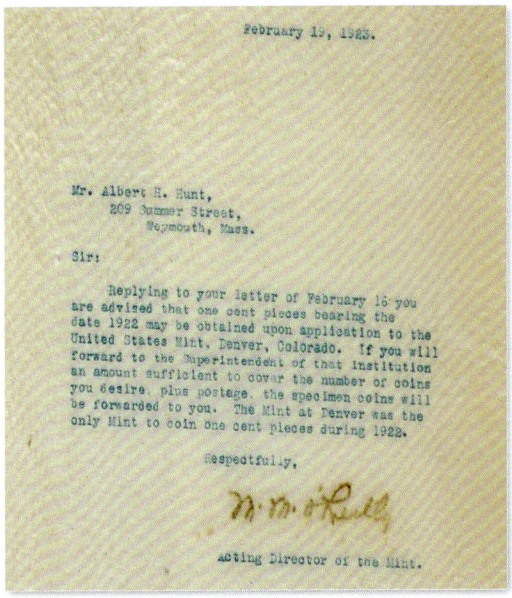

February 19, 1923.

Mr. Albert H. Hunt,
209 Summer Street,
Weymouth, Mass.

Sir:

Replying to your letter of February 16 you are advised that one cent pieces bearing the date 1922 may be obtained upon application to the United States Mint, Denver, Colorado. If you will forward to the Superintendent of that institution an amount sufficient to cover the number of coins you desire, plus postage, the specimen coins will be forwarded to you. The Mint at Denver was the only Mint to coin one cent pieces during 1922.

Respectfully,

Acting Director of the Mint.

A Feb. 19, 1923 letter from the Acting Director of the Mint on how to get 1922-D cents. Officially the request should have been referred to the Office of the Treasurer. From the National Archives, RG 104, E-235, Vol. 452, thanks to researcher and author Roger W. Burdette.

denomination was delivered, and these supplies could be used to fill orders for years to come. I once bought in a date run of S-Mint dollars from the 1921-S Morgan to the 1928-S Peace coin, along with the cover letter to the collector who ordered them in 1929, IIRC.

Despite this official change in procedure, I am quite certain that there must have been some method, official or unofficial, by which 1922-D cents could be obtained in small quantities directly from the Denver Mint, probably in person at the cash window. Even the Director's office continued to direct collectors directly to the Denver Mint, as seen in these two letters from 1922 and 1923. Then there are various "lucky piece" encased 1922-D cents that appear to have actually been issued in 1922. More on the lucky pieces near the end of the book.

The backlog of older coins that caused the general embargo on 1922-D Cents was caused partly by the Independent Treasury Act of May 29, 1920, which recognized that the sub-Treasury system created in the 1840's had been made redundant by the Federal Reserve Act of 1913. It ordered all of the sub-Treasury system's facilities closed prior to July 1, 1921, which necessitated the redistribution of a large quantity of circulated and uncirculated coins into the custody of the Federal Reserve Banks and/or the three Mints,

SUBTREASURY FUNCTIONS ACQUIRED.

With the closing of the subtreasuries in the latter part of 1920 the principal institutions of the Mint Service acquired large additions to their stocks of coin, and are also being used as storage places for reserve stocks of paper money. Considerable stocks of coin which formerly would have gone to the subtreasuries have been returned from circulation to the mints for storage. These operations have added materially to the work of the mints.

At the New York assay office it became necessary to inaugurate the making of cash payments for bullion since the Subtreasury (next door to the assay office) was no longer available for the cashing of its checks. The large stock of gold bullion temporarily stored in the New York Subtreasury building has been transferred to the vault in the new assay office building.

Notice in the 1921 Mint Report mentioning that some of the functions of the Subtreasuries, and their stocks of coins, had been acquired by the Mint Service. Image courtesy Newman Numismatic Portal.

which then became *de facto* sub-Treasuries for the Federal Reserve Bank districts they serviced. The first significant batch of 1922-D cents was thus probably not released into actual circulation until early 1924, by which time they were "old news."

(The flow of used coins to the Mints caused by the ending of the Independent Treasury system dragged on for many months. Once received, the coins had to be sorted by denomination if not already done, inspected for fitness for re-issue, and counted and bagged for re-issue to banks requesting coins. One piece of correspondence from the Denver Superintendent indicated that he had two people working full time processing the ex-Independent Treasury coins. The Supt's monthly request for operating funds for March of 1922 contained a line-item request for $693.90 for Independent Treasury operations.)

On top of all this there was a post-war recession which lasted from January of 1920 to July of 1921, sometimes called the Depression of 1920-1921. On April 19, 1922 the Director of the Mint wrote to the Denver Superintendent: "…there is no demand whatever upon the Treasury for coins for circulation." Other correspondence instructed Denver to get rid of the circulated coins it had received back before distributing any new coins.

(There were of course exceptions made by order of the Director's Office. Decades ago many banks liked to have new coins on hand at Christmas time for customers who wanted to give gifts, and in December of 1922 the Denver Mint shipped $50,000 in new half dollars to the FRB of New York, and another $25,000 to the FRB of Boston. One of the NY bags was rifled while in the Postal System, and the correspondence file showed that that bag had contained 1921-D halves. If all $75,000 worth were 1921-D halves, that would represent almost 3/4th of the total 1921-D mintage! $50,000 in new dimes were sent to the FRB of San Francisco, potentially almost half of that 1921-D mintage.)

According to Mint Reports, Denver had about 3.18 million cents on hand at the end of the fiscal year on June 30, 1921. It then struck 7.16 million 1922-D cents in the first two months of 1922, but because of the inflow of circulated coins from the Independent Treasuries and/or the Federal Reserve Banks it had about 20.25 million cents on hand on June 30, 1922. By June 30, 1923 this stockpile had grown to over 21 million cents. Then in late 1923 the Economy began picking up, and by June 30 of 1924 the stockpile had fallen to 5.78 million cents, presumably all or mostly all 1922-D coins. 2.52 million 1924-D cents were struck in the second half of CY1924, and by June 30 of 1925 the stockpile was down to 4.86 million cents, presumably mostly 1924-D and 1925-D coins.

Despite the trickle of 1922-D cents available from the Philadelphia Mint starting in November of that year, as well as the original trickle of coins which could be obtained directly from the Denver Mint's own Cashier from January 1922 onward, contemporary mentions in *The Numismatist* of 1922-dated cents are virtually non-existent.

The first I could find was in the published notes for the September 1925 meeting of the prestigious New York Numismatic Club, which included a mention by member Howland Wood that for several months he had been keeping track of the dates of all the cents he had seen, and that "None bearing the date 1922 had been met with in the East." A distinguished numismatist, he did mention that all had been struck in Denver.

The April 1927 *Numismatist* contained several reports of National Coin Week activities from all around the country. From Willimantic, Conn. it was reported that the Union Shoe Company on Main Street had displayed an extensive collection of United States coins. A small bag of coins bore the label "This bag of money free to the first boy finding a 1922 Lincoln penny during Coin Week." No girls allowed, I take it, and no indication as to whether or not the prize was ever collected.

WILLIMANTIC, CONN.—An exhibit was arranged by J. Z. Mathieu in one of the windows of the Union Shoe Company, on Main street, in which was displayed an extensive collection of United States coins. The window was most tastefully arranged, with a large placard announcing that it was a part of Coin Week observance. A feature of the exhibit was a small bag of coins, labelled, "This bag of money free to the first boy finding a 1922 Lincoln penny during Coin Week." Another display of coins was made by John T. Ashton in the window of his store at 856 Main street.

Brief item in the April, 1927, issue of The Numismatist, among other National Coin Week news coverage, stating that in Willimantic, Conn. a merchant offered the prize of a bag of coins to the first boy to find a 1922 cent. Whether or not the presence or absence of a mint mark mattered was not given. Reprinted with permission of *The Numismatist*, the official publication of the American Numismatic Association (money.org)

An article by Robert H. Lloyd on the irregular mintages of various date and mint mark combinations in the 1920s, which appeared in the June 1927 *Numismatist*, stated: "The 1922 cent from the Denver Mint is in demand, and although the coinage of 7,160,000 pieces would indicate that there are plenty to go around, they are much sought after and are difficult to find in circulation." No mention was made of the alleged "P Mint" coins.

The earliest ad I could find offering the 1922-D cent for sale, by the Arcade Stamp and Coin Co. of Cleveland, reading: "1922 Cent, D Mint. Unc. .40" appeared in the October 1927 *Numismatist*. William Rabin of Philadelphia began the first of many offerings of them in the January 1928 issue, at 35 cents in Uncirculated condition. To appreciate that that price indicated a scarce coin, the same ad offered 10 different date large cents for $1 total, and half dollars over 100 years old (i.e., the Capped Bust type) for 65 cents apiece!

1922 Grant Half Dollar. Unc.	1.25
1922 Grant Half Dollar, star. Unc.	4.50
1922 Cent, D mint. Unc.	.40
10 Different Store Cards	1.25
10 Different Hard Times Tokens	1.25
25 Different Civil War Cents	2.00
10 Foreign Silver, dollar size	8.25
10 Half Dollars, 100 years old	6.75
100 German Notgeld Notes, all different	1.65
200 German Notgeld Notes, all different	3.00
10 Different World War Coins	.75
10 Liberty Seated Dimes	1.45
10 Old Half Dimes	1.25

THE ARCADE STAMP AND COIN CO.,
357 Arcade, Cleveland, Ohio.

The earliest ad I have been able to find offering a 1922-D Cent for sale, at 40 cents in Unc., by the Arcade Stamp and Coin Co. of Cleveland, O. From the Oct. 1927 issue of The Numismatist. American Numismatic Association (money.org)

(In February of 1926 Rabin had offered a set of "Small Cents 1857-1925 Complete set of all dates minted, Uncirculated and Proof $12.50" which should have had a 1922-D in it, but it was not specified.)

With this uptick in interest in the cents of 1922, some collectors must have noticed that while most had a D mint mark, some scarcer pieces had no mint mark. A brief note in the March 1928 *Numismatist* began with the headline: "Are there Any Philadelphia Mint Cents Of 1922?" After the Editor's note that "Mint records say that cents of 1922 were coined only at the Denver Mint," he quotes A.S. Bailey of Jamaica, NY as asking: "I have a cent of 1922 that seems to have been coined at the Philadelphia mint. Under the date, where the mint mark should be, it is just as clear as any Philadelphia mint coin. I have had it under a magnifying glass, but cannot find any trace of a mint mark. Can this be explained?"

ARE THERE ANY PHILADELPHIA MINT CENTS OF 1922?

Mint records say that cents of 1922 were coined only at the Denver mint. A. S. Bailey, 11029 164th street, Jamaica, N. Y., writes as follows:

"I have a cent of 1922 that seems to have been coined at the Philadelphia mint. Under the date, where the mint mark should be, it is just as clear as any Philadelphia mint coin. I have had it under a magnifying glass, but cannot find any trace of a mint mark. Can this be explained?"

The earliest mention of a 1922 Cent without a mint mark (current variety number unknown) that I have been able to find, by A.S. Bailey of Jamaica, NY. From the March, 1928 issue of The Numismatist. American Numismatic Association (money.org)

Chalmers R. Roberts of Pittsburgh quickly responded in the May issue, in a letter he wrote March 19. Under the headline "No Philadelphia Mint Cents of 1922" he stated: "In answer to the paragraph entitled … let me say 'No.' I have looked at a good many specimens claimed to be P Mint and on which no mint mark was visible, but every one was a worn specimen, and I have yet to see a red one without the mark, however faint. In a lot I picked up some time ago of about 15 new red ones, all but about two or three had very faint or poor D's. I have only one which is really sharp. It can easily be seen that with a little wear—presto! and some collector has a P mint 1922 cent. I think this to be a very true and plausible statement and would like to hear from anyone having a 1922 cent, red, with no mint mark. Why they were struck so poorly I do not know."

NO PHILADELPHIA MINT CENTS OF 1922.

In answer to the paragraph entitled "Are There Any Philadelphia Mint Cents of 1922?" on page 183 of the March number, let me say "No." I have looked at a good many specimens claimed to be P mint and on which no mint mark was visible, but every one was a worn specimen, and I have yet to see a red one without the mark, however faint. In a lot I picked up some time ago of about 15 new red ones, all but about two or three had very faint or poor D's. I have only one which is really sharp. It can easily be seen that with a little wear—presto! and some collector has a P mint 1922 cent. I think this to be a very true and plausible statement and would like to hear from anyone having a 1922 cent, red, with no mint mark. Why they were struck so poorly I do not know.

CHALMERS M. ROBERTS.

Pittsburgh, Pa., March 19, 1928.

Chalmers M. Roberts response to A.S. Bailey's question regarding 1922 Philadelphia cents. From the May, 1928 issue of The Numismatist. American Numismatic Association (money.org)

In the June issue Mr. Charles N. Cooley of Grand Rapids, Mich. disagreed with Mr. Roberts, stating: "I have seen several specimens of the cents with D mint marks, of which I have two, one struck sharp and one faint. I also have one with absolutely no mint mark at all. This cent is in very fine condition, showing only a few stains only." Taking the middle ground, the Editor used a headline "The Cents Of 1922."

THE CENTS OF 1922.

In looking over the May number of THE NUMISMATIST I read Mr. C. M. Roberts' article on Philadelphia Mint cents of 1922. I wish to state that I disagree with him on this matter.

I have seen several specimens of the cents with D mint marks, of which I have two, one struck sharp and one faint. I also have one with absolutely no mint mark at all. This cent is in very fine condition, showing only a few stains only.

CHARLES N. COOLEY.

Grand Rapids, Mich., May 7, 1928.

Charles N. Cooley's response to Chalmers M. Roberts' comments re 1922 Cents. From the June, 1928 issue of The Numismatist. American Numismatic Association (money.org)

Until somebody proves otherwise, I am going to give Mr. Bailey credit for the discovery of the 1922 "No D" cent (current die variety[s] unknown), and for starting off the hunt for them. I will give Mr. Roberts credit for the discovery of the 1922 "Weak D" cent, (current die variety[s] unknown) even though he had no idea what he had, and for the first use of the description "faint" which I am resurrecting here below. Mr. Cooley deserves an honorable mention for both.

As collectors began looking for the "Plain" 1922 cents others must have noticed that certain coins had poorly formed mint marks that were neither normal nor missing. Nobody knew what caused the "No D" or the "Weak D," cents, or indeed what to call them, but some people collected them anyways. The first ad offering a "1922 P. Mint Cent, Unc. .25" (current die variety unknown) was run by Ambrose J. Brown of Marblehead, Mass in the November 1928 *Numismatist.*

1829 Unc. 1.00
1831 V. Fine .... .75
1922 P. Mint Cent. Unc. .... .25
1871 Gold Quarter, California, Liberty Head, 13 Stars, Unc. 1.75

I am in the market to buy U. S. Coins or will sell on commission at reasonable rates.

AMBROSE J. BROWN,
8 Elm St., Marblehead, Mass.

The earliest ad I have been able to find offering a "1922 P. Mint Cent" in Unc. at 25 Cents, by Ambrose Brown of Marblehead, Mass. From the November, 1928 issue of The Numismatist. American Numismatic Association (money.org)

The September 1929 meeting report from the Dallas Coin Club, published in the November *Numismatist*, stated as follows: "G.D. Morton gave an interesting discussion of 1922 cents, describing the various die breaks and other peculiarities of that year's issue. He said it was generally agreed that the 7,000,000 cents of that year were all struck at Denver, and presumably sent to the Dallas Federal Reserve Bank, hence most of the cents of that comparatively small issue are now in this territory. He further said the average run of cents would now yield about 25 cents of the 1922 date out of every 1,000 in this district. He promised to exhibit at the next meeting the various die breaks on the 1922 cents and other current cents from his voluminous collection."

and the small envelope still bore the express company's wax seals.

G. D. Morton gave an interesting discussion of 1922 cents, describing the various die breaks and other peculiarities of that year's issue. He said it was generally agreed that the 7,000,000 cents of that year were all struck at Denver, and presumably sent to the Dallas Federal Reserve Bank, hence most of the cents of that comparatively small issue are now in this territory. He further said the average run of cents would now yield about 25 cents of the 1922 date out of every 1,000 in this district. He promised to exhibit at the next meeting the various die breaks on the 1922 cents and other current cents from his voluminous collection.

A very illuminating talk was made by J. H. Cassidy on Continental Cur-

In September of 1929 G.D. Morton gave a talk on 1922 cents to the Dallas Coin Club, including the first mention of "die breaks and other peculiarities of that year's issue." From the November, 1929 issue of The Numismatist. American Numismatic Association (money.org)

Note the casual use of "1922" in apparent reference to "1922-D" cents. In my research I have seen many such usages, which makes it impossible to know if any given "1922" usage was referring to a 1922 "No D" cent or a normal 1922-D cent. Perhaps some collectors just assumed that since all

1922-dated cents came from Denver, merely giving the year would imply the mint mark. Morton made no specific mention of the existence of the "No D" cents, and seemed to be more interested in die breaks. More on those die breaks later, though unfortunately the meeting report(s) that might have covered his followup talk were never published. (If the Dallas Coin Club still has its minutes from 1929 and 1930, I would love to see them.)

Cents dated 1922-D must have remained scarce for some time, with some people still attempting to get them from their source, as many collectors had done so from 1922 onwards. On Jan. 6, 1930, the Superintendent of the Denver Mint sent a letter to Mr. W. F. Moyer of Philadelphia: "Dear Sir: I regret to say that I am unable to send you the 12 one-cent bronze pieces of 1922 coinage as requested in your letter of the 2nd instant as these coins have long since been distributed. In this connection, please be advised that application for new coins must now be made to the Treasurer of the United States, Washington, D.C. The two-cent stamp and 12 cents enclosed with your letter are herewith returned."

On June 7 his office likewise informed Mr. Bernard McCabe of Wallkill, NY that "our entire stock of these (1922) coins is long since exhausted. ... Your money order (for 20 cents) is returned herewith." This time he referred the collector to other collectors. The desirability of the 1922-D cents was such that they were deemed worthy of mention in the "show and tell" portions of the meeting reports for the Buffalo Numismatic Association for November of 1930, and the Rochester Numismatic Society for April of 1931.

However, despite the numerous mentions above that all 1922 cents had been struck in Denver, confusion over their place of minting continued on. In 1933 budding numismatic great Lee F. Hewitt, soon to start the *Numismatic Scrapbook Magazine* in 1935, submitted a short blurb in the March, 1933 *The Numismatist*, printed under the headline "Uncirculated 1922 Cents, Philadelphia Mint." It read: "I would like to know if any collector has a 1922 Philadelphia Mint cent, an Uncirculated specimen. I've seen several advertised, (where, I wonder?—TD) but they are not mint specimens. It has always been my opinion that the mint mark has worn off the supposed 1922 cent without mint mark."

It is unknown which varieties he, and Roberts, were referring to. They could have been the Die Pair #1 & 3 coins popularized in the 1960s, ANACS's Die Pair #4 recognized in the 1980s, or any one of my several Die Pair #Zero and Die Pair #5 through #13 coins listed below. Many do appear to be horribly worn even in new condition. Once their mint red color is gone, they may look to be in no better than Very Good condition. (See the

Uncirculated 1922 Cents, Philadelphia Mint.

The "Voice of the Collector," in my opinion, is the outstanding feature of The Numismatist. I am in favor of a classified exchange department. There are plenty of collectors who would like to run an exchange ad the year round, but how many of us can afford a $1.00 ad every time?

I would like to know if any collector has a 1922 Philadelphia mint cent, an uncirculated specimen. I've seen several advertised, but they are not mint specimens. It has always been my opinion that the mint mark has worn off the supposed 1922 cent without mint mark.

LEE F. HEWITT.

Chicago, Ill., Feb. 5.

Future numismatic great Lee F. Hewitt posted a blurb in the March, 1933 issue of The Numismatist looking for an Uncirculated 1922 Cent from the Philadelphia Mint. His comment saying that the ones he had seen "are not mint specimens" may indicate that he, like other collectors of the era, did not understand that missing details can be caused by die deterioration rather than circulation wear. American Numismatic Association (money.org)

discovery specimen of the Die Pair #4B latest die state "No D" coin below.) And, it can be difficult to distinguish between a true "No D" specimen and a "Very Faint D" coin unless you have seen multiple specimens of each, as I have. See their descriptions below.

Dealer Fred Greenclay of Denver, who had been advertising 1922-D cents since January of 1931, had an ad in the March 1935 *Numismatist* offering, in a run of Lincoln cents, "1922 D only .15; same, mintmark missing .25." This is the first ad I have found that offered both the "With D" and the "No D." In the May issue his ad included the line: "U.S. Cent, 1922, D missing, rev. die break, fine, v. scarce .35." (The die break mention tells us that this was probably what is now known as Die Pair #1, or possibly its Die Pair #Zero doppelganger. See below.)

His March ad must have generated some letters, as the May issue also included an editorial blurb from Greenclay under the headline "All 1922 Lincoln Cents Struck At Denver Mint." It read: "I have received many inquiries asking if any 1922 Lincoln cents were struck at the Philadelphia Mint. There are cents of this date where the D is missing, this being the last lot struck from a very poor die and the D was worn off. In many cases the last 2 in date is very weak and hardly visible. On the reverse is a die break on some of them, starting from L down in Pluribus to O in One. This variety is struck flat, none are sharp, even in very fine condition. Those with the die break are very scarce. I am not selling coins of the Philadelphia Mint."

(Readers of *The Numismatist* back in 1922-23 would have known that all 1922-dated cents were struck at Denver, but that knowledge was lost to the average collector in the mid-1930s who did not have access to U.S. Mint Reports or back issues of *The Numismatist*. There were no standard U.S. coin

1919 S, 25c.; same, D .... .15
1920 S or D, each .... .15
1921 S only .... .25
1922 D only, 15c.; same, mintmark missing .... .25
1924 S., 25c.; D .... .15
1925 S or D, each .... .15
1926 S, 25c.; D .... .10
1927-1928 S, each .... .15
1927-1928 D, 10c.; 1929 S .... .10
10 different dates Lincoln Cents, S Mint, and 10 different dates D Mint, v. good and better, set of 20—Dates to be my own selection on these—only 1.50
Lundy Island, 1929, set of 1 Puffin and ½ Puffin, obverse Portrait of Martin Coles Harmon, Date 1929. Reverse, a Puffin Bird. Unc. v. scarce set of 2 .... .35

Harmon was deposed by the British Government, and fined 25 pounds for striking these coins, most of them being confiscated, hence their scarcity.

Postage, insurance or registration extra.

FRED GREENCLAY,
1626 Washington St., Denver, Colo.

Same, Lincoln one side, Grant on the other, Unc. .... .35
U. S. Cent, 1922, D missing, rev., die break, fine, v. scarce .... .35

U. S. Lincoln Cents, San Francisco or Denver Mints, various dates in fine condition:

1910 S, 25c.; 1911 S or D, each 15c.; 1912, S or D, each 15c.; 1913 S or D, each 25c.; 1914 S or D, each 50c.; 1915-16-17-18 S or D, each 15c.; 1919 S, 25c., D, 15c.; 1920 S or D, each 15c.; 1921 S, 25c.; 1922 D, 20c.; 1923 S, 25c.; 1924 S, 25c., D, 25c.; 1925 S or D, each 15c.; 1926 S, 25c.; 1926 D, 1927 S, 1928 S, 1929 S, 1931 S, each 10c.

Postage, insurance and registration extra on all orders under $5.00. Satisfaction guaranteed or your money refunded.

FRED GREENCLAY
1626 Washington St., Denver, Colo.

ALL 1922 LINCOLN CENTS STRUCK AT DENVER MINT.

I have received many inquiries asking if any 1922 Lincoln cents were struck at the Philadelphia mint. There are cents of this date where the D is missing, this being the last lot struck from a very poor die and the D was worn off. In many cases the last 2 in date is very weak and hardly visible. On the reverse is a die break on some of them, starting from L down in Pluribus to O in One. This variety is struck flat, none are sharp, even in very fine condition. Those with the die break are very scarce. I am not selling coins of the Philadelphia mint.

Denver, Col., April 10, 1935. FRED GREENCLAY.

In the March, 1935 issue of The Numismatist Fred Greenclay of Denver ran an ad offering 1922 cents with and without mint mark at 15 and 25 cents respectively. Obviously collectors were still confused about the "No D" coins, as he felt compelled to include a blurb about them in the May issue along with his followup ad which also had some interesting comments about die cracks. American Numismatic Association (money.org)

references at the time, and the casual collector could reasonably have assumed that any coins with no mint marks were struck at Philadelphia. Two of the earliest U.S. coin books, Wayte Raymond's *Standard Catalogue of United States Coins & Currency*, first copyrighted in 1934, and C.E. Green's *Mint Record and Type-Table United States Coins*, copyrighted in 1936, did not mention any varieties for 1922-D cents.)

CHAPTER FOUR

The 1922 Cent Varieties Get Recognized

When the first albums for collecting coins by date and mint mark were test marketed by M.L. Beistle in 1927, and mass marketed in 1928, they ignored the 1922 "No D" cents, apparently relying on the official Mint records for their entries. However, they were a bit expensive for the times (at $1 per page!), especially during the Great Depression which began in 1929, and their usage was not widespread.

The Great Revolution in coin collecting began in 1934, when collector Joseph K. Post (who worked as an engineer for a paper products company in Wisconsin) devised what became known as the "pennyboard," a stiff sheet of cardboard 14 inches tall by 11 inches wide (a standard picture frame size for possible display) with die cut holes backed by sturdy paper. Beneath each hole was printed the year, the mint mark if any, and an approximate mintage in millions. (Earliest copyright date "1934." Some dated "Jan. 11, 1935.")

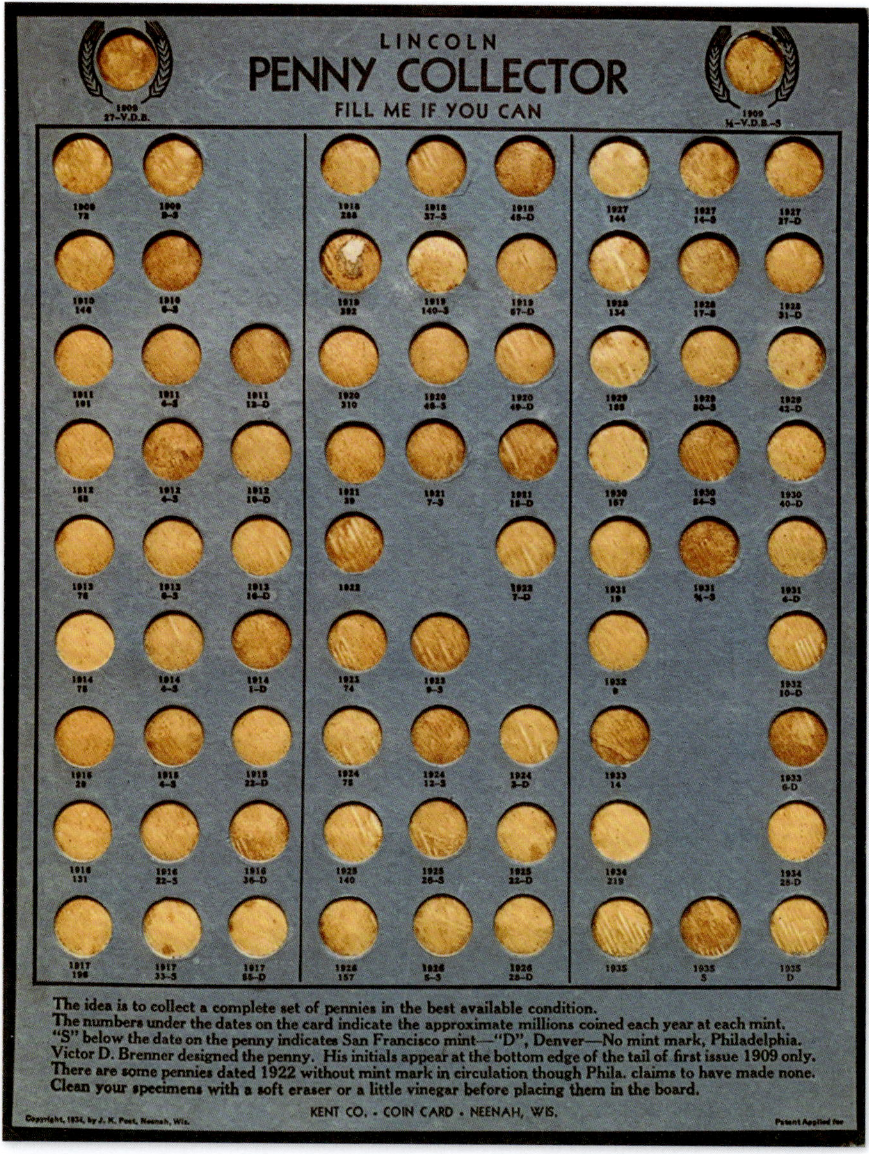

Front side of a classic Kent Coin Card, *aka* a "Pennyboard," Copyright 1934 by J.K. Post of Neenah, Wis. Patent Applied For. The invention that revolutionized coin collecting and ultimately increased the number of collectors from thousands to millions. Photo courtesy Christopher Buck.

His initial boards had three wide columns of holes arranged one line per year, three holes per line in each column for the (P), S & D coins, with holes omitted where no coins were struck, such as for 1909 and 1910 Denver coins. (By mistake, he included a hole for the non-existent 1921-D cent.) For 1922, he included a hole for a "1922" coin in line with the other Philadelphia coins, with no mintage figure or description given, as well as the "1922 D" coin with a mintage of 7 (million). Among several footnotes was the line "There are some pennies dated 1922 without mint marks in circulation though Phila. claims to have made none."

Did he include the "1922" hole because his format would otherwise have had two blank spots on the 1922 line, and he thought that might have looked bad? Or did he just like the 1922 "Plain" cents? They were out there, and some people did collect them. Regardless, he began wholesaling the "pennyboards" (to be retailed at 25 cents) in early 1935, and they proved so successful that later that year the company that printed them for him purchased the rights to them. That company, now the hobby giant Whitman Publishing, duplicated Post's layout in its earliest editions, and so demand for the "1922 Plain" coins soared. (Most collectors hate having albums with empty holes in them.)

The 1936 Edition of the Whitman penny board eliminated the one line per year format to squeeze in coins struck after 1935, as well as eliminating

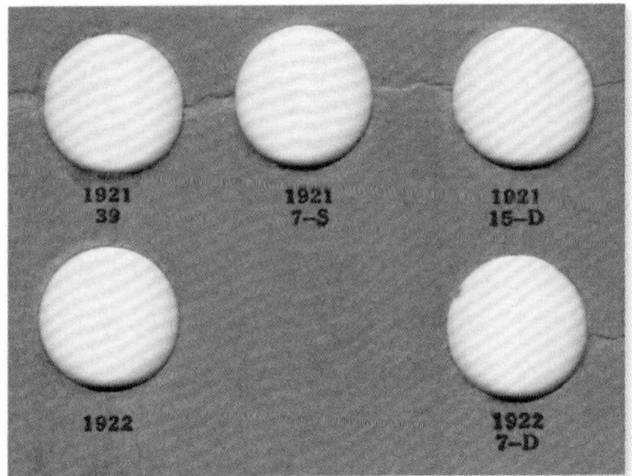

Detail of a Kent pennyboard showing holes for both 1922 and 1922 D Cents. The presence of the no mint mark hole enormously increased the demand for what is now called a "1922 No D Cent," guaranteeing its place in numismatic history and generating interest in other die varieties as well. Photo courtesy of my late friend David W. Lange, who literally wrote the book on pennyboards and was a great help in the writing of this book.

The idea is to collect a complete set of pennies in the best available condition.
The numbers under the dates on the card indicate the approximate millions coined each year at each mint.
"S" below the date on the penny indicates San Francisco mint—"D", Denver—No mint mark, Philadelphia.
Victor D. Brenner designed the penny. His initials appear at the bottom edge of the tail of first issue 1909 only.
There are some pennies dated 1922 without mint mark in circulation though Phila. claims to have made none.
Clean your specimens with a soft eraser or a little vinegar before placing them in the board.
KENT CO. - COIN CARD - NEENAH, WIS.
Copyright, 1934, by J. K. Post, Neenah, Wis. Patent Applied for

Detail of a Kent pennyboard showing a useful comment about 1922 mint marks and giving some absolutely horrible advice on the cleaning of coins. DO NOT CLEAN YOUR COINS!!!!! Courtesy David W. Lange.

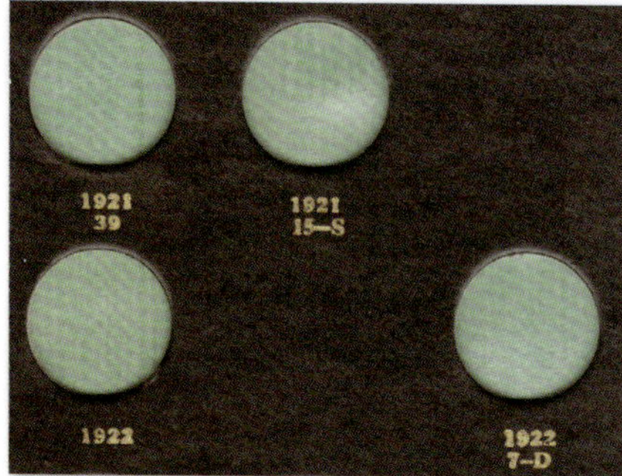

Detail of a Whitman pennyboard from 1936 eliminating the non-existent 1921-D cent but, more importantly, retaining Kent's list of 1922 dates and keeping the 1922 "No D" cent one of the great rarities of the Lincoln Cent series. Courtesy David W. Lange.

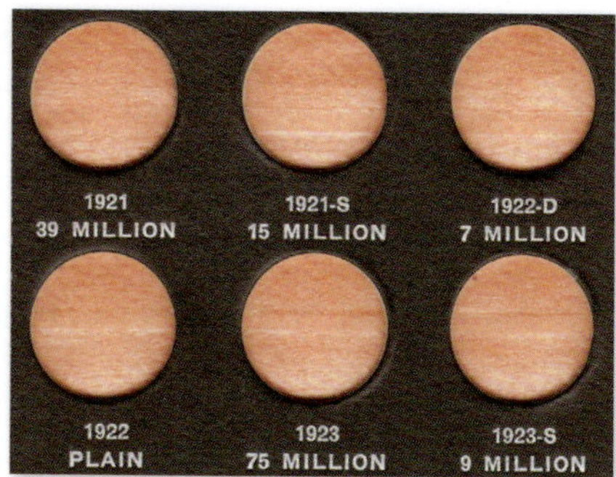

Detail of a Whitman pennyboard from 1939 with "1922 PLAIN" replacing "1922 Broken D." Courtesy David W. Lange.

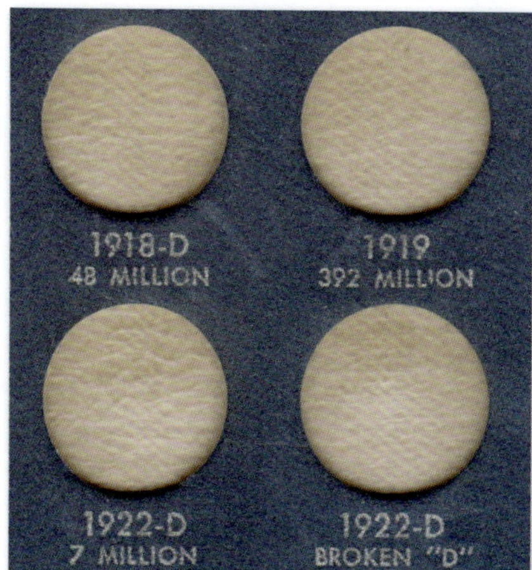

Detail of a Whitman pennyboard from 1938 with the peculiar (and inaccurate) designation "Broken D," which may have been intended to include both "No D" and "Weak D" coins to make it easier to fill in the hole. (Collectors hate empty holes!) Note also that the hole has been moved to the right of the hole for the "D" coin, which may have been done to quietly stress the fact that "No D" coins are NOT "Philadelphia" coins. Courtesy David W. Lange.

By 1940 the number of different date and mint mark combinations of Lincoln Cents struck, with three more coming each year, forced Whitman to abandon the one page pennyboard format and introduce the blue tri-fold album, Volumes One and Two. This detail from the former shows a 1940 listing with the unfortunate "Broken D" designation, which suggests that the person tasked with designing it had been given a 1938 pennyboard as a list of dates to include in it. Courtesy David W. Lange.

the non-existent 1921-D cent, but it kept the hole for the "1922" with nothing else printed under it. In the 1938 Edition, and on the earliest tri-fold "Blue Folders" introduced in 1940 because the series had outgrown the Penny board format, Whitman downgraded the 1922 "No D" entry by listing a normal 1922-D and then a 1922-D "Broken D."

(Curiously, it issued a Kent-style throwback board in 1939 only, with a "1922" hole labeled "Plain." For the complete history of pennyboards, which later included other types and denominations, see *Coin Collecting Boards of the 1930s and 1940s* by the late David W. Lange.)

So where did the term "Broken D" come from? Perhaps because the first significant release of 1922-D cents had occurred in Texas, (according to G.D. Morton), Corpus Christi jeweler, collector and part-time coin dealer Maurice D. Scharlack became obsessed with 1922 cents of all types somewhere in the 1930s. It is not impossible that he knew Morton from Dallas, or at least his interest in die cracks.

Scharlack, who had been running ads in *The Numismatist* for various coins since early 1936, began specializing in 1922 cents in June of 1937. These ran under headlines such as "Those Rare 22's" or "1922-D My Specialty," and offered such varieties as "1922 (No D) the hard-to-get one," "1922-D Cracked Die," "1922-D Rev. Cracked Die," "1922-D with 2 (or 3) Die Breaks" and the enigmatic "1922-D Dented obverse." Sometimes the die cracks were specified as "Cracked Die through 'P' (not currently known; he probably meant the L of PLURIBUS)" or "With die break thru 'OF'." The prices were typically 50 cents or a dollar, when a dollar was still serious money.

1922-D MY SPECIALTY.

Will Buy or Sell from 1 to 10,000.
'22-D, V. G., 10c. $7.50 per 100.
'22 No D, 50c.
'22-D, Rev. Cracked Die, 50c.
'22-D, with 3 cracked die, $1.00.
'22-D, Repolished (like unc.), 50c.
'22-D, Dented obverse, 35c.

MAURICE D. SCHARLACK,
Numismatist,
Corpus Christi, Texas.

A CHANCE AT THE 1922-D AGAIN

1922-D Fine, with dented profile..$ .50
1922-D Fine, cracked die thru "P" .50
1922-D Fine, with 3 die breaks ... .75
1922-D Fine, with die break thru "OF" .... .75
1922 (no D) the hard-to-get one.. 1.00
1922-D Fine, 8 for 1.00
MAURICE D. SCHARLACK
Numismatist. Corpus Christi, Texas.

Two of the many ads by Maurice D. Scharlack of Corpus Christi, TX that appeared in The Numismatist in 1937 through 1939. I love the hype such as: "1922-D My Specialty" or "(no D) the hard-to-get one." He and the pennyboards that came out around the same time helped make the 1922 cent varieties famous. Reprinted with permission of *The Numismatist*, the official publication of the American Numismatic Association (money.org)

He even influenced his brother-in-law, a printer, to issue a knockoff pennyboard with a hole for the 1922 cent with the comment "NONE REPORTED" below the hole. (See the Lange Pennyboard book.) In a letter to *The Numismatist* in July of 1937 he bragged about having accumulated over 25,000 1922-D cents, and suggested, a bit uncertainly, that the "sans D" cents might have resulted from the mint mark area having broken off the die. This is of course ridiculous, as such a hole or void in the die would have left a corresponding raised bulge on the coins struck from it rather than a smooth field, but it may explain the term "Broken D" used by Whitman and others.

THE NUMISMATIST, July, 1937 645

"PENNIES FROM HEAVEN" IN 1922.

In the interest of throwing a little more light on the much discussed 1922 Lincoln cent, I am jotting down these notes. The United States mint record shows a coinage of only 7,160,000 coined from the Denver mint only. This is a comparatively small issue, and the writer feels confident that these pennies will increase in value as time goes on and collectors begin to take notice of their absence from circulation. I have 25,000 of them packed away in a little wooden chest, and in all due modesty I honestly believe this is the largest collection of this one cent.

There is an interesting little fact I want to bring out. I said above that the 1922 Lincolns were minted only at the Denver mint. Yet you will occasionally find a 1922 plain Lincoln cent (which ordinarily means they were minted at the Philadelphia mint). In this particular instance I do not believe that is the case, but the only explanation I can give is that the die might have broken or worn off and thus coined a 1922 sans the D. I have in my lot some specimens showing no signs of wear, yet no D is visible, even under a lens.

There is one other interesting thing about these 1922 cents. In my search of these cents for many years I have come across broken-die items. There are four types of breaks. The first has a break from the L of Pluribus into the O of One. The second is the same as the first, except that it has an additional break across the top portion of the right-hand wreath. The third is the same as the second, except that it has an additional break between the left-hand edge of the left-hand wreath and the edge of the coin. The fourth has only one break, which is from the left edge of the coin across the stem of the left-hand wreath to the O in Of.

MAURICE D. SCHARLACK.

Corpus Christi, Texas, May 25, 1937.

"Pennies From Heaven in 1922," a self-promoting blurb by Maurice D. Scharlack in the July, 1937 issue of The Numismatist. It is particularly interesting for his comments on the reverse die crack varieties. Like many a collector after him, he confused the single, jogging die crack through the O of ONE found on Die Pairs #1 and #Zero below with the straight die crack through the O of ONE found on Die Pair #10 below. Die Pair #10 is the one found with either two or three die cracks on the reverse. The die crack through the O of OF can be found on some variants of Die Pair #11 below. He was obviously unaware of my (scarcer) Die Pair #12 with the die crack though the second S of STATES. American Numismatic Association (money.org)

The October 1939 issue of *The Numismatist* reprinted a talk on small cents in general given to the California Coin Club by Wesley R. Hauptman on August 1 of that year. After repeating various unsubstantiated and/or scurrilous rumors that the 1922 "No D" cents were surreptitiously struck by Philadelphia Mint employees in that year for sale for a profit, he launched into a technologically laughable mish-mash about how the Denver Mint workers did not replace the electrotype copy of the master die soon enough after the mint mark wore off of it. Ignore him.

In 1942 Whitman copyrighted the First Edition of the *Handbook of United States Coins* (the Blue Book) by R.S. Yeoman, Lee F. Hewitt and Charles E. Green. It listed the premium on a "1922 (Without D)" cent at 25 cents in Good and 50 cents in Fine. For comparison, the 1909-SVDB cents listed at 25 cents and 75 cents in the same grades, and the 1914-D at 15 cents and 30 cents. 1931-S cents listed at four cents in either grade. 1909-S cents without the VDB listed at two cents and three cents.

LINCOLN CENTS

Date and Mint Mark	Quantity Minted	Good	Fine
1915 D*	22,050,000	$.01	$.01
1915 S*	4,833,000	.02	.04
1916	133,833,677	.01	.01
1916 D	35,956,000	.01	.01
1916 S	22,510,000	.01	.01
1917 *	196,429,785	.01	.01
1917 D	55,120,000	.01	.01
1917 S*	32,620,000	.01	.01
1918	288,104,634	.01	.01
1918 D	47,830,000	.01	.01
1918 S	34,680,000	.01	.01
1919	392,021,000	.01	.01
1919 D	57,154,000	.01	.01
1919 S	139,760,000	.01	.01
1920 *	310,165,000	.01	.01
1920 D	49,280,000	.01	.01
1920 S*	46,220,000	.01	.01
1921	39,157,000	.01	.01
1921 S	15,274,000	.02	.04
1922 D*	7,160,000	.02	.03
1922 (Without D)		.25	.50
1923 *	74,723,000	.01	.01
1923 S	8,700,000	.02	.04
1924	75,178,000	.01	.01
1924 D*	2,520,000	.04	.07
1924 S*	11,696,000	.02	.04
1925	139,949,000	.01	.01

1922-D Cent listings in the First Edition (1942) Bluebook. Photo by the author.

Following the Lincoln cents was a page entitled "Die-Cracks And Other Varieties of Lincoln Cents," with an introduction "Varieties of Lincoln Cents probably due to broken dies, dirt or some other cause. Variations from perfect coins are sought by many collectors. Prices paid are recorded in this list. Number in existence not known."

DIE-CRACKS AND OTHER VARIETIES OF LINCOLN CENTS

Varieties of Lincoln Cents probably due to broken dies, dirt or some other cause. Variations from perfect coins are sought by many collectors. Prices paid are recorded in this list. Number in existence not known.

Date and Mint Mark	Good	Fine
1909 Double edge	$.15	$.30
1909 V.D.B. Die, bar between right leaf and rim	.25	.35
1910 S Letter S tilted	.10	.20
1911 First 1 missing and mere dot of metal where mint letter should be	.15	.20
1911 S Thin extra rim on obverse	.15	.30
1913 D Mint letter off center	.30	.45
1914 S Mint letter tilted	.12	.25
1915 D Mint letter tilted	.10	.20
1915 S Mint letter tilted	.25	.45
1917 Off center	.05	.10
1917 Second 1 has root shaped foot to left	.15	.20
1917 S Mint letter off center	.10	.20
1920 Apparently this date last two figures run into little rough mound of metal	.15	.20
1920 S Mint letter tilted	.05	.10
1922 According to Mint records no cents from Philadelphia so those without Mint letter are evidently freaks from Denver	.25	.45
1922 D Reverse die crack line over right wreath	.08	.15
1922 D Mint letter tilted	.15	.25
1922 D Several varieties of die cracks on reverse	.15	.25
1923 Very thin	.30	.65
1924 D Line from U of Union to N of One	.05	.10

Excerpt from a full page list of various "Die-Cracks and Other Varieties of Lincoln Cents" from the First Edition (1942) Bluebook. Photo by the author.

Amidst ephemera such as "1917 Second 1 has root shaped foot to left" and "1924 S The famous Goitre, Obverse die break" there are these entries:

"1922 According to Mint records no cents from Philadelphia so those without Mint letter are evidently freak from Denver … .25 … .45"

"1922 D Reverse die crack line over right wreath … .08 … .15"

"1922 D Mint letter tilted … .15 … .25" and

"1922 D Several varieties of die cracks on reverse … .15 … .25"

All 1922 Cents Struck at Denver

An explanation of this variety was printed in the May, 1935, issue of Numismatist. Apparently the die from which these coins were struck became worn and the D beneath the date did not appear on several hundred coins that were released for actual circulation.

The amount of coins released without the mint mark was very small and therefore they command many times more than the coins with the mint mark showing.

★ ★ ★

Beginning of a full page section on general information about Lincoln Cents, from the First Edition (1942) Bluebook. Photo by the author.

I have no idea what the "Mint letter tilted" refers to. Following this page is a page of general information about coins, which begins: "All 1922 Cents Struck at Denver." "An explanation of this variety was printed in the May, 1935, issue of *Numismatist* (the Greenclay note—TD). Apparently the die from which these coins were struck became worn and the D beneath the date did not appear on several hundred coins that were released for actual circulation. The amount of coins released without the mint mark was very small and therefore they command many times more than the coins with the mint mark showing."

Curiously, the First Edition of the *Guide Book of United States Coins* (the Red Book, copyright 1946, by Yeoman only) completely ignores the 1922 cent varieties. This probably indicates that the die crack listings in the earlier Blue Book were promoted by Green (listed as a contributor to the new Red Book) or by Hewitt (not listed as a contributor).

Collectors may have complained about the omission of the significant varieties, as the Second Edition Red Book included both a "1922D (broken D)" and a "1922 Plain (No D)." In the Seventh Edition this was changed to "1922D (Part D)" and "1922 Plain (No D)." In the Eighth Edition the "Part D" variety was dropped.

In 1952-54 collector E. V. Wallace published a series of articles on Lincoln cents in Hewitt's *The Numismatic Scrapbook Magazine*, that were reprinted once finished in a pamphlet grandiosely entitled *A Numismatography of the Lincoln Head Cent*. The first few chapters are well researched treatises on how the coins were made, but Chapter V devolved into mind-numbing descriptions of what error collectors of the day called "FIDO's" for Freaks, Irregularities, Defects and Oddities.

SMALL CENTS

Lincoln Head Type
1909 to Date

Victor D. Brenner designed this cent which was issued to commemorate the hundredth anniversary of Lincoln's birth. The designer's initials VDB appear on a limited quantity of cents of 1909. The San Francisco mint produced the smallest issue before the initials were removed, creating the scarcest and most sought-after Lincoln Head Cent. The initials were restored, in 1918, to the obverse side as illustrated below. This type cent was the first to have the motto "In God We Trust."

	Fine	Unc.	Proof
1909 V D B	$ .05	$ .25	$ 7.00
1909 S, V D B	10.00	16.50	

Same as the preceding type, but VDB omitted from the reverse.

	Fine	Unc.	Proof
1909	$.05	$ .30	$3.00
1909S	1.00	4.00	
1910	.05	.65	3.00
1910S	.25	1.25	
1911	.05	.60	3.00
1911D	.35	2.50	
1911S	.35	3.50	
1912	.05	.60	3.00
1912D	.50	5.50	
1912S	.35	4.50	
1913	.10	.60	3.00
1913D	.40	6.50	
1913S	.30	5.50	
1914	.15	3.00	6.00
1914D	4.50	15.00	
1914S	.35	6.50	
1915	.15	3.50	7.00
1915D	.25	1.75	
1915S	.30	4.00	
1916	.05	.50	8.00
1916D	.20	2.00	
1916S	.20	3.50	
1917	.05	.50	
1917D	.20	2.75	
1917S	.20	2.75	

Designer's Initials Restored

	Fine	Unc.	Proof
1918	$.05	$ .50	
1918D	.20	4.00	
1918S	.20	5.50	
1919	.05	.50	
1919D	.20	1.50	
1919S	.10	1.50	
1920	.05	.50	
1920D	.20	2.50	
1920S	.20	4.50	
1921	.15	2.00	
1921S	.25	13.50	
1922D	.35	3.00	
	Good	V.G.	
1922D (broken D)	1.25	3.00	
1922 Plain (No D)	2.50	3.50	
1923	.05	.50	

[82]

Page from the Second Edition (1948) Redbook showing 1922 Cent listings. Note that the varieties are listed in much lower grades than normal coins, perhaps reflecting the fact that the variety coins were typically struck from badly deteriorated dies. Photo by the author.

Basically they were any coin less than 100% perfect. Some of the errors so described and listed were significant type of errors, but many were not. (Full disclosure: I began collecting such coins out of circulation in the early 1960s, and learning about *how* they happened helped make me the numismatist that I am today. But I moved on.)

In a section titled "Condition of the Dies," subtitled "Defects due to Debris and Waste" he described how various foreign substances could obscure various parts of the design. He then stated: "The most famous and widely known product of an unclean die is the 1922 Lincoln Cent specimen from the Denver Mint which is minus the Mint designation letter 'D.' "

A Numismatography of the Lincoln Head Cent

By E. V. WALLACE

CHAPTER V—Contd. Freaks, Irregulars, Defects and Oddities (Fido's)

b. Defects due to Debris and Waste.

The presence of oil or grease on a die, metal slivers, oily or greasy cotton waste or lint, and numerous other kinds of debris, is another media responsible for coins looking different from its otherwise intended design. Much of the debris which collects on the die is more than likely brought to them on the planchets. If the waste moves on with the newly stamped coin only one specimen is affected. If it sticks—then numerous succeeding coins may bear similar irregular markings or deletions. However a die may have become dirty the effect is the same on the coin. The effect may be deletion of some of the intended letters, or numerals, or alteration of them. The effect may be to alter the figures, or the effect may be to add miscellaneous markings, lines etc.

The most famous and widely known product of an unclean die is the 1922 Lincoln Cent specimen from the Denver Mint which is minus the Mint designation letter "D." The U. S. Bureau of the Mint records for the year 1922 show that Lincoln Cents were only manufactured at the Denver Coinage Mint that year. Therefore coins bearing the date 1922 without the Mint letter D can only be explained by the presumption that the Mint letter in the die became filled with some foreign substance, possibly oil or grease, thereby ruining its embossing effect. Specimens can be found with descending order of perceptibility of the "D" which lends credence to the presumption. This oddity should not be confused with the broken "D" irregular, which will be discussed later in this chapter.

An excerpt from E.V. Wallace's article "A Numismatography of the Lincoln Head Cent," serially published irregularly in Numismatic Scrapbook Magazine during 1952-1954 and subsequently republished in pamphlet form. The series contains many interesting theories on the causes of the different varieties found on the cents of 1922. Some of them are both correct and useful. Image courtesy Newman Numismatic Portal.

After explaining that only Denver struck cents in 1922, he went on: "… coins bearing the date 1922 without the Mint letter D can only be explained by the presumption that the Mint letter in the die became filled with some foreign substance, possibly oil or grease… Specimens can be found with descending order of perceptibility of the "D" which lends credence to the presumption. This oddity should not be confused with the broken "D" irregular(sic), which will be discussed later in this chapter."

Wallace is to be credited with being the first to suggest mint grease clogs as "a" cause of a "No D" cent, but he was wrong to state that it was "the only" cause. Mint grease only obliterated the D on Die Pairs #1 & 3, and not impossibly (though none are currently known) on some #Zero and/or #4B coins, where the D was already severely weakened by die erosion and/or die polishing.

Later, under the section "Defects due to Normal Die Wear," he first covers "die cracks," (where the die metal is broken but still all present), of which there are four such dies listed for 1922-D cents. In a section on die "breaks," (which are more severe because metal has left the die), he listed a 1922-D Obverse thusly: "This specimen is truly the broken 'D'.* The die, at the bottom part of the mint letter seems to have sloughed off or chipped away. The result is that the bottom right of the D is not elevated, i.e., the coin surface goes directly to the hole area in the 'D'."

This may have been a reference to Die Pair #4B described below, on which the field around the D was eroded unevenly by natural die erosion, causing the lower right side of the D to gradually fade away. However, it may also refer to one or more of the new varieties I have added below on which the lower right side of the D fades away. (See Die Pairs #5 through #13 below.) I strongly disagree that any metal broke away from any die in the mint mark area. As I said above, a void in the die steel would result in more raised metal on the coins struck from such a die, not less.

The asterisk leads to a discussion about the term "Broken D," as some people at that time were apparently claiming that "Broken D" was an abbreviation for "Broken Die," even though "Broken D" was never used with a period, and the word "Die" was arguably too short to bother abbreviating. Indirect reference is made to Scharlack's ads, which intermingled "No D" coins with cracked die coins. The discussion is useful if only because it illustrates the dangers of using nicknames for errors rather than correct technical descriptions.

CHAPTER FIVE

Towards Enlightenment – The Craig Numbers

Modern 1922-D cent researcher Alan D. Craig published a groundbreaking, if a bit flawed, article entitled "The 1922 No D Cents" in the November 1962 issue of *The Numismatic Scrapbook Magazine*. He began by citing Wallace's attribution of the missing mint letter to a clogged working die, but then was the first to suggest that multiple dies were involved. He noted: "Firstly, two dies apparently struck no-D cents, and a formless, micro spot where the D tried to come up is sometimes seen on strikes from both no-D dies." He was almost right on the first part (there were actually at least four, from three different causes), but wrong in saying that a "micro spot" was sometimes seen on Die Pair #2.

Numismatic Scrapbook Magazine

PUBLISHED MONTHLY BY
HEWITT BROS., 7320 MILWAUKEE AVENUE, CHICAGO 48
SUBSCRIPTION $4.00 PER YEAR: CANADA $4.50: FOREIGN $4.50
SECOND CLASS POSTAGE PAID AT CHICAGO, ILLINOIS

VOL. XXVIII No. 11 NOVEMBER 1962 Whole No. 321

The 1922 No-D Cents

By A. D. CRAIG

(Rights reserved by author)

EACH YEAR millions of coin collectors spend $millions by the scores on everything from "gems" to freaks. While nothing mass produced is faultless, the public seldom notices rare American coinage mishaps. But misstrikes excite coin collectors because they're collectors—not because they mean to belittle our mint's work or its art. The wonder of collecting money oddities is no mere ignoble fad — consider all the commercially embossed, mounted, filigreed, engraved and bejewelled money novelties — and consider the fact that in medieval Japan, people prized misprinted coins as "lucky" pieces.

Today, thanks to our mints' devo- auctions; phony-rarity detections and decades national distribution negate 1922 no-D's as altered or counterfeit. This writer knows of three explanations for this mintage.

VIEW #1: "A Numismatography of the Lincoln Head Cent" by E. V. Wallace attributes the missing mint letter to a **clogged working die.** The mints use soap, cream-of-tartar and oil to remove grease, grime, lint and metal shavings from flans. Such stuff can and has filled nooks and crannies in coin dies; Wallace lists no less than 59 examples in 42 P, D, S cent mintages from 1913-51.(1)

In support of the clogged-dies theory for no-D cents, it is noted:

Beginning of Craig's first article on the 1922 "No D" Cents, from the Numismatic Scrapbook Magazine, Nov. 1962. Image courtesy Newman Numismatic Portal.

(Craig was a credible numismatist best known for his work on the coinage of Korea and the Far East, publishing the reference book *The Coins of Korea, and an Outline of Early Chinese Coinages* in 1955. He also published the journal *Far Eastern Numismatic Digest*, which began in January of 1957 and lasted for a few years. Born in 1930, he served in the Korean War, joined the ANA in 1953, served on the Newell Audio-Visual Education Committee [which prepared slide sets] and contributed to the first edition of the *ANA Grading Guide* [1977]. He died shortly before the turn of the Millennium.)

His second point merely mentioned the fact that obverse dies were typically the upper die in a press, where they were hard to see and a problem might be overlooked, followed by the more significant "Thirdly, other little vagaries happened to the 1922-D cents; poor D's, clashed-together and worn dies, die breaks, tilted coin faces" (and etc.) Note the reference to die clashes.

He then rightly dismissed Hauptman's 1939 "electrotype" and "Philadelphia Mint conspiracy" balderdash, and raised the very valid point that had a new obverse die been used under any scenario that had never had a mint mark punched into it, "…there should be some sharply struck D-less coins from new dies and there seemingly aren't. **(The same should go if the working dies involved were not at first given good D's or any D's at all.)**" (Emphasis his.) Scharlack is not mentioned by name, and only alluded to as "the late '1922 Cent King' of Corpus Christi" during a brief comment that no other hoard of 1922 cents was known but his (Scharlack's).

The article then goes on to describe the two varieties known to him at the time. His "First Die," which he called the "1922 Plain," is essentially the Die Pair #2 coin described below. However, he also states that "… in a late stage of this die, a corner of the D and more beard bristles come up." This is refuted today, so perhaps he was confusing a late die state of one of the DeLorey Die Pairs listed below, which he was not familiar with, with a late state Die Pair #2 coin. Some have reverse dies stronger than those seen on Die Pairs #1 & #3, which appear to have been the only other dies that he was familiar with.

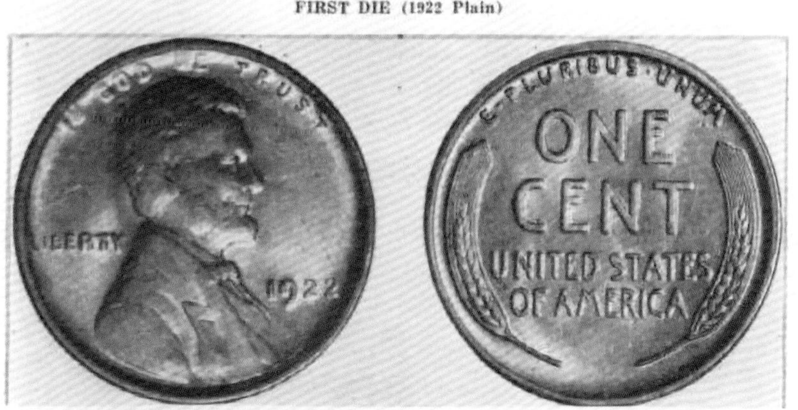
FIRST DIE (1922 Plain)

TRUST sharper than IN GOD WE; LIBERTY-L touching rim and I small; usual die break joining RT; little or no trace of V.D.B. Obverse die: fairly nice to weak strike. Reverse: sharp and weak. The first die is called "Plain" because most of its strikes are completely plain. However, in a late stage of this die, a corner of the D and more beard bristles came up. (Die cleaning?) (Heavier striking?)

SAY YOU SAW IT IN THE NUMISMATIC SCRAPBOOK MAGAZINE PAGE 3083

Craig's Illustration of his "FIRST DIE (1922 Plain)." (Modern DP#2.) Image courtesy Newman Numismatic Portal.

(It is also remotely possible that he was referring to the newly discovered DeLorey Die Pair #5 [see below], which has as its obverse an earlier die state of the die used for D.P. #2 but before the D was completely polished off the die. This is unlikely, as the LIBERTY on D.P. #5 is clearly in an earlier die state than the LIBERTY on D.P. #2, and D.P. #5 is only known paired with a well-worn (not strong) reverse die, but anything is possible when it comes to the cents of 1922.)

His "Second Die," which he called a "1922 No-D," is the Die Pair #1 described below. He finished with two pictures that give contradictory explanations for the term "Broken D." The first shows the Three Die Crack reverse below (DP #10, DeLorey-2210) and mentions that it has gone under the name of "1922 Broken D(ie)." The second shows what is probably a 1922-D "Weak D" (traditional terminology) Die Pair #8C coin with the caption "1922-D's with poor but actual D's are called 1922 'Broken D' cents." He also included a suggestion that it would be a good idea to interview Denver Mint employees who might have made the cents in 1922.

(*Scrapbook* received several letters from readers concerning Craig's article, and he answered four of them in the "Questions and Answers" section of the April 1963 issue. Nothing very important is contained therein, but one person's coin was declared by Craig to be a "removed-D," the first mention of such an alteration. As the 1922 "No D" coins became more and more popular, and valuable, this type of alteration became increasingly common. You can still find "removed D" 1922 cents in online auction venues today. I own one such coin erroneously slabbed as a "No D" coin by a major TPG.)

As a followup to the 1962 article, Craig published another in the July 1964 issue of *The Whitman Numismatic Journal*, based in part upon a series of conversations that he had had with retired Denver Mint workers during the 1963 ANA Convention held in Denver. This article ill-advisedly claimed that the plugged (i.e., grease-filled) die theory was exploded, and offered a new explanation for the "No D" and "Weak D" cents.

The workers were shown pictures of various defective 1922 cents. One worker commented: "The LIB and 22 on both coins are weak because the impression resulting from clashed dies needed to be rubbed out by abrasive implement." Another worker said "These were not plugged dies, but dies so heavily worn as to obliterate the D." He also said "Dies were used as long as any kind of imprint would come up -- only so many dies to use."

The article is imperfect because, contradicting his 1962 article, it also suggests that one obverse die may have been received from the Philadelphia Mint without a mint mark. At least one Mint worker seemed to confirm that

SECOND DIE (1922 No-D)

TRUST, GOD sometimes sharper than IN, WE; TRUST's first T sharp and jutting out, die break joining LIBERTY-RT, little or no trace of V.D.B. Obv. fairly nice to weak strike. (The prominence of such details runs with the state of die wear and circulation wear.)

Craig's Illustration of his "SECOND DIE (1922 No-D)." (Modern DP#1.) Image courtesy Newman Numismatic Portal.

Another 2-3 reverse die-cracks 1922-D variety has gone under the name of "1922 broken D(ie)." (E. V. Wallace Collection.)

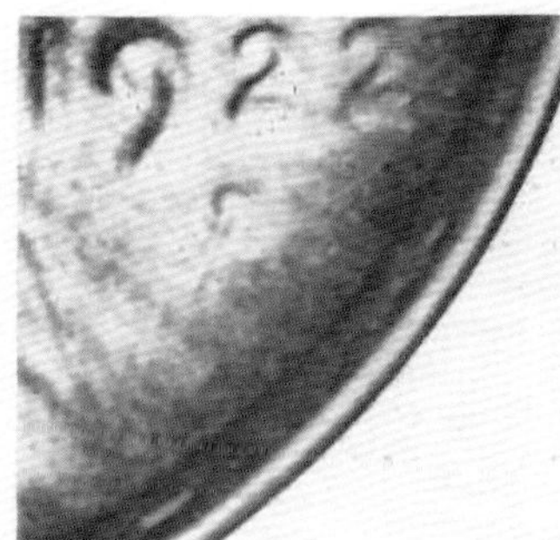

1922-D's with poor but actual D's are called 1922 "Broken D" cents.

So here it is, folks, glamourized by listing in ads, auctions, folders and books, legendary stories; by scarcity in any grade and rarity in

Craig's Illustrations of what I say are conflicting explanations for the term "Broken D." On the left is the reverse of DP#10 with die cracks irrelevant to the mint mark, and on the right is a bad picture of what is probably DP#8C. Image courtesy Newman Numismatic Portal.

this was so, but I wonder if Craig might have asked him a question in such a way as to lead the witness to that answer. To repeat what Craig said in 1962, there is no such thing as a 1922 "No D" coin from otherwise new and perfect dies.

The 1964 article also erred by saying that the plugged die theory was exploded in favor of the abraded die theory, and/or the possibility that a die had been received without a mint mark. The reality is that the plugged die theory (Die Pairs #1 and #3); AND the overpolished die theory (Die Pair #2); AND my new "the mint mark finally just wore off of the die" theory (Die Pair #4B, but only in the XXLDS obverse die state) are all three correct, but for several different dies. Only the "One Die Never Had a Mint Mark" theory is utterly false, as proven by the existence of DeLorey Die Pair #5, the obverse of which DID have a mint mark before the die was ground down again and used, without a mint mark, on Die Pair #2.

Nevertheless, it did explain that most if not all of the 1922-D obverse dies were badly overused, and that one or more of them may have been ground down to remove defects, such as (perhaps) clash marks, citing the 1937-D "Three-Legged Nickel" (which some of the Mint workers interviewed were allegedly familiar with from first-hand experience) as a similar example.

CHAPTER SIX

The Common Knowledge Challenged

Before I began working on what became this book, I had always presumed that all of the various defective 1922 "No D" and "Weak D" and "Weak Reverse" cents were coined in the last several days of February, 1922, before a telegram to the Superintendent of the Denver Mint dated March 3rd ordered the stoppage of the one cent coinage thusly: "Discontinue as promptly as possible coinage one cent pieces confining operations to silver dollars./ Baker/ Director." (Work on the Cents had actually stopped at the end of February because the Peace Dollar production had begun, but this made it official. It also prevented any potential striking of 1922-D nickels, for which the Denver Mint did have dies on hand, and for which that Mint had requested extra dies just a few days earlier.)

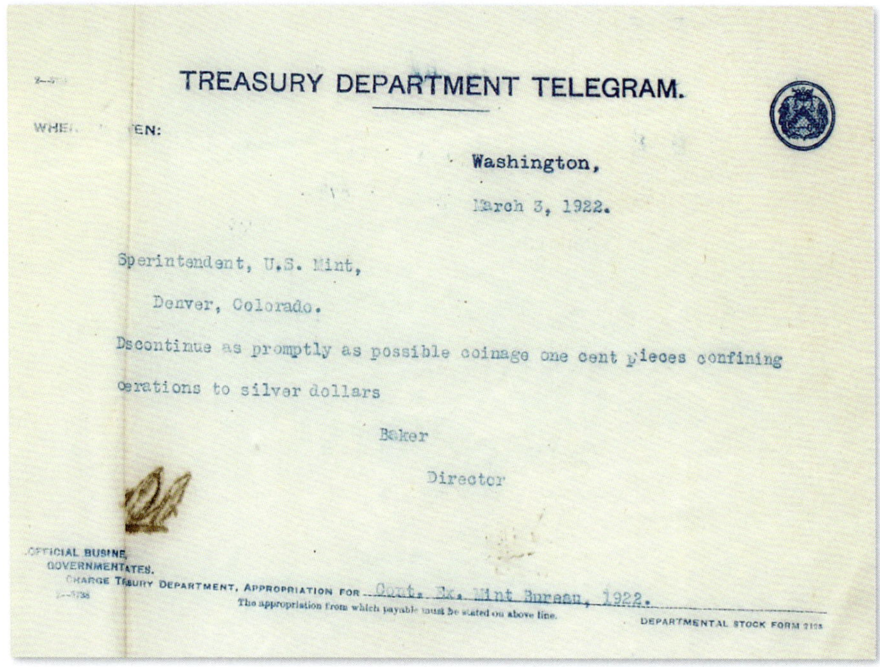

TREASURY DEPARTMENT TELEGRAM.

WHE... EN:

Washington,

March 3, 1922.

Sperintendent, U.S. Mint,

Denver, Colorado.

Dscontinue as promptly as possible coinage one cent pieces confining

oerations to silver dollars

Baker

Director

OFFICIAL BUSINE
GOVERNMENT...TES.
CHARGE TREASURY DEPARTMENT, APPROPRIATION FOR Cont. Ex. Mint Bureau, 1922.
The appropriation from which payable must be stated on above line.
DEPARTMENTAL STOCK FORM

March 3, 1922 telegram from the Mint Director to the Denver Superintendent: "Discontinue as promptly as possible coinage one cent pieces confining operations to silver dollars." U.S. Archives RG 104 E-235 Vol. 450 Denver, Courtesy Jeffrey Sam.

I was working in *Coin World's* Collectors Clearinghouse Department (one of the leading sources of error and die variety research) in the 1970s, and I believe that this assumption was fairly widespread in the hobby in that era. Walter Breen's 1988 *Encyclopedia*, which relied heavily upon Craig's 1964 article for the 1922 Cent listings, states this as gospel.

It was not unreasonable for us to assume that as the supply of decent obverse and reverse dies dwindled throughout the month of February, the Coiner and/or the Die Setter would have looked through all of the worn out and used up and retired cent dies sitting in the die vault and picked out the best ones that they had left of both sides to finish the production run with. They would then have proceeded to do whatever they had to do with files, brushes and polishing wheels to make a few of them fit for usage, artistic integrity be damned.

However, I now believe that the 1922-D cent coinage was struck during two somewhat separate (though overlapping) coinage periods, Tuesday, Jan. 3 to Monday, Jan. 23 (or so), and Jan. 23 (or so) to Tuesday, Feb. 28. Those "or so" qualifiers recognize the fact that some of the first batch obverse dies still in the presses when the second batch of obverse dies arrived were left there to continue striking coins until there was hardly anything left of them. Though eight of the first 10 1922-D obverses had been retired by Saturday, Jan. 21st, meaning that some of the presses had been sitting idle that week for lack of dies, the last two first batch obverses remained in use until Jan. 26th and 28th.

I suspect that the Die Pair #3 coins, with their badly eroded obverse and notoriously worn out "weak reverse," were coined, along with various other "mushy die" coins, before or just immediately after the second batch of obverse dies arrived on Jan. 23rd. Then, once the Die Setter no longer felt it was necessary to keep frugally using up the ten reverse dies hubbed in late September of 1920 while the first ten 1922-D obverse dies were being beaten to death, the last of the (inferior for reasons which will be explained below) late September 1920 reverses was condemned on Jan. 24th.

Why Were The 1922-D Cent Dies So Badly Overused?

Elsewhere in his 1964 article Craig discussed an examination he made of the Denver Mint's older records, graciously allowed to him during his extended visit to the city. (The current Denver Mint is not so gracious, completely ignoring my FOIA request to re-examine these records.) The records he examined included the Denver Mint's *Record of Coinage Dies* volume covering the years 1911-1925. Guided to it by Craig's reference to it, and with the invaluable help of Leonard Augsberger, I have studied the scanned copy of it in the Newman Numismatic Portal (NNP).

(Obviously a similar book had been put into use when the Denver Mint began striking only silver and gold coins in 1906. However, with the start of cent coinage in 1911, and perhaps in anticipation of the start of nickel coinage in 1912, this new book was started with ample room for dies of both denominations, plus certain other denominations but not Dollars, since they were not being struck in 1911.

Roger W. Burdette has seen archival notes dating from 1938 which make reference to three such Denver die books. As the records for Silver Dollar, Quarter Eagle and Half Eagle dies are missing from the NNP copy referenced above, it is possible that the Quarter Eagle and Half Eagle dies were simply continued in the missing Book One, while the Silver Dollar and certain of the nickel and half dollar pages are in the missing Book Three. If anybody can ever achieve access to either of these die books, or any of the Philadelphia, Denver or San Francisco Mint die books for any years, be sure to make copies of them for both Burdette and the NNP.)

An examination of the existing die book shows that near the end of each calendar year it was customary for the Philadelphia Mint's die shop to ship

U. S. MINT SERVICE.
Form No. 864.
10 x 14.

RECORD OF
Calendar Yea[r]

Denomination: One Cent

DATE.	Obverse: Number of Obverse Dies.	Die Number.	Number of Pieces Struck.	Condemned. Date.	Reverse: Number of Reverse Dies.	Die Number.		Number of Pieces Struck.
1922					1922			
Jan 3		11	300000	1-10	Jan 3	786	1920 Dies Retained	250000
		12	350,000	-11		787		260,000
		13	360,000	-12		788		270,000
		14	400,000	-13		789		250,000
		15	400,000	-14		790		250,000
		16	350,000	-16		791		230,000
		17	300,000	-19		792		300,000
		18	350,000	-21		793		300,000
		19	340,000	-26		794		250,000
		20	360,000	-28		795		250,000
23		21	514,159 (4,034,159)	-31		11	1921 Dies Retained	260,000
		22	300.000	2-6		12		270,000
		23	300,000	-9		13		260,000
		24	400,000	-11		14		240,000
		25	400,000	-15		15		260,000
		26	300,000	-18		16		124,159 (4,034,159)
		27	400,000	-24		17		300,000
		28	300,000	-24		18		300,000

INAGE DIES.

22

nomination: One Cent

verse | Reverse

Die Number.	Number of Pieces Struck.	Condemned. Date.	Number of Reverse 1922	Die Number.	Number of Pieces Struck.	Condemned. Date.
29	300000	2-27	Jan 3	19	200000	2-9
30	512,508 7,236,667			20	200000	-11
				21	300,000	-15
				22	300,000	-17
				23	300,000	-20
				24	300,000	-24
				25	300,000	-25
				26	300,000	-27
				27	412,508 7,236,667	-28
				28		
				29		
				30		

1921 Dies Retained

One Cent 1922.

	Obverse	Reverse.
tal Pieces	7236667	7236667
es Used	20	27
rage Pieces	361833	268025

The 1922 Cents Page from the Denver Mint's "Record of Coinage Dies" for the years 1911-1925. A wonderful source of information, some of it even true. Note the reverse dies retained from previous years, a normal practice. The numbers of coins struck per die are, unfortunately, mere guesses. Image courtesy the scan of the book in the Newman Numismatic Portal.

Denver (and San Francisco as well as confirmed by other sources) a small number of dated obverse dies for every denomination from cent through half dollar that might possibly be struck in the new calendar year, and if necessary undated reverse dies for inventory. This was typically done in December, though occasionally the package arrived after New Year's Day.

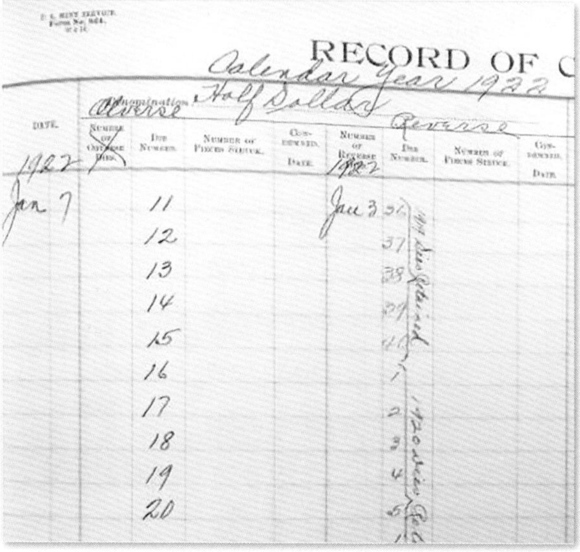

Except from Denver Mint Die Register showing 1922-D Half Dollar Obverse Contingency dies numbered 11-20, the same number run as the 1922-D One Cent Obverse Contingency dies. Image courtesy Newman Numismatic Portal.

The larger gold coin dies were apparently only shipped if actual gold coinage was anticipated, but this did include obverse and reverse dies for 1917-D Eagles and Double Eagles that never happened. The un-mintmarked Double Eagle reverse dies received in 1917 were eventually used for the 1923-D coinage. The mintmarked 1917-D Eagle reverse dies were still being "Retained" when the ledger was replaced in 1925. Never used, they might not have been destroyed until 1933 or 1934.

I call these dated early bird dies "Contingency Dies," as it was cheaper in the long run for each of the Mints to have potentially unnecessary obverse dies of the new year on hand on January 2nd (or 3rd) just in case they *were* needed. The alternative was to run the risk of having no dies on hand for several days while working men stood around getting paid for doing nothing, if one or more Mints' production plans suddenly changed, as did indeed happen in 1922.

In most normal years the majority of these dated obverse contingency dies would end up getting used sooner or later. If they were not, oh well.

(Non-gold dies were typically shipped in sequentially-numbered batches of ten or multiples of ten, though multiples of five or a dozen did sometimes occur. The dies for each side of each denomination were numbered from 1 to whatever within each year regardless of which mint they ended up at, with dated obverse dies being destroyed at the end of a calendar year and undated reverse dies being "retained" for use at the start of the next year that that same design was coined.)

Dan Owens has uncovered in the S.F. Mint's correspondence file a carbon copy of a note, dated Dec. 27, 1921, acknowledging receipt of ten each 1922-dated Half Dollar, Quarter Dollar, Dime, Five Cents and One Cent Obverse dies, all numbered 1-10. The assignment of early numbered dies to a particular Mint in any particular year seems to have followed a pattern. For cents in the 1912-1924 period, Denver typically started out with both obverse and reverse dies numbered 21 to 30 or 35 or 40, though in slow years it might only get numbers 11-20. I would assume this to mean that in such a slow year San Francisco routinely got numbers 1-10, with Philadelphia routinely getting numbers 21-30.

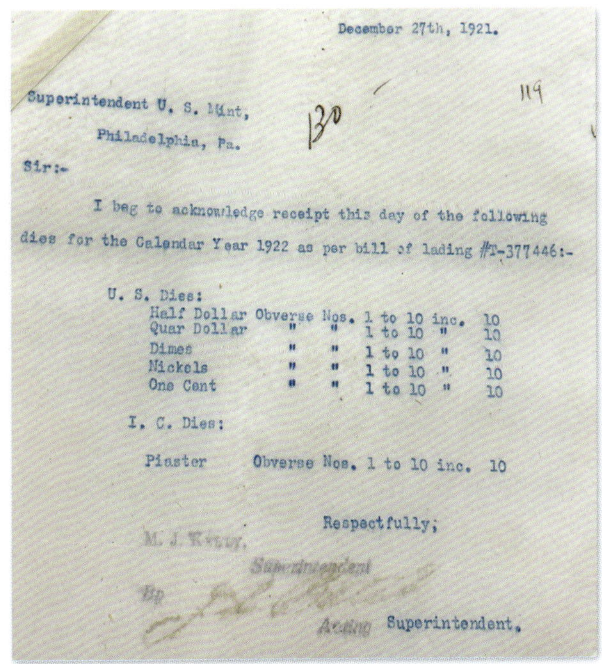

December 27th, 1921.

Superintendent U. S. Mint,
Philadelphia, Pa.

130 119

Sir:-

I beg to acknowledge receipt this day of the following dies for the Calendar Year 1922 as per bill of lading #T-377446:-

U. S. Dies:

Half Dollar	Obverse Nos.	1 to 10 inc.	10
Quar Dollar	" "	1 to 10 "	10
Dimes	" "	1 to 10 "	10
Nickels	" "	1 to 10 "	10
One Cent	" "	1 to 10 "	10

I. C. Dies:

Piaster	Obverse Nos.	1 to 10 inc.	10

Respectfully;

M. J. [illegible],
Superintendent
By
Acting Superintendent.

S.F. Mint letter to Philadelphia Mint dated Dec. 27, 1921 acknowledging receipt of many 1922 dies numbered 1-10. Note that this included Indo China (One) Piaster Obverse dies, which fortuitously gave S.F. something it could strike to keep busy while the new Peace Dollar dies were being worked on. From the U.S. Archives courtesy Dan Owens.

Because dies had to be shipped via rail, it would be logical in normal years to ship San Francisco (which had the longest travel time from Philadelphia, besides being senior to Denver) the first batch of dies finished and numbered 1 to whatever. As more dies were produced over the next few days, Denver would be sent the second batch starting at whatever +1, with Philadelphia retaining the third batch for itself, numbered sequentially after Denver's, simply because their dies required no travel time.

To support this theory, I refer you to the 1920 Mint Report, which mentions that the San Francisco Mint was undergoing significant internal renovations during the Fiscal Year which ended June 30, 1920, which of course included the first half of calendar year 1920. With San Francisco thus temporarily out of action during the rollout of the 1920 dies, the Denver Mint received cent obverses 1-20 and cent reverses 1-10 on Dec. 16, 1919, a unique happening during the years covered by this Denver die register. (It likewise received dime and quarter obverses and reverses starting at #1.) Denver still had a number of cent reverses retained from 1919, which per custom were used up before the newer cent reverses were put into use a few weeks into the year. Its second batch of cent reverse dies received in 1920 was numbered 151-190.

RECORD OF COINAGE DIES.

Calendar Year 1920

Date	Number of Obverse Dies (Denomination One Cent, Obverse Dies)	Die Number	Number of Pieces Struck	Condemned Date	Number of Reverse Dies (Reverse Dies)	Die Number	Number of Pieces Struck	Condemned Date	Number of Obverse Dies (Denomination One Cent, Obverse Dies)	Die Number	Number of Pieces Struck	Condemned Date
1919 Dec 16		1	500000	1-5		1444	500000	1-5	1919 12-16	19	500000	1-27
		2	500000	5		1445	500000	1-5		20	500000	28
		3	400000	10		1446	400000	13	1920 1-24	161	600000	28
		4	600000	7		1447	600000	7		162	400000	29
		5	600000	13		1448	600000	13		163	400000	29
		6	500000	13		1449	500000	13		164	400000	30
		7	500000	15		1450	500000	15		165	850938	30
		8	500000	15		1451	500000	15		166	400000	2-5
		9	600000	17		1452	600000	17		167	300000	5
		10	400000	17		1453	400000	17		168	400000	7
		11	600000	20		1454	600000	20		169	300000	9
		12	600000	20		1455	200000	20		170	500000	9
		13	500000	21		1456	500000	21	1-26	171	600000	13

The Denver Mint Die Register's first page for 1920-D Cents showing that in that particular year, when the San Francisco Mint was closed for an upgrade, Denver got Obv. dies #1-20. To me this is proof that the lowest numbered Contingency dies were sent to the Western Mints each year before Philadelphia kept some for itself. Image courtesy Newman Numismatic Portal.

By coincidence, on Dec. 27, 1921, the Superintendent of the Denver Mint sent the Director of the Mint a telegram asking "Have dies for new year been forwarded?" He was probably only concerned about dollar dies, since Denver was still striking that denomination, and he expected to strike nothing else in 1922. As we now know the Philadelphia Mint was frantically getting ready to begin strike Peace Dollars on the 28th.

However, he might have been prudently inquiring about the 1922 Contingency Dies. An examination of the Denver Mint's railway freight charges shows that it paid for a box of unspecified 1922 coinage dies shipped from Philadelphia on Dec. 28, 1921. A separate box of half dollar dies was shipped on Jan. 3rd. (Monday, Jan. 2, 1922 was the observed holiday for New Year's Day.)

A box of 10 Peace Dollar dies (presumably five slightly modified High Relief obverses and five normal High Relief reverses of the type of 1921) was shipped on Jan. 6, but returned to Philadelphia on Jan. 12, no doubt because of the unresolved design relief problems. Another box of 10 1922-D obverse cent dies was shipped on Jan. 19.

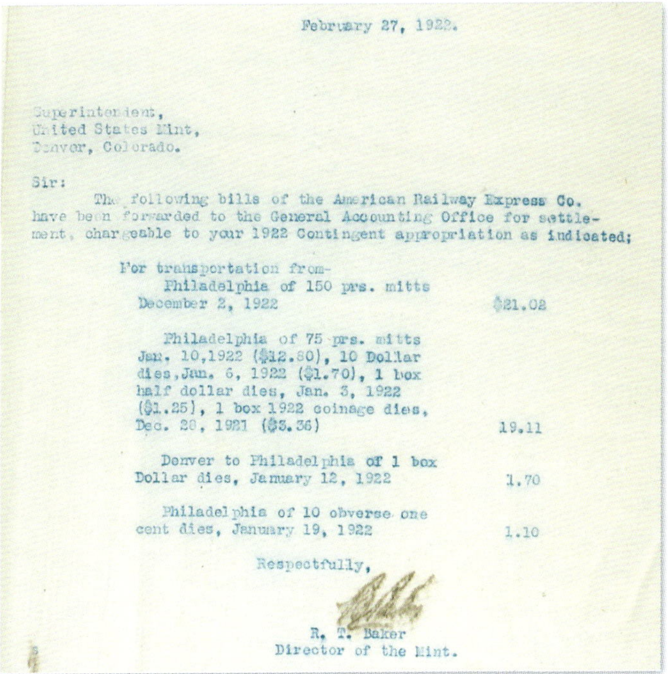

February 27, 1922.

Superintendent,
United States Mint,
Denver, Colorado.

Sir:

The following bills of the American Railway Express Co. have been forwarded to the General Accounting Office for settlement, chargeable to your 1922 Contingent appropriation as indicated;

For transportation from-
Philadelphia of 150 prs. mitts December 2, 1922 — $21.02

Philadelphia of 75 prs. mitts Jan. 10,1922 ($12.80), 10 Dollar dies, Jan. 6, 1922 ($1.70), 1 box half dollar dies, Jan. 3, 1922 ($1.25), 1 box 1922 coinage dies, Dec. 28, 1921 ($3.36) — 19.11

Denver to Philadelphia of 1 box Dollar dies, January 12, 1922 — 1.70

Philadelphia of 10 obverse one cent dies, January 19, 1922 — 1.10

Respectfully,

R. T. Baker
Director of the Mint.

Feb. 27, 1922 Letter from Mint Director to Denver Superintendent detailing Denver Mint's railway shipping charges, including for cent dies shipped Jan. 19, 1922, for the period of Dec. 1921 through Jan. 1922. From the National Archives, RG 104, E-235, Vol. 450 Denver, courtesy of Jeffrey Sam.

The die book shows that 10 1922-D cent obverse dies were received on Jan. 3, 1922. They were numbered by the Philadelphia Mint's die shop for inventory purposes as obverse dies number 11-20, and recorded in the Denver Mint's die register as such. The ten 1922-dated dime and quarter obverses also received on Jan. 3, as well as the 10 1922-dated half dollar obverses received on Jan. 7, were likewise each numbered 11-20. (Alas, the records for the Buffalo Nickel dies after 1917 and the half dollar dies before 1922 are not in this book, or they simply were not scanned.)

I presume that the Philadelphia Mint likewise made contingency obverse dies for itself for 1922, even though the die shop was in house. After all, it takes time to partially hub, anneal, re-hub and harden each working die, and the point of contingency dies was that might be needed upon a moment's notice. If San Francisco and Denver each got ten hardened 1922-dated obverse dies even though absolutely no cent coinage was planned for 1922, then it is almost a certainty that Philadelphia made ten hardened 1922-dated obverse dies, without mint marks, for itself as well. This will become extremely important later.

DIES MANUFACTURED.

For—	Unused.	Issued to mint at— Philadelphia.	San Francisco.	Denver.	Manila, P. I.	Total prepared.
Domestic:						
Regular gold coinage	20	210	120			350
Regular silver coinage	280	835	280	270		1,665
Regular minor coinage	210	20	20	30		280
Memorial—						
Grant gold dollars and silver half dollars		50				50
Pilgrim half dollars		20				20
Missouri half dollars	15	20				35
Alabama half dollars	3	15				18
Philippine coinage	50				144	194
Venezuela coinage	13	161				174
Colombia coinage	20	100				120
Costa Rica coinage		20				20
Indo-China coinage			55			55
Cuba coinage	70					70
Salvador coinage	7					7
Peru coinage	10					10
Total coinage working dies	698	1,451	475	300	144	3,068
Master dies and hubs manufactured for:						

Table from the 1922 Mint Report showing the dies manufactured in FY 1922. Philadelphia and San Francisco each received 20 minor coinage dies, logically 10 One cent obverses and 10 Five Cents obverses, while Denver received 30, logically 20 One Cent obverses and 10 Five Cents obverses. The Philadelphia One Cent obverses were logically numbered #21-30, and yet Denver received One Cent obverses numbered #21-30 on January 23, 1922. To me this is proof that the 1922 Philadelphia One Cent obverses were altered by adding mint marks to them and then being sent to Denver. Image courtesy Newman Numismatic Portal.

Burdette's research into the Denver Mint's incomplete correspondence records produced a file copy of a telegram from the Superintendent to the Director's office (originally dated January 4th, but crossed out and re-dated the 5th), requesting "Please forward ten obverse one cent dies as soon as convenient," eventually followed by a January 18th telegram asking "Have dollar dies been shipped? If not please forward ten obverse one cent dies ordered fifth instant as soon as possible." These ten obverses were shipped on the 19th and received on the 23rd. They were numbered in the Denver die register as obverse dies 21-30.

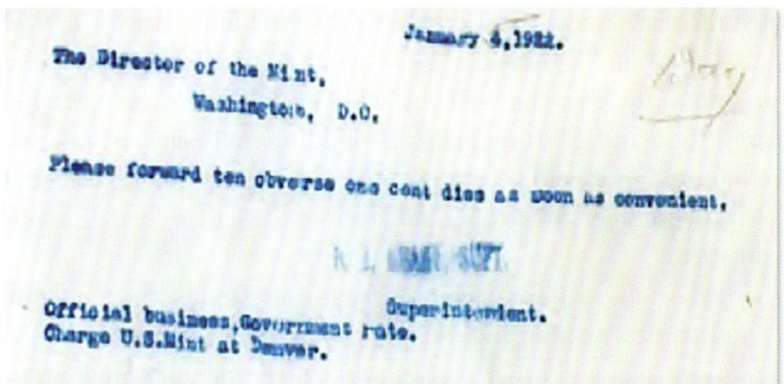

January 4,1922.

The Director of the Mint,
Washington, D.C.

Please forward ten obverse one cent dies as soon as convenient.

Superintendent.

Official business,Government rate.
Charge U.S.Mint at Denver.

Sender's copy of telegram from Denver Superintendent to Mint Director, originally dated Jan. 4, 1922 but pencil corrected to Jan. 5, stating: "Please forward ten obverse one cent dies as soon as convenient." Marked to send at day rate rather than usual cheaper night rate, presumably because of the urgency of the need for extra dies. From the National Archives, RG 104 Denver E-23 Box 5b, courtesy of Roger W. Burdette.

NIGHT LETTERGRAM

January 18,1922.

Superintendent, U.S.Mint,
Philadelphia, Pa.

Have dollar dies been shipped? If not please forward ten obverse one cent dies ordered fifth instant as soon as possible.

Grant
Superintendent.

Official business,Government rate.
Charge U.S.Mint at Denver.

Sender's copy of Jan. 18, 1922 Night Lettergram from Denver Superintendent Grant to the Superintendent of the Philadelphia Mint asking "Have dollar dies been shipped? If not please forward ten obverse one cent dies ordered fifth instant as soon as possible." From the National Archives, RG 104 Denver E-23 Box 5b, courtesy of Roger W. Burdette.

23	21	514,159	-31
	22	300,000	2-6
	23	300,000	-9
	24	400,000	-11
	25	400,000	-15
	26	300,000	-18
	27	400,000	-24
	28	300,000	-24

Except from Denver Mint Die Register showing 1922-D Cent obverse dies #21-30 rec'd Jan. 23. Image courtesy Newman Numismatic Portal.

Because of the severely limited 1921 production of coins smaller than one dollar, there were plenty of retained reverses for most of these denominations. For the Denver cents of 1922, these included ten reverse dies hubbed and/or shipped in late September of 1920 and received on 10-2-1920 and numbered 786-795 in the 1920-D coinage die section, and 20 reverse dies received on 12-17-1920 and numbered 11-30 in the 1921-D coinage die section. That coinage never happened, and the dies were "retained" into 1922. (See notes in Record of Coinage Dies image.)

The cent die ledger lists an alleged "number of pieces struck" for each of the 20 obverse and 27 reverse dies actually used in 1922, as well as the date that each die was condemned by the Die Setter, but most of the numbers struck are very rounded off and obviously estimates. (Before 1915 the entries were precise to the coin, but starting in 1915 they began being rounded to the nearest thousand. Starting in 1917 rounding to the nearest ten thousand or even hundred thousand became common. Craig did not appear to understand that the numbers struck per die given in the ledger for 1922 were only approximates.)

Only the last die used for each month, as indicated by the condemnation dates, shows a precise (but highly suspect) number of gross strikes (which includes mis-strikes and other pieces later culled out and remelted) for that die, with the total number of gross strikes for the month (Jan. or Feb.) penciled in below that. The ledger page ends with a note added later that the total number of gross strikes for the year was 7,236,667, for an average of 361,833 strikes per obverse die and 268,025 per reverse die.

(Averages are deceptive. At least one of the obverses is known to have failed spectacularly, as indicated by the large die cud at TRUST illustrated below as DP #14, DeLorey-2214 and Die Crack variety DC-6. The presence of the V.D.B. on Lincoln's shoulder and overall sharp detailing indicates that it failed in an early die state, and so every other die had to strike all the more coins to attain these averages.)

No internal Mint records survive to tell us what happened during this two-month production run, but we can speculate. The Denver Mint's Superintendent was under orders to find something for the working men to do. He couldn't strike gold, because he had no refined gold to work with. He had silver, but he couldn't strike dollars because he had no dies, and he did not know how long it would be before the revised dollar dies would be ready. At best he could keep the melting, rolling, blanking, upsetting and annealing departments busy preparing dollar planchets, to be struck when the dies for them eventually arrived.

That left the coining and counting departments, which could either strike and bag cents or go polish the Mint's brass doorknobs and spittoons. There were (apparently) millions of cent planchets on hand, perhaps made for the 1921-D coinage that never happened, but only the ten 1922-D contingency obverse dies sent just in case of unforeseen problems such as this. I can just hear the Superintendent telling the Coiner: "Make 'em last!"

To illustrate how long cent dies normally lasted, the 1918 Mint Report lists the average strikes per die for all coins for CY1917. For the 1917-D cents, there were 442,190 gross strikes for each of 127 Obverse dies, and 387,297 gross strikes for each of 145 Reverse dies. Lange's Lincoln cent book makes the following comment about the 1917-D issue: "...most D-Mint cents of this date were coined from overused working dies which ranged in condition from obviously tired to absolutely terminal. In short, 1917-D cents are mushy, with blurred date, mintmark and mottos being the rule. The wheat stems are frequently merged with the reverse border."

In other words, just like the 1922-D coinage, the difference being that Philadelphia did not strike cents in 1922, and the existence of 1922 Denver cents without mint marks created something collectible. If there are 1917-D "No D" cents out there, we will never know, and probably never care.

(The 1917 die usage figures also confirm that Denver tended to use more reverse dies than obverse dies, just as Denver used 20 obverse and 27 reverse dies in 1922. The main difference is that with such a smaller total number of dies, the early failure of just a few of the 1922 dies would have resulted in the remaining dies having had to produce a substantially higher number of strikes per die to produce the averages indicated above.)

In 1918, a busy year because of the War but one in which the Denver Mint knew it could get all the cent dies that it would need, Denver's Die Setter retired six obverse dies and eight reverses by January 5th, a Sunday. (Because of the die usage patterns I suspect that Denver had six presses striking cents in 1918, but I cannot prove this. This may or may not have been the number of presses striking cents in 1922.) The last of the first 20 1918-D contingency obverses was retired on Jan. 16th, along with the first die from the second batch of obverses, which had been received and presumably put into use on Jan. 12th. Also by the 16th 24 reverse dies had been retired.

The first 1922-D obverse die was not retired until Jan. 10th, and the sixth obverse not until the 16th. During this same time period nine reverse dies were retired. Because of this deliberately flagrant overuse, the condition of the first ten 1922-D obverse dies must have deteriorated well below normal quality standards long before the second batch of obverse dies was received on Jan. 23rd. I believe that the coins struck from the most worn obverse dies, such as Die Pair #3, were struck during these first three weeks of January, along with most of the other overly worn obverse and reverse die strikes.

As mentioned above, virtually every cent die used in 1922 struck a massive number of coins. The numbers listed are averages, which invariably means that some dies must have struck even more coins to make up for any die which failed utterly and had to be discarded, such as the obverse cud die

Normal 1920-D cent from new dies. Courtesy Bob Campbell.

1920-D Cent from well worn dies showing die wear patterns very similar to many 1922-D cents. Courtesy Hurst Barbee.

previously mentioned. Besides Die Pair #3 there are other 1922-D cents known that show horribly excessive die wear, such as the obverse of Die Pair #4B in its late die states, but in many cases it is not in the mint mark area where everybody cares about it.

(I doubt that any 1922-D cents were rejected due to poor die quality. According to the "Percentage of Good Coin Produced to Pieces Struck" chart in the 1922 Mint Report, 7,236,667 gross strikes were made in 1922, of which 98.94% were accepted as good coins. This corresponds to the 7,160,000 coins delivered to the Cashier, 4,000,000 in January and another 3,160,000 in February, during which month the deluge of silver dollars began anew.

The actual number of spendable coins may have been a little bit higher, since the Mints liked to deliver coins in round number batches and play games with the odd lot leftovers that could not fill up a solid bag. Any left-overs might have been remelted, or they may have just been quietly mingled in with the 1924-D coinage. See my article in the July, 2019 issue of *The Numismatist* about the non-existent 1873-S Seated Liberty Dollars, which were presumably leftover 1872-S coins delivered in 1873.)

These dies received heavy use out of necessity, but the Coining Department may have had some good reason to expect them to hold up to that use. The Denver Mint's Record of One Cent Coinage Dies for 1920 had shown amazing die durability in the earliest part of that year, with pieces struck per die often hitting (in rounded numbers) 500,000 or 600,000 coins per die, and one stalwart obverse being credited with 850,000 strikes!

However, something drastic may indeed have then happened to the quality of the die steel used for cents throughout the rest of 1920. I would speculate that a very bad batch of die steel was received from the Mint's supplier, though I suppose that we must allow for the remote possibility that the people at the Philadelphia Mint's die shop responsible for competently hardening dies either died or retired.

(As yet another possible consideration, the 1920 Mint Report mentions the very heavy demand upon the die shop for dies for military decorations and other items related to World War One. Though the actual stamping of the decorations was typically done by private mints, the U.S. Mint had to make the dies for them. This *could* have affected the processing of coinage dies.)

According to the Denver die register, reports of cent strikes per die in the 140,000 to 160,000 range were common for the rest of 1920, with a few as low as 120,000. The last obverse used in 1920 only struck just over 110,000 coins, but that may have been just because it was still in the press when production ceased for other, ordinary reasons.

The last ten obverses used in that year averaged just under 178,000 strikes per die. Because of those exceptional early dies, the obverse average for the year was deceptively higher, at just under 272,000 strikes per die. Using the first average (178,000), the 20 obverses used in 1922 should have produced just under 3,560,000 coins. Using the second average (272,000), the 20 obverses should have produced just under 5,440,000 coins. They produced over 7,200,000 coins.

The last ten reverse dies used in Denver in 1920, #776-785, did somewhat better with an average of just under 245,000 strikes per die, compared to the annual average of over 273,000 strikes per reverse die. The Denver Mint began its 1922-D cent production with the remainder of this same die batch, reverse dies #786-795, which had been hubbed in the Fall of the problem year of 1920. It then continued with 1921 contingency reverse dies #11-30, which were received on December 17, 1920 for the 1921-D coinage that never happened. It did not receive any reverse dies during calendar years 1921 or 1922.

During the 1922-D cent production run both the obverse and the reverse dies fared little better than they had in the second part of 1920. They wore down quickly, several reverse dies cracked, and both design details and lettering became badly deformed. At least one obverse die formed a RAISED vertical ripple or wave ABOVE the original surface of the die in front of Lincoln's face, caused by the sideways displacement of die metal under repeated hammer blows. This raised wave on the die left a corresponding depression, or trough, on the coins struck from that die. I suspect that this represents Scharlack's "dented obverse" variety. See DP #8C for the best example of this "dent."

Several other dies developed tiny blobs of RAISED metal around the D mint mark, some larger and more significant than others, perhaps a result of the die steel in that area being weakened when it was resoftened and then rearranged by the mint mark punch. I call the tiny depressions left on the coins by these raised blobs on the dies "Dimples." The two most interesting examples are listed as Die Pairs #8 & #9 below. There are several other dies that show minor dimples which are not included here.

These various raised blobs on the dies slowly deformed and/or grew through die erosion, and sometimes lengthened into relatively straight or relatively curved raised lines, which left corresponding depressed lines on the coins struck from them. I am assuming that sometimes these

A 1922-D Cent struck from distorted obverse die that had a raised ridge on it in front of Lincoln's face, which in turn left a depressed "gutter" in the coins struck from it. This is probably Scharlack's "Dented Obverse" variety. Courtesy Stack's Bowers Galleries auction archives.

deformations became so noticeable on the coins coming off of the presses that the dies were removed from their presses and ground down in the mint mark areas, removing the raised blobs from the dies and also some of the field that defined the mint marks.

One obverse die (used for #4A&B) developed a series of scallop-shaped "dimples" along the rim below the word LIBERTY, which were eventually removed from the die by a die polishing tool of some sort that left the field slightly beveled in that area. Other obverse and reverse dies that developed severe die erosion near their rim were treated the same way, in at least one case removing the tops of some of the letters in E PLURIBUS UNUM.

A different obverse die (my #5 in this die state, always found with a Weak Reverse) was ground down until the mint mark became thin and of reduced height above the field (what I am calling a "Faint D"), presumably to remove dimples from the mint mark area. I have proven through die erosion characteristics that it was then ground down so deeply that the die steel which defined the D was completely removed from the die. Paired with a different, new reverse die, this is "No D" ANACS Die Pair #2 below.

I have not been able to determine why that last grinding took place, but the latest die state known of the obverse of Die Pair #5 shows no clash marks such as have long been speculated to be the cause of Die Pair #2. Perhaps the reverse die of Die Pair #5 needed to be replaced, and while they were doing that they gave the obverse die another lick!

Two other obverses and two other reverses became notoriously "mushy," with the mint marks on the obverses so weak that they were occasionally obscured by the grease commonly seen on coining presses. These "Weak Reverse" coins will be described as Die Pairs #1 & #3 below. Other mushy obverse dies became various of the "DeLorey Varieties."

It is highly likely that various of the obverse dies were taken out of their respective coining presses and temporarily moved to a workbench for repairs. It is reliably reported that this was done to the 1937-D Buffalo Nickel reverse die that became the "Three-Legged Variety."

While the various obverse and reverse dies were out of the presses, the presses might have sat idle waiting for their return, or different obverse and reverse dies might have been installed in the presses and production resumed for a short while or a long one. See the triple die marriages of Die Pair #8. This might have depended upon the availability of alternative usable dies at that exact moment. The important thing is that such shuffling of dies may have resulted in other die matings not reported here. The author would love to hear of them.

I have discovered that the obverse die used in a famously late die state to strike Die Pair #1 coins both with and without a mint mark, either variety being best known for its "jogging die crack" through the O of ONE on the reverse, had been re-installed in a coin press that already had that used and cracked reverse die in it. That reverse die had previously been paired, both before and after it cracked, with a different obverse die that has often been confused, in its later die states, with Obverse #1 due to the common reverse. This new "Worn D" to "Very Faint D" (depending on die state) obverse die will be listed below in the "DeLorey Varieties" as Die Pair #ZeroB.

To recap the above, the first ten 1922-D one cent obverse contingency dies were received on Jan. 3rd, and the Denver Mint telegrammed the Director of the Mint's Office on the 5th asking for ten more. None were included with the half dollar dies received on Jan. 7th, which were already *en route* when the request was made, or with the dollar dies shipped on Jan. 6th.

That Jan. 6 package could have included additional 1922-D cent obverse dies if any more had existed on that date, and if Philadelphia knew that Denver needed more cent obverse dies. (As a rule all correspondence between two Mints had to go through the Director's Office in Washington, D.C. and be relayed, so it is possible that the Dollar dies were shipped before Philadelphia knew that Denver needed more cent dies.) Nevertheless, the fact that none were included in the Jan. 6 package, or sent by themselves in a separate package in the next few days, (as had been done with the half dollar dies,) strongly suggests that no such additional 1922 D-Mint cent dies existed on that date or immediately thereafter. This gets very important in a minute.

There are no further notes in the correspondence files until Jan. 18, when Denver telegrammed the Director's Office asking if the new dollar dies were on their way yet, and oh, by the way, if the dollar dies are not coming, could you please (emphasis mine) send the ten one cent obverses requested on Jan. 5! Those obverse dies, numbered 21-30, were shipped on Jan. 19th and received on Jan. 23rd.

(The Director's Office had to approve everything that the Denver Mint did. The Denver correspondence file shows copies of three letters to Washington requesting permission to spend less than $40 to fix a leaky roof, and three letters requesting permission to replace a typewriter with a different one with a wider carriage to be used to fill out forms.)

So, for 20 days the Denver Mint's Coiner had to assume that he had exactly 10 obverse dies to miraculously strike seven million plus planchets with, with no guarantee that he would ever receive more obverses. He must have rode those obverses hard, while keeping the inferior reverses retained from October of 1920 in the presses as long as possible as well. He knew that if he ever *did* receive more 1922-D obverses, he would need most if not all of those 1921-intended reverses to go with them, and so he and/or the Die Setter held their noses and allowed the absolutely horrible Die Pair #3 coins to be struck, along with various other well-worn die coins.

Once the ten extra obverse dies were in hand, the Coiner and/or the Die Setter could have begun using those dies plus the reserve supply of reverse dies originally made for the 1921 coinage. The Die Pair #2 coins, struck from decidedly NOT-mushy dies, were probably struck during the second coining period, after something (I strongly believe dimpling; see below) caused the area below the date to be ground down to the point that the mint mark completely disappeared forever. After these "repairs" to the obverse die were completed, a new (or possibly nearly-new) reverse die was available to use with it.

The Die Pair #4B coins, also struck with one of the better reverse dies to begin with, could have been struck near the end of February, as the supply of new obverse dies ran out for a second time and once again the Mint was forced to overuse an obverse die. I suspect, but cannot prove, that this was the obverse die number 30 which both Craig and Breen speculated was the obverse of Die Pair #2. Alas, we shall never know for sure.

What we do know for sure is that the Denver Mint had three unused reverse dies on hand at the end of 1922, which were retained until 1924 before finally being used. With these unused dies available to use in February, there would have been absolutely no reason to use the ghastly "Weak Reverse" dies late in that month. To me, this is very strong evidence that Die Pair #3 coins, and many other horribly weak reverse coins, were struck in January.

CHAPTER SEVEN

A Shocking New Theory on Why So Many 1922-D Cent Dies Failed

When the cent through half dollar contingency dies were made for all three Mints for 1922, there was zero expectation that any of them would be used. The Treasury Department had very definite plans to strike nothing but Silver Dollars and Double Eagles in 1922, not counting of course commemorative coins. We know that San Francisco got cent obverse contingency dies numbered 1-10. We know that Denver got cent obverse contingency dies numbered 11-20. Therefore, it is extremely probable that cent obverse contingency dies numbered 21-30 were prepared for use in Philadelphia, without mint marks!

However, on Jan. 23rd, the Denver Mint, after having asked (politely) for the second time in the month for more obverse dies, received ten one cent obverse dies numbered 21-30, with D mint marks! There are only two possible explanations for this. The first, and highly implausible, explanation is that the Philadelphia Mint's die shop had made **twenty** 1922-D obverse contingency dies numbered #11-30 in December of 1921, with no plans to see any of them used, but for some inexplicable reason refused to ship the second 10 D-mint obverses until Jan. 19th. We know that no cent obverse or reverse dies were shipped to Denver between the 5th and the 18th, even though a box of dollar dies that they might have gone into was shipped on Friday, Jan. 6th.

The second, and much more plausible, explanation is that the Philadelphia Mint's die shop simply ignored the Jan. 5th request for it to make more 1922-D cent obverse dies for as long as possible, in the not unreasonable expectation that that first batch of 1922-D Peace Dollar dies shipped on Jan. 6th (presumably five obverses and five reverses) would render the need for more cent dies moot. Under this scenario, while that box was in transit nothing would have been done about the request for cent dies. However, on Tuesday, Jan. 10, Acting Director O'Reilly ordered a halt to the work on the first version of the 1922 dollar coin dies. (See Burdette.) That first box of dollar dies was shipped back to Philadelphia on Thursday, Jan. 12th.

If those additional 1922-D cent obverse dies numbered #21-30 had already existed on January 10th, this would have been an absolutely splendid time to rush them off to Denver in a box all by themselves. However, nothing happened with cent obverse dies for another nine days! Therefore, I don't think that any unused D-Mint dies, numbered #21-30 or anything else, existed on January 10th.

Work was quickly begun by Chief Engraver George T. Morgan on a new, second revision to the Peace dollar design with lower relief, but the dashing young hero of the 1878 dollar competition was out of his league when faced with the design technology of 1922. According to Roger W. Burdette's *Renaissance of American Coinage, 1916-1921:*

"The relief-reduction were not going well and by January 19 the situation must have looked bleak. (Philadelphia Mint Superintendent) Styer wired Denver Mint Superintendent Grant: 'Unable to say when dollar dies will be shipped. Forwarded one cent obverse dies today.' It was clear that the artists could not be given control over production matters, however it was equally clear that the mint's revised design was not acceptable. Acting Director O'Reilly again ordered all work stopped on January 20."

A beautiful example of a 1922 Matte Proof Peace Dollar, struck from Chief Engraver George T. Morgan's second attempt at modifying the relief of the Peace dollar design. Because the relief was still too high to strike up well under normal production conditions, the Philadelphia Mint's Engraving Department hastily rushed a second batch of 1922-D Lincoln Cent obverse dies to Denver so that it could continue striking them rather than the Dollars it was hoping would be ready. I believe that this second batch of Cent dies were the dies originally made for the Philadelphia Mint without mint marks. Photo courtesy of the current owner of this coin.

I think that what happened was that the Philadelphia Mint's die shop, frantically trying to get the all-important dollar dies revised, could not be bothered with the mundane task of hubbing and mint-marking more 1922-D cent obverses after they were requested on Jan. 5th. I think that what it eventually did do, as Morgan's second revision to the Peace dollar design was crashing and burning all around him, was to hastily re-soften its own ten contingency one cent obverse dies, logically numbered #21-30, punch D mint marks into them, and reharden them for shipment to Denver.

If this happened, it would have been a totally non-standard procedure for the Mint, and neither of the two metallurgists with whom I have consulted (both of whom are also numismatists) could guess what effect this would have upon both the hardness and the durability of the ten dies. Both agreed that it was possible that such a course of action might have caused something like my hypothetical dimples to have raised up in the areas around the mint mark, but neither knew how I could prove it.

There are very few examples of this ill-advised procedure, the un-hardening, punching something new into, and then re-hardening of a previously-hardened working die, at the U.S. Mint. There was one cluster of them in 1806 when one each Quarter Dollar, Half Dollar and Quarter Eagle obverse previously used to strike normal coinage in 1805 was softened and overdated as 1806/5. The very fact that this non-standard procedure was only used for business strike dies in 1806, despite thousands of hardened but unused dies being disposed of in other years over many decades, speaks volumes about the potential problems that this procedure must entail. (FWIW the Mint hired an Assistant Engraver in 1807.)

The other known example is the 1827/3/2 Quarter Dollar obverse, the die having previously been used to strike a very limited number of 1823/2 quarters. However, the late Karl Moulton made a good case that the purpose of this re-overdating process was to strike fewer than ten specimen pieces very late in the year for distribution to Mint insiders, so die durability was probably not a concern there.

This radical new theory of mine could be proven, or disproven, if the Philadelphia Mint's Die Register(s) for the years 1921-1923 could ever be located. If you can find it (or them), please let me know.

(There is no point in asking the Mint what it did back then. Today's Engraving Department has no idea what its ancestors did a hundred years ago, and even if there were written records of such an act the Mint would never share them. It might embarrass them, you see!)

CHAPTER EIGHT

Some Thoughts on the Terminology Used to describe 1922-D Cents

Let me begin by acknowledging that for all intents and purposes there is technically no such thing as a true "die variety" among the cents of 1922, at least not in the classical definition of a die variety, where one die is made significantly different than another die when both are new. Such die varieties can be major or minor or somewhere in between.

For example, in the early years of the U.S. Mint where dies were individually made by hand, there was an instance where the Engraver hand punched "UNITED STATED OF AMERICA" into a die, realized his error, and punched an "S" over the errant "D" before the die was hardened. Certain warped individuals, such as myself, find such major die variations fascinating.

Major varieties also include overdates, where the dates on unused dies that had been finished but never hardened were updated in a later year by punching new digits over one or more of the original digits, such as the spectacular 1800/1798 cent. Other die varieties might be more subtle, be it the presence or absence of a leaf or a hair curl where neither variant is artistically wrong, just different. Even the random placements of letters and numbers on hand-punched dies that are otherwise absolutely correct can create eagerly collected "varieties." The important thing is that the dies were made different from each other, and can be collected based upon those differences.

With the Cents of 1922, on the other hand, all dies apparently started out perfectly normal and identical to each other, except for some relatively slight differences in the position of the mint mark. I did not make up a chart of mint mark positions, such as has been done with 1909-SVDB cents or 1916-D Mercury dimes, because I did not think that the average collector could tell one from another on the 1922-D cents. Where relevant as a diagnostic I will mention the mint mark position relative to the date, as on D.P. #5.

Instead, these are collectible "Die States," and people have been collecting 1922-D cents by certain of these "Die States" since 1928. Some of these "Die States" show zero trace of a mint mark, some show remnants of a mint mark generically called "Weak D's," and others show essentially normal mint marks. This is part of the reason why the cents of 1922 are usually described as "Die Pair #2" or whatever rather than "Variety #2." That said, per common usage I will sometimes be using the term "Variety" to describe classes of coins such as "The ANACS Varieties" and "The DeLorey Varieties."

The Redbook has a variety (no pun intended) of popular and collectible "Die State Varieties" other than the 1922 "No D" and "Weak D" cents, such as the 1937-D "3-Legged" nickel, the 1807 "Bearded Liberty" Capped Bust half dollar, the 1812 and 1814 "Single Leaf" half dollars, and the 1861-O "Cracked Obverse" half dollar where the die crack proves that the otherwise normal die pair was struck by the CSA. Within some collecting fields such as large cents and early half dollars the collecting by die state can get quite spirited.

Work on this project began when Bill Fivaz asked me, in 2019, to clarify the differences between 1922 "No D" and "Weak D" cents. One of the major TPGs had recently changed its policy regarding the "Weak D, Weak Reverse" coins and the "No D, Weak Reverse" coins, un-recognizing the latter and lumping them in with the former, to the considerable consternation of many collectors who owned the latter. I set out to write a 3,000 word article for *The Numismatist*, but after five+ years of work and study and some 60,000 words later, all I can say for sure is that the term "Weak D" has become meaningless.

The reality is that the mint marks found, or not found, on 1922-D Lincoln cents typically exist, or do not exist, along a continuum that runs from 100% present to 0% present, as can be seen on Die Pairs #4A&B. Die Pair #2 has the only obverse known with the mint mark completely gone in all known die states for *that* die pairing, though I have identified an earlier die state of that obverse die that shows a "Worn" or "Faint D" while it was paired with a different reverse die. (See Die Pair #5.) Die Pairs #1 & #3 are only known with their mint marks already significantly impaired, though continued research might trace their obverses back to when they were new or nearly so, as I have done with Die Pairs #4A&B and new Die Pairs #ZeroA&B, #8A,B,&C, #9, and #13A&B.

You must remember that every obverse and reverse die started out strong and faded over time, to various degrees, sometimes paired with a new or lightly used opposing die, and sometimes paired with a scandalously worn or overly-polished opposing die. Sometimes both dies are scandalously worn or over-polished. I will be presenting some new die pair combinations below where the fading is more or less extreme, which I hope you will find interesting. More on them later.

In a world where the cents struck in 1922 were often consigned by the spacing practicalities of numismatic publishing into a mere three categories, "1922-D," "1922-D Weak D" and "1922-D No D" at three significantly different price levels, there was always a strong pressure among collectors and dealers alike to try to push any coin with a bit of weakness on the D noticeable to the naked eye into the "Weak D" category to make it worth more. It's called Human Nature. Look it up.

At the other end of the continuum we had the Third Party Grading Services, starting with ANACS long ago, certifying 1922 cents from Die Pairs #1 & 3 as "Weak D" coins when the D was mostly gone but still visible, no matter how slightly, and as "No D" coins if, in good faith, they could not detect a D on the coin.

In my opinion as a former professional Senior Authenticator and Grader who has dabbled in the whys and the wherefores of the 1922 cents for literally half a century, this is how the "No D" coins can and should be attributed, IF and only IF the coin is undamaged and in a high enough condition to verify that the mint mark area bore absolutely "No D" when the coin was struck.

It must be acknowledged that some coins fall below this level of certainty because of damage or wear. Such coins should, or at least could, be returned with "No Decision" as to their attribution as a "No D," or perhaps they could be certified as "1922-D Genuine - Too Worn to Attribute Mint Mark Status." I am open to suggestions. (I have also seen images of a few Die Pair #4B coins certified by ANACS decades ago as "No D" coins, and I assume that they were certified in good faith, though ANACS does not currently recognize a "No D" coin from their definition of a Die Pair #4 coin. That said, I have a high grade Die Pair #4B coin with literally no mint mark, which I will be showing below.)

Unfortunately, within the past decade or so, two of the three major TPGs, spooked by having discovered that over the years they had, in good faith, incorrectly certified a small number of D.P. #1, #3 & #4B coins (often lower grade ones) with traces of the D as "No D" coins, have stopped certifying *any* D.P. #1, #3 & #4B coin as a "No D" coin, even if the coin is in a high enough grade to be absolutely certain that it was made without a mint mark. Though I too made mistakes in my days as an Authenticator/Grader, this is, in my humble opinion, unfair to both the legitimate "No D, Weak Reverse" coins and to their collectors.

Two of the three TPGs now certify such D.P. #1, #3 & #4B coins (and the Die Pair #Zero coins that they thought were D.P. #1 coins, because they did not realize that they were from a different obverse die) as "1922-D Weak

This 1922-D DP #1 coin appears to be a "No D" variety with a tiny random contact mark where the mint mark should be, but how can you tell for sure? Such coins from any die pair must be regarded as un-attributable due to condition. Photos by Robert Kelley courtesy of the American Numismatic Assoc.

A 1922-D Faint D Cent. DP #ZeroB VLDS/LDS. This coin does not appear to have a mint mark, a situation not known to exist for this die pair in this die state, but the coin is too worn to legitimately attribute as having either a No D or a Faint D. In such situations it is best to assume the lesser variety. Author's coin.

D" coins, lumping them in together with coins that were certified as "1922-D Weak D" coins under the 1982 ANACS system. This has rendered the term "Weak D" totally meaningless. If you buy a "Weak D" coin sight unseen today, you have absolutely no idea what sort of mint mark you will be getting.

I propose a set of new terms, starting with "1922-D Faint D," for undamaged coins in a high enough grade to properly attribute where the D shows 10% or less of its original volume. If the coin shows 2% or less of the original D, but not 0%, it is a "1922-D Very Faint D." If you even think you see a trace of the mint mark, it is a "Very Faint D" and not a "No D." Period.

It is my intent that these two terms correlate to what the TPGs currently require for a "Weak D" status, with the understanding that any decades-old standards for a "Weak D" label are now obsolete. I would hope that the "Faint D" and "Very Faint D" coins would be priced along the lines of "Weak D" coins of the strict recent standards.

If it shows more than 10% of the original D, but less 25%, I propose the term "1922-D Well Worn D." If it shows more than 25% but less than 50%, I propose the term "1922-D Worn D." Any coin where the D is more than 50% present is just a normal 1922-D cent. I would hope that the "Worn D" and "Well Worn D" coins would be worth a modest advance or two over the "Normal 1922-D" prices, once they are properly recognized for what they are, with the strict understanding that they do not qualify for the modern "Weak D, Weak Reverse" prices.

How do you determine these percentages? Good Faith leavened with Experience, plus as much Time as is necessary to actually stop and think about the coin. These things worked before when well-trained Authenticators were not afraid to use them.

However, it is commonly known that the TPGs like production line output speeds on most coins for the sake of meeting production quotas. That works on Morgan dollars, but obviously it will not work on 1922-D cents where a reasoned study of the mint mark is required. This will require the TPGs to treat 1922-D cents as varieties requiring variety attribution, and charged for accordingly, unless the submitter specifically requests that the status of the mint mark be ignored and the coin be certified as a generic 1922-D cent.

Eventually somebody may invent a machine that can scan a mint mark and calculate the volume of the metal above the level of the field and compare that to the volume of the D on a new die coin, but I won't hold my breath. (I have seen preliminary results from a machine that can accurately measure the height of a mint mark above the field, which holds great promise.) In the meantime I will trust in Good Faith and Experience, aided by Time and a few good pictures.

CHAPTER NINE

How and Why do Dies Deteriorate?

A coining die is basically a cylindrical piece of steel with various holes in one end of it. The holes can be large, such as Lincoln's bust; medium, such as the two wheat ears; or small, like the date, the mint mark and the lettering. Put two dies in a coin press along with a steel collar (sometimes called the third die) and mechanically deposit a blank planchet atop the lower die. This lower die is called the anvil die; the upper die is called the hammer die. For most of the 20th Century Lincoln cents were struck with the reverse die as the anvil die.

(Other denominations were sometimes struck with the obverse die as the anvil die just because certain designs struck up better that way. From error coins that I have seen I can say that the 1921 Peace dollars were struck obverse up and the 1922 Peace dollars obverse down. Modern coin presses strike sideways rather than up and down, but the die imparting the force is still the hammer die. This discussion will concern itself with the technology used to make cents during the 1920s.)

After the feed fingers push away the previously struck coin and deposit a new blank planchet atop the anvil die, they separate and withdraw and go back to the feeding tube and re-close to grab the next planchet. Each planchet must be slightly smaller than the hole in the collar so that it can easily drop down inside it. As the hammer die descends and transforms the planchet into a coin, the planchet expands slightly to completely fill up the collar, giving our coinage virtually uniform diameters.

After the strike the hammer die withdraws and then the anvil die raises up to push the coin up and out of the collar it is now tightly wedged into, so that the feed fingers can then knock it away and the cycle can repeat itself, roughly 100 times per minute, though that varies.

To accommodate this high-speed process, the struck coins must easily separate from the dies. For this reason every design element on a coin is tapered somewhat, lest each letter or number be as tightly wedged into that character in the die as the coin is in its straight-sided collar.

The D mint mark on a struck coin is a three-dimensional object with three axes, basically right to left, top to bottom and the height above the field. To simplify this, think of it as a tiny, slope-sided flower pot turned upside down on a table, which represents the field of the coin. The widest part of the pot now represents the base of the D touching the field of the die. Both the pot and the D get narrower as they taper upwards. The new top of the pot, the part furthest away from the table, is noticeably smaller than the new base. Ditto with the top of the D.

As the metal in each planchet is struck, some of it has to do that expanding outwards towards the collar. As the metal in the center of the planchet is too busy filling up the bust or eagle or shield or other design elements, the metal in the outer parts of the planchet has to do that expanding. As it does, it scours the field of the die a tiny bit. The scouring of one strike is negligible. The scouring of 100,000 strikes is not. If your die steel is not hard enough to withstand that scouring, it can wear away.

As the field of the die wears away, the tapered holes in it slowly get smaller because of that tapering. Go back to that flower pot we imagined earlier and use a grinder to remove a half an inch of it at the wide end to simulate wear to the surface of the die. When you put it back on the table upside down it now covers a smaller footprint. It, and the D it represents, got smaller in length and width. It also got smaller in height above the field. Grind some more off of the field end of the mint mark and it gets smaller still. Grind enough field away and the mint mark disappears.

This type of die wear can develop from the outward expansion of planchet metal across the fields of the die. However, that is only one type of die wear. It can easily be simulated if a Mint worker takes a worn and/or damaged die out of a press and over to a work bench to repair it with a file or some sort of grinding machine. He might just be smoothing out some ordinary roughness that has developed from die erosion, or he might be trying to remove a clash mark. Clash marks result when two dies hit each other without a planchet in between them, and parts of the design elements of one or both dies are struck up on the other die(s).

Grind off the raised areas on the die, typically on the field, and you remove the unwanted design element. Of course, you also run the risk of removing a desired design element, such as one of the forelegs on a 1937-D Buffalo Nickel.

Some grinding was not as severe. In the listings below you will see references to things such as a raised bulge in the field of the die in front of Lincoln's face that left a depressed valley on the coins struck from it (Scharlack's "dented obverse"); "scalloped" die erosion near the rim below LIBERTY or in among the letters of E PLURIBUS UNUM; and raised "dimples" on multiple dies near the D mint marks. In normal times such deteriorated dies might simply have been retired. In 1922 the Denver Mint was desperate to keep these dies in use for as long as possible, and if that meant grinding them down and slapping them back in a press, they did so.

However, there is a third type of die erosion that must be mentioned. During a strike you not only have radial expansion of the planchet outward into the collar, you also have the planchet metal simultaneously trying to move up into the hammer die or down into the anvil die to fill in the design elements of the dies. This leads to situations where you have metal initially flowing up or down into a letter or a number, only to be dragged back out of it, kicking and screaming, towards the collar.

This movement of planchet metal into and back out of a character can cause a different type of scouring of the die steel, actually widening the character at its base as the original angles where the character met the field erode away. Thus the characters can end up both broader in length and width but shorter in height than they were when the die was new. (Occasionally a character might disappear completely from a die due to die erosion, such as the I of LIBERTY on a few dies and the D mint mark on the final die state of Die Pair #4B, but that will be discussed later.)

This erosion tends to be somewhat coarse and ragged or lined, and varied from one die to the next. I call this type of die erosion (which broadens a character) "feathering." The best term I can think of to describe such characters is "mushy." Curiously, because of the mechanics of metal movement when a planchet with an upset rim is struck, it seems to affect characters in a circular zone in from the rim a bit, affecting the 9's in the dates more than the last 2's, and the R's of LIBERTY more than the I's. The 2's and the I's are more likely to just get shorter and narrower.

On the reverse of 1922-D cents this zone of scouring sometimes greatly deteriorated the details of the two wheat ears, weakening or even eliminating the parallel lines normally used to grade Lincoln Wheat Ear cents. This makes the grading of 1922-D cents quite difficult. The best thing to do is to grade the coin based on whichever side of the coin was struck from a relatively new die, if there is one. If there isn't, experience is the only answer. Try to find pictures of how that die looked in that die state when your coin was struck, and see what might have worn away.

Important: Because of the way that certain dies were worn down, polished down, and/or otherwise repaired before being pressed back into use, many of the significant die characteristics that will be described below will only appear on certain intermediate or later die states of that particular die.

Not every numbered Die Pair or particular die characteristic described below is a significant collectible die state. This is a highly technical, and I hope scholarly, study of many discernable die characteristics. I hope that by covering all of the most identifiable dies this work will help you to understand the significant ones all the better. It will also help future Authenticators in their identification of the significant 1922 die varieties, while at the same time helping them identify altered coins, of which there are many, by showing die characteristics of dies that never struck a "No D" or a "Faint D" coin!

CHAPTER TEN

On The Numbering of The Varieties, Old and New

For the sake of clarity as to which dies are being discussed, I have been referring to the four traditional 1922-dated obverse dies in this study, and their respective reverse dies, as Die Pair #1, #2, #3 or #4. These are also known as "The ANACS Varieties." This "canon" is recognized by most serious die variety specialists but not by all certification services, some of which tend to lump Die Pairs #1 and #3 together just because the Cherrypickers' Guide does, and/or ignore the very late die states of my Die Pair #4B, which is recognized by ANACS as their traditional #4.

As a rule I have tried to leave the "canon" unchanged to avoid confusion. However, the new Die Pair numbers added by me will begin with a necessary addition to the "canon," a previously unknown and unlisted "Faint to Very Faint D" obverse die listed as part of Die Pair #Zero, because it is die-linked via a very well-known cracked reverse die to Die Pair #1. It is also included in the "canon" because it is so similar to D.P. #1 that I am quite certain that many specimens of D.P. #Zero have been mis-identified as D.P. #1 coins over the years, and (presumably) been mis-certified as such accordingly.

(Note: As mentioned above, not all die states of every die are significant. Some of them are basically just normal coins. D.P. #Zero can be traced back to die states long before the mint mark deteriorated to first a significant "Faint D" status and then to an even more significant "Very Faint D" status. While the earlier die states are certainly collectible as such, it MUST be remembered that such die states do not qualify for what the TPGs currently consider "Weak D" status, and as such are not to be considered a part of the "canon." Let's call them "pre-Canon die states." Likewise the obverse die of Die Pairs #4A&B can be traced back to basically normal mint mark status with a normal truncation of the bust of Lincoln, followed by several "pre-Canon" intermediate die states leading up to the "Canon die states" recognized by ANACS.)

Two new varieties that I consider to be very collectible in their "Faint D" die states are Die Pairs #5 and #9. The obverse of D.P.#5 is the same obverse die as the obverse used to strike D.P.#2 in a later die state without a mint mark, paired with a different reverse die. Die Pair #9 is the best example of what I call "Dimpling" around the mint mark, and "Exhibit A" in my case that ten 1922 Philadelphia Mint obverse dies were re-softened, punched with mint marks, and re-hardened with D mint marks of questionable durability.

Two other new "Very Faint D" and/or "Very, Very Faint D" obverse dies that I consider to be totally equal in significance to Die Pairs #ZeroB, #1, #3 and #4B (all in their final die states) will be presented as Die Pairs #6 and #13B. The terminal die state of Die Pair #13B also shows extensive crumbling of the obverse rim, which is why it is catalogued here with other broken dies. After D.P. #6 I will present the interesting but much less significant D.P. #7 just because it is a doppelganger of D.P. #6 in its middle die states, and you should not confuse the two.

In my opinion, Die Pairs #6 and #13B, in their respective extreme die states, deserve as much respect as Die Pairs #ZeroB, #1, #3 and #4B do now, because they show the same thing that made those other dies famous, a greatly deteriorated mint mark. I can only assume that they were never recognized as part of the "canon" because they are rarer, though I will bet you that some of you have one or all of them in your collections now. Go look! I'll wait.

Another "Worn D, Dimpled Mint Mark" variety will be listed as Die Pairs #8A, #8B, and #8C. As with D.P. #9 I believe that the dimpling of this obverse die in the mint mark area is related to my new theory that ten 1922 Philadelphia Mint dies, Mint inventory numbers 21-30, were re-softened, punched with D's, and re-hardened for use in Denver. Please note that there are other 1922-D cent dies with other "dimples" around the mint mark, but these are just the two best ones that I have seen. Have fun looking for the others.

An assortment of generally minor varieties caused by die cracks and/or rim cuds will be introduced by me as Die Pairs #10, #11A & #11B, #12, and #13A & #13B just to create reference numbers for them, as the die cracks at least were collected as such in earlier years by Scharlack and others. Only Die Pair #13B develops a very significant mint mark in its terminal die state. See above and the listing below.

One highly desirable (but rare to the point of being Non-Collectible) variety with a major die break (*aka* large cud) at the word TRUST will be listed as Die Pair #14. An assortment of very, very minor die varieties with anomalies such as die scratches, which are included because they can be useful to Authenticators, will follow as Die Markers 1, 2 & 3.

That said, it is possible that additional die pairings exist because of an old Mint practice called die-chaining. The obverse dies tended to last longer than the reverse dies, and so logically a hypothetical new Obverse Die A put into a press with a new Reverse Die A would have been struck together until Reverse A wore out, at which point Reverse B would be installed and this "used Obv. A/ new Rev. B" combination used until Obverse A wore out, at which point new Obverse B would be mated with used Reverse B until Reverse B wore out, etc.

Die Pair #4A was only discovered after more than four years of research, and after the "finished" manuscript had already been submitted to the publisher. Please keep an eye out for new die pairings of any of the listed dies, and report them to me care of the publisher. Do not send coins unless asked.

Because three different numbering systems have been used for the cents of 1922 over the years, two of them obsolete, I have adhered to the following formatting in all references to them to help you keep the enumerations straight:

Craig's 1962 system, "First Die" and "Second Die." Now obsolete.

Craig's 1967 system, "Variety 1," "Variety 2," etc. Now obsolete, though parts of it incorporated into the following.

Modern ANACS system mostly used since the early 1980's, with hashtags added by me to denote that they constitute the modern system: "Die Pair #1," "Die Pair #2," "Die Pair #3" and "Die Pair #4." (Note: DP #4 was not added by ANACS until the late 1980s.)

Any Die Pairs numbers listed before #1 or after #4 are my own invention introduced in this work, but please feel free to use them with proper attribution. Because we will have the longhand designation "ANACS Die Pair #1" (or D.P.#1) through "ANACS Die Pair #4" followed by "DeLorey Die Pair #Zero" and "DeLorey Die Pair #5" through DeLorey Die Pair #14, I thought it best to overlay these designations with a shorter universal numbering system suitable for slab labels. To avoid confusion with the DeLorey-1, 2, 3 & etc. numbers already used to denote the tokens and medals issued by Thomas L. Elder (see *The Numismatist*, June & July, 1980), "ANACS Die Pair #1" will also bear the shorthand designation "DeLorey-2201," where the "22" refers to a cent struck in 1922. "DeLorey Die Pair #5" will be listed as "DeLorey-2205," etc.

The listing of the varieties below will begin with Variety 2, or Die Pair #2, or DeLorey-2202, the one with absolutely no trace of a D on the obverse and a "strong reverse die." This is the best one, the Redbook "No D" variety that everybody wants, and the only one which certain certification services will recognize today as a "No D" coin. Why is it Die Pair #2 you ask, not unreasonably? It is a long story. Pour yourself another cup of coffee if you like and kick your shoes off.

In the August 30 and September 6, 1967, issues of *Coin World*, the Collectors' Clearinghouse page published a third article by Craig entitled "Research Uncovers Four '22 Plain Cent Varieties." In that article he listed as his "Variety 1" a coin that he claimed was struck from an earlier die state of his "First Die" (No D) obverse from 1962, paired with a worn-out or weak reverse die.

Such a pairing was plausible because of the die-chain sequencing described above, but no such coin is known today, without a mint mark and with a worn-out reverse die, except for my newly-discovered Final Die State Die Pair #4B. Because its obverse is so totally different than what we now call Die Pair #2, we can be certain that that is not what Craig was calling his

"Variety 1. Besides, we now know that an earlier die state of the Die Pair #2 obverse, with a Faint D and a worn-out reverse die, is listed by me below as Die Pair #5.

His "First Die Obverse/new Strong Reverse" combination from 1962 (the traditional "No D" die combination) became his Variety 2. That enumeration survives as our modern Die Pair #2.

His "Second Die" from 1962 (mushy obverse and reverse) became his "Variety 3" in 1967, and a similar mushy obverse and reverse combination was revealed as his "Variety 4" in that same year. These are the similar but different "weak reverse die" varieties that will be discussed below as Die Pairs #1 & #3.

Craig may have supposed that his Variety 1 must have existed because the Denver Mint die usage record book showed that the last obverse die used, Serial No. 30 (the 20th obverse die used that year in Denver because dies #1-10 were sent to San Francisco), had produced a whopping (albeit alleged) 512,508 gross strikes, while the last reverse die used, No. 27, which it was paired with "most of the time" (as per the explanation above) only produced (an alleged) 412,508 gross strikes.

He presumably thought that Obverse Die No. 30 must have been paired with a different and well-worn reverse die, perhaps No. 26, for its first 100,000 (or so) strikes, creating his Variety 1. Unfortunately, Craig's Variety 1 was known to him by only a single corroded specimen, and to the best of my knowledge, and every other Authenticator I have consulted with, neither this nor any other specimen of his Variety 1 (with no mint mark from this particular obverse die and a weak reverse) is known today.

It was certainly plausible that the Mint's obverse Die No. 30 could have struck a number of "Worn to Faint to Very Faint D" coins in an initial usage with the D mint mark still showing (in diminishing amounts) on the obverse while paired with a worn out reverse die. My new DeLorey Die Pair #5 fits that bill perfectly. However, I have never seen a DeLorey DP #5 with the mint mark completely missing, or an ANACS DP #2 with the weak reverse.

If something had happened to one or both of the dies (such as perhaps clashing together, as Craig suggested in 1962) to cause the obverse die to be further polished down, there is no intermediate die state known that shows both the characteristics of Die Pair #5 AND any sort of die damage. I don't think that any such die damage ever occurred, though I must admit that I have not seen every 1922-D cent. If you find such a coin, please let me know.

I think that Craig's lone Variety 1 specimen was one of my DeLorey DP #5 coins with a Very Faint D obscured by the corrosion that he mentioned. For some unknown reason the obverse die of DeLorey #5 was taken out of the coin press and polished one more time, completely removing its Faint mint mark. It was then put back in the press with an unused reverse die, which the die vault still had a few examples of, to create the "1922 No D, Die Pair #2."

(One important lesson from all of this is that it is impossible to definitely match up one of our Die Pairs with the die record book, as Craig and Breen claimed to be able to do.)

The Craig 1967 system remained the standard for variety collectors for many years. *Coin World* Collectors' Clearinghouse Editor Jim Johnson referred to it in a column on June 20, 1973. He retired in early 1974, Ed Fleischmann was promoted from Assistant Editor to replace him, and I joined Clearinghouse as Ed's Assistant Editor. We used Craig numbers in our columns and in our letters to subscribers who sent us 1922-dated cents for attribution, as well as phrases such as "mushy obverse" and "weak reverse."

ANACS began authenticating coins in Washington, D.C. in early 1972. Because the Director and sole original Authenticator, Charles Hoskins, was uncomfortable making a call on some of the "mushy obverse" No D coins, ANACS began declining to certify "No D" cents in 1972 and 1973 after apparently mislabeling a few.

When F. Michael "Skip" Fazzari joined ANACS in February of 1974 he was skilled enough to make that call, and ANACS resumed certifying coins without mint marks as "US 1922 Plain 1c." To the best of my knowledge ANACS in D.C. never put a variety number on a certificate, though in modern correspondence with this author Fazzari has shown that he and ANACS were indeed familiar with Craig's work.

In late 1976 Fleischmann joined the ANACS staff as it was being moved to Colorado Springs, bringing his familiarity of the Craig system with him from *Coin World*. I have seen some of Ed's 1977 internal and/or photographic notes from the ANA Museum archives, and he made notes of specimens being photographed as being "Craig Var. 3" or "Var. 2" or whatever. There are no instances of a Craig "Var. 1" being noted. However, Colorado Springs likewise did not put variety numbers on certificates, nor did it say things like "weak reverse" except on internal notes.

From the Fall of 1976 to the Summer of 1977 the 1922 cents with absolutely no trace of a D, whether they had the strong or a weak reverse, were certified as a "USA 1922 1c." Perhaps because this looked like the standard designation of a Philadelphia Mint coin, the designation was changed to 'USA 1922 "No D" 1c' in the Summer of 1977. Where appropriate, other coins were certified as "Weak D" pieces.

I joined ANACS in late 1978 as an Authenticator. Over the years we saw a lot of 1922-dated cents of all sorts, partly because of the large number of "removed mint mark" coins on the market. An ANACS column which ran in the January 1976 *Numismatist* ranked altered 1922 cents as number eight on the top ten list of false coins seen by the service. You can still find them today on a popular online auction site which shall remain nameless.

Eventually we decided in 1982 that Craig's "Var. 1" did not exist, and a new "ANACS System" was created by a committee of Authenticators. Because we had been telling people for years at coin shows and in Summer Seminars that "Variety 2" was the best "No D" coin to have, we left it as "Die Pair #2" to avoid confusion. Unwisely, we moved Craig's "weak reverse" Variety 3 die pair, known to come both with and without a D, to the "Die Pair #1" position for the sake of numerical completeness, rather than just leaving #1 blank as we should have done. His "weak reverse" Variety 4 die pair, also known to come both with and without a D, then became our "Die Pair #3."

ANACS published a "1922 'No D' Cent Die Study" in *The Numismatist* in July of 1982. It was written by Authenticator Mike Fahey based in part upon Craig's and Fleischmann's earlier work, plus input from fellow Authenticators such as myself, future PCGS President Rick Montgomery, and others. Between us we had many years' worth of observations to draw upon, and almost ten years' worth of records of coins submitted to ANACS to study.

That said, the correct (and rather scarce in the very late die states) "Die Pair #4" was not recognized by ANACS as a separate die until 1988, though photographic evidence in the early ANACS files reveals that several had been certified by ANACS as "Weak D" and even "No D" specimens over the years. Like Craig in 1962, we may have assumed that Very Late Die State "Die Pair 4" coins were a (non-existent) VLDS of "Die Pair #2." (There is a VLDS of DP #2, but the lapel just fades away without elongating.)

The Cherrypickers' Guide to Rare Die Varieties of United States Coins, Sixth Edition, Volume 1, by Bill Fivaz and the late J.T. Stanton, recognizes Die Pair #2 as a "No D" variety and assigns it number FS-01-1922-401, commonly abbreviated on slab labels as FS-401 since the denomination, 01, and date, 1922, appear elsewhere on the label. Die Pairs #1&3 are unfortunately listed together as "Weak D" varieties under the common number

FS-01-1922-402, while acknowledging that the D is sometimes completely obliterated on them. Die Pair #4 is not mentioned in the CPG. It should be, just as Die Pairs #1&3 need separate listings.

USA 1922 "No D" Cent

In our opinion this is a genuine original item as described.

ANACS No: E-4416-I Grade: N/A

Registered To: 5-22-81

Old ANACS paper certificate showing the then not yet recognized 1922-D D.P.#4B Cent in the extremely rare "No D" XXLDS/VLDS die state. The Author was an ANACS Authenticator from November of 1978 to June of 1984. Certificate courtesy ANA Museum Archives.

CHAPTER ELEVEN

The ANACS Varieties, Die Pairs #2, #1, #3 & #4A&B

And now, *finally*, back to **ANACS Die Pair #2 (DeLorey-2202). GSID-2330, aka GSID-376706 if with FS-401 designation. No D. Strong reverse. Class Two.**

The traditional wisdom, based presumably upon Craig's 1962 and 1964 articles, was that a pair of dies clashed together so strongly that the obverse die was taken out and heavily ground down to remove the clash marks, so much so that the field around the mint mark was removed as well. The clashed reverse die was simply discarded, and a new reverse die installed to replace it.

1922 No D Cent, Strong Reverse, DP #2. PCGS MS62BN. TrueView courtesy West Coast Coins of Toledo, Oregon.

1922-D Cent, Very Faint D, Weak Reverse, DP #1. Author's coin, Photo by Robert Kelley Courtesy of the American Numismatic Assoc.

1922-D Cent, Faint D, Weak Reverse, DP #3. True View courtesy PCGS

1922-D Cent, Very Faint D, Weak Reverse, DP #4B, VLDS/LDS. Note the lobes extending down from the lapel, and know that this die exists in many different die states as described in the text, and that only the next two die states after this one are currently recognized by the current ANACS as Die Pair #4. Courtesy Heritage Auctions, (www.HA.com)

A nice example of a 1922 No D Cent, Strong Reverse, DP #2, LDS/EDS. Note feathering on the 9 and the R, and the weak lapel. Photos courtesy PCGS Coin Facts.

1922 No D Cent, Strong Reverse, DP #2. Closeup of date. Note the distinctive sharp second 2 compared to the more normal first 2, and how the 9 is starting to feather out into the field. Closeup courtesy West Coast Coins of Toledo, Oregon.

However, I hereby declare this traditional wisdom to be false. To the best of my knowledge, the only 1922-D cents known to actually exhibit *any* clash marks on their obverses are Die Pairs #ZeroB & #1, and neither of these show clash marks in the date/mint mark area. In over 50 years of studying errors and varieties on U.S. coins, I do not recall ever seeing a clash mark in the date area on a Lincoln wheatback cent. The curvature of the convex die faces strongly discourages this. The lowest spots on the coins are the back of Lincoln's neck and the indent under his jaw, and the high points on the dies, which strike these low areas, are where clash marks would happen.

Die Pair #ZeroB (DeLorey-2200B) shows various light clash marks along the back of Lincoln's head, the most prominent of which can be identified as fragments of the base of the C of CENT from the reverse die, the N from UNITED and the O from OF. As those clash mark seems to come and go, usually just showing the C from CENT, they probably represent repeated clashings that each disappeared over time from continued die use. The obverse die was not taken out and polished down.

Some D.P. #1 coins (DeLorey-2201) show a marginally stronger clashing of that C in a slightly different position due to die rotation before the clash. However, either obverse die shows too much overall deterioration in its later die states for either of them to have been a predecessor of the relatively normal D.P. #2, the obverse of which is always seen in an earlier, less worn die state than the obverse dies of Die Pairs #1 & #3.

The Three Die Crack Reverse variety (see Die Pair #10 below) shows three different light clashings over the life of the reverse die (q.v.), but each was apparently allowed to wear away from continued natural die erosion. This tells us that light clash marks were tolerated. Curiously, the normal mint mark obverse die always seen with this triple-cracked reverse die remained miraculously unaffected by these multiple clashings, and was never swapped out over their long usage together. It may have been hardened much better than the reverse die was, and thereby resisted any damage from clashing.

I don't think that clash marks ever affected the obverse die of Die Pair #2. As noted above, this same die is known in an earlier die state as the obverse die of my Die Pair #5, which always shows at least a Faint D. In that die pair's latest known die state, which resembles (through similar die erosion on IN GOD, LIBERTY and the back and front of Lincoln's coat) the earliest known die state of Die Pair #2, there are no indications of any die clashing between the two pairings.

Matching die erosion on the back of Lincoln's coat on an early DP #2 coin (left) and a late die state DP #5 coin (right). Note the prominent spike directly below the Y of LIBERTY when viewed upright. The presence of this spike on a coin with a strong reverse can be used to authenticate a DP #2 coin. DP #2 coin owned by J.P. Martin of ANACS, photo by the author. DP #5 coin by the author.

For whatever reason, the obverse die of D.P. #5 was taken out of the press and ground down *again*. The field below the date was selectively and evenly lowered so much so that the three-dimensional hole in it which formed the mint mark was completely obliterated. (Picture a sand box with a D-shaped hole in the sand, three inches deep. Now remove four inches of sand from the box. The hole disappears.)

Die Pair #2 shows three different obverse die states (see below), a fact curiously overlooked in all previous writings on this variety. In none of them did the coins struck from this (now) obverse die #2 ever show even a trace of the missing D. Craig was wrong when he said that it did. It is possible that he was confused by a Late Die State of my Die Pair #5, or some other die

Another nice example of a 1922 No D Cent, Strong Reverse, DP #2, in the fairly scarce MDS/EDS. These were struck AFTER the mint marks was completely polished off of the Obverse die and that die was paired with a new Reverse die (See DP #5 for previous pairing with worn Reverse die.) Note early die erosion on R of LIBERTY. The lapel was weakened by the die polishing that removed the mint mark from the die, but its outline is still intact. Courtesy Heritage Auctions (www.HA.com)

1922 No D Cent, Strong Reverse, DP #2, MDS. Closeup of date. Enlarged from the obverse photo courtesy Heritage Auctions (www.HA.com).

1922 No D Cent, Strong Reverse, DP #2, MDS. Closeup of LIBERTY and die erosion on back of coat (see below). Enlarged from the obverse photo courtesy Heritage Auctions (www.HA.com).

pair, or he simply tried to make his observations fit his pre-conceived notions. He would not be the first researcher to fall into that trap. The cents of 1922 are strange and magical things. If you study them long enough, you start seeing things and hearing voices.

Obverse #2 always shows a weak lapel on Lincoln's coat adjacent to the mint mark area, but this is not diagnostic. The lapel fades out completely on the latest die state coins struck from this obverse. The fading could have been caused by additional polishings, or by simple die erosion. While still visible the bottom edge of the lapel is a smooth curved line, with only a few tiny die erosion spikes, unlike Die Pairs #Zero & #4B.

1922 No D Cent, Strong Reverse, DP#2. The fairly scarce MDS/EDS. The "Rosetta Stone" specimen that proved that this earliest known Obverse die state of the traditional DP #2 is actually a slightly later die state of the Obverse of my new 1922-D Very Faint D DP #5. See the closeups of the die erosion lines on the back of Lincoln's coat below. Coin owned by J.P. Martin of ANACS. Photos by the author.

1922 No D Cent, Strong Reverse, DP #2. Date with perfectly smooth field below. Coin owned by J.P. Martin of ANACS. Photos by the author.

1922 No D Cent, Strong Reverse, DP #2. LIBERTY with beginning of feathering on R, die erosion down coat. Coin owned by J.P. Martin of ANACS. Photos by the author.

Ignoring the earlier die states of this obverse die found under its Die Pair #5 usage (with mint mark, and paired with a different, weak reverse), I am calling the earliest known die state of the D.P. #2 obverse a **Mid Die State** (MDS). It is identified by some noticeable die erosion doubling on the tops of IN and GOD, which gives the letters sort of a stepped appearance. This doubling fades as the letters erode more and become rather blob-like.

1922 No D Cent, Strong Reverse, DP #2. The earliest known Obverse die state of DP #2, with erosion doubling on the tops of IN, GOD and WE, but not TRUST (ignore the random scratch thru the I.) The latest known Obverse die state of DP#5 has the same erosion doubling, though it later disappears on the more common die states of DP #2. Perhaps the obverse die of DP #2 received yet another polishing after the mint mark was already gone. Coin owned by J.P. Martin of ANACS. Photos by the author.

The date does not look too bad, though the 9 is feathered out into the field in all directions. The first 2 is almost normal, with just a tiny bit of feathering where the sides of the 2 meet the field. The second 2 is noticeably thinner than the first 2, the field under it (and any feathering that might have been there) presumably having been polished away by the same polishing that removed the last of the mint mark. This does give the outline of the 2 a very crisp, sharp look.

The R of LIBERTY is starting to feather out to the right and to the left, but the rest of LIBERTY is basically intact. The L touches the rim (as seen on many 1922-D dies), though the rim is slightly higher than the L on high grade specimens. The foot of the L begins to fade. This die state (**MDS Obv./ EDS Rev.**) is fairly rare, and I would estimate that it constitutes perhaps 5 to 10% of the D.P. #2 population seen by me.

The "normal" (i.e., how usually seen) "1922 No D" D.P. #2 has a weak lapel, IN GOD WE softer, the I of LIBERTY starting to fade and the R of LIBERTY fatter and merged with the T, which itself develops a fattened upright. I am calling it a **Late Die State** (LDS) obverse, though it is probably a bit stronger than the average LDS 1922-D cent found in this study just because the die abrasion in the date area was so localized. The reverse is basically unchanged. This **LDS Obv./ EDS Rev.** probably constitutes around 85% of the "No D, Strong Reverse" coin universe, plus or minus 5%.

1922 No D Cent, Strong Reverse, DP #2. A pleasing example of the more normal LDS/EDS die state. PCGS MS62BN. Courtesy West Coast Coin of Toledo, Oregon.

The **Very Late Die State** (VLDS) Obverse coins with the 9 heavily feathered out, the first 2 softer and the lapel virtually gone is significantly scarcer, perhaps 5% of the total population. LIBE can also get rather weak, but the R is broad and heavily feathered. The tops of RUST are eroded outwards towards the rim, making the first T look significantly shorter than the R next to it. The reverse of the **VLDS Obv./ EDS Rev.** die state remains basically unchanged.

As indicated above, once the mint mark was totally gone, the "abridged" obverse die was then paired up with an unused (or possibly very slightly used, though I doubt it) **Early Die State** (EDS) Reverse die that retained this EDS status through each of the three obverse die states. It must have been very well hardened. Together this die pair was used to strike many,

1922 No D Cent, Strong Reverse, DP #2, in the significantly scarcer VLDS/EDS. Apparently the obverse die received yet another polishing, while the seemingly invincible reverse die remained unchanged. Note the missing coat and the very weak IN GOD WE. The die erosion lines on the back of Lincoln's coat may be harder to see in this die state. Photo courtesy of Heritage Auctions (www.HA.com)

many thousands of "No D" coins with a "Strong Reverse," probably several tens of thousands. The First Edition Blue Book was wildly wrong as to quantities.

In the modern ANACS classification system this die pair is designated as Die Pair #2. The following comments were made about it in the 1982 ANACS die study:

"Second 2 in date is sharper than first 2. All letters in TRUST are sharp. WE is only slightly mushy. Reverse is sharp." It goes on to state: "Two theories pertaining to this variety have been advanced in the past, both of which are subject to debate. One of the theories contends that a die intended for the Denver Mint was never punched with the 'D' mint mark. This theory can be easily refuted by the fact that no genuine 'No D' cents are known to have been struck from a new obverse die with normal details."

(Before I wrote this work no certification service considered the "Never had a mint mark" theory to be plausible, though it had to be addressed for the sake of thoroughness. However, the identification of DeLorey Die Pair #5 as being an earlier die state of this obverse die, *with* a mint mark, destroys that theory for good.)

The article continued, after a discussion of the Die Pairs #1 & #3 coins (see below) and how they came to be, with:

"Die pair 2 evolved in a different manner. A pair of dies producing normal 1922-D cents clashed together, shattering the reverse die, and a new reverse die was put into service. The obverse die, though worn, was still considered usable, and was taken out of the press, reworked and polished, and put back into service. This procedure removed sufficient metal from the die to erase any trace of the mint mark. Every coin examined by ANACS from this die pair has been the 'No D' variety."

(This theory was more plausible than the "never punched" theory, and virtually every error and variety expert at the time [including myself] believed that it was true, but there was always a troubling lack of physical evidence to support it. The reverse of Die Pair #10 (DC-2 below) does show clashing and cracking, but I would not call it "shattered," as it produced quite a few coins after cracking, and its obverse die never changed.)

(Also, there was the troubling reality that the severe die polishing on the obverse of D.P. #2 is localized to the area below the 1922 date and on Lincoln's lapel, not areas where clash marks typically appear on Lincoln Wheat Reverse cents. The hypothetically normal obverse clash mark sites (behind Lincoln's neck above the Y of LIBERTY and under his jaw) look quite normal in fact.)

In more modern times in other publications, Fahey expanded upon the characteristics of Die Pair #2 thusly: "…in the date, the first three digits are a bit weak and blurry, while the last '2' is crisp and sharp. 'LIBER' is weak, while 'TY' is sharper. In the motto IN GOD WE TRUST, the letters in 'IN GOD WE' are indistinct, while the letters in 'TRUST' are sharper and more distinct." I certainly agree with him there, though towards the very end of this obverse die's tenure the tops of RUST do erode towards the rim.

1922 No D Cent, Strong Reverse, DP #2, LDS/EDS. Die Pair #2 coins are always graded by the reverse of the coin, which received excellent detailing from the Strong Reverse die. This coin would typically be graded as an EF-40. Author's coin, Photo by Robert Kelley Courtesy of the American Numismatic Assoc.

"There are no diagnostics that can be used on the reverse ... However, you should immediately notice that the reverse is sharper than the obverse. On a circulated example, the reverse typically appears to grade one to two full grades higher than the obverse. The major grading services typically grade a 1922 "No D" Die Pair #2 cent by the remaining details on the reverse."

"One last diagnostic that you can use is the alignment of the two sides. Every genuine (Die Pair #2—TD) "No D" cent that I have inspected over the last 35 years has the two sides almost perfectly aligned. If you have the obverse aligned with the right edge of the 'W' of 'WE' at exactly 12:00, then flip the coin over, the left edge of the 2nd 'U' in 'PLURIBUS' will be at the 12:15 position." (I have found Fahey's die alignment notations to be quite precise for all of the ANACS Canon dies.)

I firmly believe, but cannot yet prove, that the "Faint D" obverse of Die Pair #5, later reborn as the "No D" obverse of Die Pair #2, resulted from one of the second batch of obverse dies (Serial #21-30) developing raised "Dimples" around the mint mark and being firmly ground down to remove said dimples. The grinding was beveled slightly towards the rim rather than being parallel to the field, so that the mint mark was first weakened and then removed and the lapel weakened without the date being significantly weakened. I likewise believe that D.P. #1 was treated the same way for the same reason, although in that case the mint mark was never 100% removed. (See Die Pairs #ZeroB, #5, #8, #9 and #13B below.)

ANACS Die Pairs #1 & #3—Are they Fraternal Twins (or Triplets with Die Pair #Zero)?

Obverse Dies #1 & 3 had long been assumed to have had similar origins, with both obverses having been polished down so much that the overall details of both dies became seriously degraded and the D mint marks became very weak, but never completely gone from the dies. It was a part of their shared heritage that these two obverse dies were always paired up with well used "Weak Reverse" dies, the first one cracked and the second one notably weaker than the first.

In the course of their usages, they were subject to oil and grease dripping down from the working parts of the coin presses, possibly the same coin press, which along the way got mixed with dirt and powdered metal, the resulting sludge occasionally coating the surfaces of the dies. On Obverses #1 & 3, this occasionally filled in the shallow mint marks so that when the dies struck planchets the bronze in the planchets could not be embossed into those mint marks in those dies. I have seen high grade Die Pair #1 & 3 coins where the mint mark area is quite smooth, with zero trace of a "D," and have certified them as "No D" coins without reservation.

However, after a number of strikes in this "No D" condition some of the grease could have worn off the mint mark area through routine striking erosion, allowing a "D" of varying faint strengths and/or shapes to reappear. The latest die state Die Pair #1 coin that I ever saw, while I was working at ANACS, had a very faint "D" on the obverse and a longer than normal jogging die crack on the Reverse.

It is also possible that the random reappearances of the D's on Die Pairs #1 & #3 were caused by the press operator(s) occasionally stopping their press(es) to lubricate them as necessary, and while they were stopped taking a greasy rag to the faces of the dies to wipe off accumulated oil and sludge. In modern times planchets have been routinely coated with a light machine oil to facilitate their passage through the press feeding mechanisms, and something similar may have been routine in 1922 as well. We don't know.

The selective polishing of the mint mark areas on Die Pairs #1 and #3 (and #Zero) sounds like what happened to the obverse die found on Die Pairs #5 and then #2, but the results do seem somewhat different. For a long time I was hesitant to say that #1 and #3 were produced during the second coining period, if only because of their always weak reverses. I just couldn't tell, in part because I was unable to definitely identify an earlier die state of either obverse, as I have been able to do with Die Pairs #2 and #4 (and #Zero).

Now, however, I am fairly confident that the original weakening of the mint marks on the Obverses of Die Pairs #1 and #3 (and #Zero) was caused by selective die polishing by the Coiner and/or the Die Setter. I say this because the earliest known obverse die states of D.P. #Zero, which precedes D.P. #1, show both a fairly normal D AND dimples around it.

The rapid diminution of the D on D.P. #Zero, which happened way faster than the other wear which accumulated on the die, was logically caused by an attempt to remove raised dimples from around the mint mark on the die, though this is speculation and we must admit that the selective polishing may have been for some other reason. Compare the appearances of these mint marks with that seen on D.P. #5 below, which also resulted from selective polishing, as compared to the mint marks seen on Die Pairs #6 and #7, which appear to be the result of simple die erosion with heavy feathering around the D.

Though Die Pairs #1, #3 and #Zero have certain things in common, it seems to me to be a bit of an injustice for certain reference guides and/or

TPG's to lump them in together in their listings and/or attributions. They are not the same thing, and they deserve to be collected individually. With the identification of Die Pair #Zero here, now would be a fine time to rewrite the Cherrypickers' Guide to give all three separate listings, as well as Die Pair #4B and certain other new varieties included in this book.

ANACS Die Pair #1 (DeLorey-2201). Die Crack 1-B. GSID-310760, Class Three with Very Faint D; or GSID-1871, Class Four with absolutely No D.

1922-D Cent, Very Faint D, Weak Reverse with Jogging Die Crack, DP #1, LDS/LDS. Note that WE is weaker than GOD. Author's coin, Photos by Robert Kelley Courtesy of the American Numismatic Assoc.

Seen with either "Very Faint D" due to die polishing or "No D" due to grease filling the Very Faint D in the die. Always seen with well-worn "Jogging Die Crack" reverse die previously used on Die Pair #ZeroB (DC-1A), though the die crack is occasionally faint.

1922-D DP #1 Jogging die crack and die erosion in EPU. Author's coin, which happens to have had the D mint mark crudely removed!

Rarely seen in a **MDS Obv./ LDS Rev.** with a Very Faint D but with a mostly clear date. There is minimal feathering on the 9, and the 1-22 are nearly normal. The D is very faint due to die polishing that also weakened the lapel of Lincoln's coat. Seen with remnants of the VDB on the truncation of the shoulder, but I would not rely on this characteristic.

1922-D Cent, Very Faint D. DP #1, MDS/LDS. Obv. and Rev. In PCGS XF-45 slab as Weak D. Author's coin, Photos by Robert Kelley Courtesy of the American Numismatic Assoc.

The "MDS" designation is somewhat speculative, and may be considered merely relative to the next die state. Presumably this obverse die had an earlier life, probably paired with a different reverse die, but I have not yet been able to identify any coins from it due to the massive discontinuity caused by the polishing. For whatever reason, it was taken out of a coin press after that earlier life, "repaired" in the mint mark area, and eventually put back in a press in a notably deteriorated condition along with the well-used **"jogging die crack"** reverse die previously used to strike Die Pair #ZeroB coins (see the DeLorey Varieties below). I have no idea what the earlier obverse die state, or the previous reverse die, looked like.

Most of the I of IN, all of GOD, most of TRUST and all of LIBERTY are still present, along with the inner wheat lines on both sides of the reverse. The word WE is noticeably weaker than the word GOD, the opposite of what is seen on Die Pair #Zero.

The back of Lincoln's head is very normal in this die state with no signs of die clashing in the field, so a possible explanation for the "repairs" just to the mint mark area would be to remove dimples that had raised up around the D.

I would estimate that less than 5% of the original D remains due to the aggressive die polishing, perhaps as little as 2%. Had the polishing gone just a little bit deeper into the die we would have had two unquestionable and relatively common "No D" dies in the ANACS Canon, but it did not. A "No

D" strike caused by grease obscuring this remnant of the mint mark in this die state is certainly possible, as happened off and on with the next two die states, but it is not currently known for this die state.

1922-D Cent, Very Faint D. DP #1, MDS/LDS. Closeup of date and almost missing mint mark. Author's coin, Photos by Robert Kelley Courtesy of the American Numismatic Assoc.

(The only other "No D" die in the ANACS Canon where the mint mark is completely gone from the die, as opposed to being filled in with grease, only appears on the very rare, extremely final die state of DP #4B. That die state is introduced to the World below, and it awaits the World's acceptance.)

D.P. #1 is more commonly seen in an **LDS Obv./ LDS Rev.** with GOD, the R-S of TRUST and the ER of LIBERTY fading, though the I of LIBERTY remains sharp, unlike D.P. #Zero. It can legitimately be found with either a Very Faint D or No D, the latter reality caused by grease accumulations that come and go in the very shallow mint mark area. There are variations within this die state as the surface of the die continued to erode from surprisingly long use, so don't be surprised if you see a bit more or less detail than typically seen in the two 2's, or in random characters in IGWT. For example, the feet of the R of TRUST are sometimes bold with the rest of the letter weak.

1922 No D Cent, Weak Reverse with Jogging Die Crack, DP #1, LDS/LDS. A legitimate "No D" coin, though some slabbing services would insist on calling it a "Weak D" coin because this obverse die sometimes produced coins with a Very Faint D. Purchased by me from GN Coins of Lemont, IL. Their pictures, used with permission.

One piece in this die state seen with the die crack rather faint, perhaps due to grease on the reverse die. Still identifiable as the jogging die crack reverse via the extensive die erosion "fingerprints" seen through E PLURIBUS.

1922 No D Cent, Weak Reverse with Jogging Die Crack, DP #1, LDS/LDS. Date area with absolutely no mint mark. Author's coin and picture.

Rarely seen in a **VLDS Obv./ VLDS Rev.** die state with either a Very Faint D or a No D, with GOD weak, R-S almost gone and the U weak, and BER faint. The I of LIBERTY is still strong. May come with a strong clash mark from the C of CENT above the letter Y of LIBERTY, but this is NOT diagnostic because D.P. #Zero (see below) is sometimes seen with a variety of clash marks from the "C" of CENT above the letter Y of LIBERTY, all a bit higher and weaker than the "C" clash mark seen here.

1922 No D Cent, DP #1, VLDS/VLDS. Obv. and Rev. Author's coin, Photos by Robert Kelley Courtesy of the American Numismatic Assoc.

All die states of D.P. #1 show the **"Jogging Die Crack"** on the reverse which runs from the L of PLURIBUS through the O of ONE. The original ANACS study mentioned that it was always found on the reverse of a Die Pair #1 coin unless obliterated by excessive wear.

This raised line begins under the right side of the upright of the L of PLURIBUS, and follows the line of the L down to the outside of the upper left curve of the O of ONE. It reappears on the inside of the curve of the O a few degrees counterclockwise of the outer line (the jog), runs to the center of the O and takes a slight bend to the right before continuing on to the inside of the lower right curve of the O.

On the seldom seen VLDS coins this die crack continues weakly along the same slight curve a bit past the O of ONE to the top of the E of CENT, about 70% of the way from the upper left corner of the E to the upper right corner of the E. As ANACS said, it can be difficult to see in low grades.

Also per the 1982 ANACS study: "Second 2 in date is weaker than first 2. First T in TRUST is smaller and more distinct than the other letters. WE is very mushy. Reverse is very weak, usually with no lines in the wheat ears." Fahey was describing the typical LDS/LDS D.P. #1 coin, but it does have the sub-die states described here.

In Fahey's later published comments he says: "1) The two T's in TRUST are both sharp, the U is slightly weak, and the remaining letters of IN GOD WE TRUST are very weak and blurry, due to die wear. 2) All of the letters in LIBERTY are weak, with BER having the most distortion. 3) In the date, the 19 is very weak, the first 2 is sharper, and the 2nd 2 is thinner than the first 2, and more clear."

1922 No D Cent, Weak Reverse with Jogging Die Crack, DP #1, LDS/LDS. IN GOD, WE and TRUST. Note that WE is weaker than GOD, and the R & S of TRUST are fading. Author's coin. (Pictures not part of Fahey's comments.)

"4) The bottom of Lincoln's jacket is a clear curved line all the way around, not ragged or distorted towards the rim. 5) (here there is a description of the jogging die crack—TD) 6) The letters in E PLURIBUS UNUM are very weak and fuzzy. ONE CENT is reasonably sharp, but some of the letters of USA are blurry. Heavy die erosion lines can be seen around the lower half of the left wheat stalk. I have never seen a genuine Die 1 example that exhibited all of the upper lines in the wheat stalks, even in high grade."

As to the rotation of the dies, Fahey states that if you flip the coin as described under Die Pair #2, the left edge of the 2nd U of PLURIBUS will be at the 11:30 position.

(To all of these characteristics I would add a new diagnostic that unfortunately can only be seen on coins above a certain grade. This is that the left obverse rim is always wide with a curved, depressed line basically splitting it in two from about 6 o'clock to about 11 o'clock. This will disappear on lower grade coins once the rim has worn down past the depth of the depression. I am not 100% positive as to what caused this effect, though it seems to be some sort of collar clash. In the bad old days of nicknames Scharlack might have called it a "Doubled Rim." What is really interesting is that a very similar curved, depressed line appears on DP #ZeroB coins! See them.)

Craig's description of his Variety 3 (ANACS D.P. #1) mentioned: "On some specimens the reverse will show a light die crack from L of PLURIBUS to O of ONE, and there is generally a strong Ghost of Lincoln." He did not mention the Strong D variety known for this year with a straight die crack from the L through the O, causing considerable confusion in subsequent years. More on that die later as Die Pair #10, DeLorey-2210, the three die crack reverse.

1922 No D Cent, Weak Reverse with Jogging Die Crack, DP #1, LDS/LDS. LIBERTY and rim with collar clash usually seen on DP #1 coins of high enough grade. Note the strong LI and the weak BER, as compared to what is seen on the later stages of the Obverse die of DP #Zero. That die had a similar Obverse collar clash while it was paired with this same Reverse die with the Jogging Die Crack. Use this picture to tell if your DP #1 coin is actually a DP #Zero. Author's coin.

(The "Ghost of Lincoln" that he mentioned is just a peculiar form of die erosion found on wheatback Lincoln cents of many years. The technical term for it is "Internal Metal

Displacement Phenomenon," or IMDP, though us old coin geezers just call it "ghosting."

When two opposing dies strike planchets, the pressure on the planchets is greater in some areas than in others depending upon the relief of the dies. As this pressure is transmitted through the planchets to the surfaces of the opposing dies, the dies erode differently in those different areas. This sometimes caused a vague outline of Lincoln's head to develop on the reverse dies opposite the void that formed the head on the coins' obverses. Other 1922-D cent dies show similar die erosion, so it is not a reliable diagnostic.)

Die Pair #1 coins are relatively common in circulated grades, but much, much rarer in Mint State than Die Pair #2 & 3 coins. A search of Heritage Auctions' prodigious auction records, which naturally tend to include higher grade pieces, will produce many Mint State DP#2 and #3 coins but no DP#1 or DP#4A or B coins. I am proud to own the AU-50 DP #1 coin seen at the beginning of this die pair, removed from a major TPG slab for photographic purposes. I also own a PCGS AU-58BN coin with a CAC sticker, possibly the finest Die Pair #1 coin I have ever handled!

As mentioned above they can be found with either a "Very Faint D" or with absolutely no trace of a mint mark due to the mint grease. The very latest die state coin that I ever saw did have a "Very Faint D" on it, so it never did go completely away on the die.

During my research I initially confused Die Pair #Zero coins that had the jogging die crack with Die Pair #1 coins simply because "everybody knew" that all 1922-D cents with the jogging die crack were from Die Pair #1. That's what we thought we knew 40 years ago. However, sometimes "everybody" is wrong. I am sure that there are many D.P. #Zero coins out there labeled D.P. #1 because of this long-held incorrect assumption.

Because I wish to keep the four ANACS varieties at the head of these listings with their traditional numbers, I will list this new discovery below as "Die Pair #Zero" at the start of "The DeLorey Varieties." The alternatives would be to renumber all of the varieties yet again, and I don't think that that would be a good idea. Just know that "Zero" comes before "One," and that the Die Pair #Zero coins, by rights, should be a part of the ANACS canon because collectors have been mistaking the ones with the die crack for Die Pair #1 coins for over four decades.

ANACS Die Pair #3 (DeLorey-2203). GSID-310766, Class Three with Very Faint D; or GSID-310763, Class Four with absolutely No D.

1922-D Very Faint D Cent, Extremely Worn Reverse, DP #3, LDS/VLDS. True View courtesy PCGS.

Seen with "Faint D" or "Very Faint D" in later die states due to die erosion, or with "No D" due to grease filling the remains of the mint mark in the die. Always seen with very well-worn reverse die, aka "Weak Reverse," though on DP #3 we should probably say "Very Weak Reverse."

1922 No D Cent, Extremely Worn Reverse, DP #3, LDS/XLDS. Courtesy Heritage Auctions, (www.HA.com)

The 1982 ANACS die study had this to say: "Second 2 in date is weaker than first 2. TRUST is weak but sharper than IN GOD WE. Lower left part of O in ONE begins to spread into the field as the die deteriorates." The

1984 update added "Normally struck from slightly rotated dies," which Fahey states that if you flip the coin as described under Die Pair 2, the left edge of the 2nd U of PLURIBUS will be at the 11:00 position.

1922-D Very Faint D Cent, Extremely Worn Reverse, DP #3, LDS/VLDS. Note weak IN GOD WE, strong TRUST. From Mike Sokoloff.

In Fahey's later published comments he states: "1) IN GOD WE is weak and mushy, while TRUST is sharper. 2) LI in LIBERTY is very weak, the R is blurry, and BE and TY are sharper. 3) The 19 in the date is slightly distorted, the first 2 is sharp, and the 2nd 2 is weaker."

"4) On the reverse, the wheat stalks are extremely worn and blurry, with few details visible. 5) E PLURIBUS UNUM is very weak and distorted. 6) The left side of the O of ONE is distorted into the field. On many pieces the left side of the O appears twice the thickness of the right side."

The obverse and reverse dies recognized as D.P. #3 must have struck many more coins than the dies recognized as D.P. #2, (ignoring any and all earlier incarnations of either die pair,) as they show much more die deterioration in the coins known from them. They quickly produced only a Faint D coin, and intermittently showed absolutely no trace of a mint mark due to mint grease.

At the end of this die pair's lifetime they have one of the worst reverse die states of all of the 1922 cents, regardless of whether they are "Faint D," "Very Faint D" or "No D" coins. It was insane that this very well worn reverse die was left in the coin press while there were still brand new reverse dies sitting in the die vault, but it was. I can only assume that the silver dollar remodeling situation was so dire at this point that the Denver Mint had absolutely no idea when it might stop striking 1922-D cents.

MDS Obv./ LDS Rev. Faint D. Weak Reverse. Unlike their so-called "fraternal twins" the Die Pair #1 coins, Die Pair #3 coins can be found, at least in this die state, with a fairly visible but **Faint D**, fully outlined but thin and in low relief above the field. In the earlier end of this die stage range I would estimate that it contains about 10% of the volume of a normal D, just qualifying for my "Faint D" status, but it does continue to fade and lose a few more percentage points while continuing to remain a naked eye "1922-D" coin. I have not yet seen a "No D, Weak Reverse" coin from the Middle Die State of this obverse, but it remains a possibility.

LIBERTY and IGWT are relatively normal, though the latter is starting to show a bit of erosion towards the rim. This can first be seen at the top of the G of GOD. Later on within this MDS range that erosion extends to all of IN GOD, with a visible "scallop" developing in the field between the I and the N. Sometimes there is a smaller "scallop" to the left of the top of the I of IN.

1922-D Faint D Cent, DP #3, MDS/LDS. Date and mint mark. Author's coin.

The date and the lapel of Lincoln's coat are fairly normal, so it is difficult to say what caused the weakening of the mint mark. If indeed it was die polishing, which remains to be seen, the polishing must have been a bit more selective than that seen on Die Pairs #1, #2, #ZeroB and #5 (below). In contrast, the back of Lincoln's coat shows extremely heavy die erosion extending well out into the field. This can often be easily spotted in photographs.

In the old days this very definitely qualified as a "Weak D" in the eyes of the TPGs. I have one in an NGC slab labeled "Weak D," with no indication of die variety. It was net graded as F 12 BN because of the weakness of the wheat ears, though the obverse is at least a VF 30 using normal Lincoln cent grading standards.

The reverse die is in the classic "Weak Reverse" range, but remember that there were several "Weak Reverse" dies used in 1922. On this die the wheat lines are gone on the outsides of the tops of the wheat ears, a bit more so on the left. The sides of the wheat stalks are feathering out into the fields, more so on the left. Both of these conditions, and others, continue to worsen over the remaining life of this die pairing.

The lower left side of the O of ONE is just starting to feather out into the field. Though typically used as the diagnostic of D.P. #3, it can be a bit difficult to see early in this die state. Look for the features mentioned above and below for confirmation of the variety.

The feathering may be a result of the so-called "ghosting" of the back of Lincoln's coat caused by excessive die wear, as the swale can be seen continuing down and through the right inside of the C of CENT, where it bends to conform to the angle at the back of Lincoln's neck on the obverse. (Remember the above-mentioned die erosion on the back of Lincoln's coat.)

As the ghosting gets worse it makes the UN of UNITED, the TES of STATES, the O of OF and the CA of AMERICA enlarged, weak and fatty. The remaining letters of USA, closer to the centerline of the reverse, remain normal. (Remember that ghosting appears on other reverse dies used in 1922.)

There is considerable erosion in and among the letters of EPU. The E has lost its two upper crossbars, and resembles a blurry L. The P has lost the hole in its upper loop, as well as the inner angle where the underside of the loop meets the upright. You might say it is starting to resemble an ice cream cone a bit lopsided to the right. The holes in the tops of the R and the B eventually fade away.

Faint scalloping caused by die erosion begins to show between certain letters of URIBU. This gets much worse as the die wear progresses. The letters of UNUM feather out sideways and develop a ghost-like doubling at their tops, getting weaker than PLURIBUS, but its scalloping is never quite as pronounced. (NOTE: many 1922-D reverse dies show heavy erosion in EPU, sometimes involving scalloping, so do not rely upon just this characteristic for die attribution.)

LDS Obv./ VLDS Rev. Very Faint D. Very Weak Reverse. Struck intermittently with

LDS Obv./ VLDS Rev. No D. Very Weak Reverse.

These are the more traditionally collected Die Pair #3 coins, the D having gotten even weaker than the previous die state, probably from normal die use, though one can never be sure on a cent of 1922. I would estimate the remaining volume of the D to be less than 2% of the original D, and perhaps even 1%.

On a decent grade coin this is still visible, either with a magnifying glass or with a well-trained eye. You must turn or wobble the coin under your light source to see if there is anything there in the normal mint mark area. If there is, it is not a "No D" coin, period! It is a "Very Faint D" coin, or as some of the TPGs prefer to conservatively call it, a "Weak D." The fact that it is significantly weaker than the "Faint D" found on the MDS Obverse is ignored by some of the TPGs.

1922-D Very Faint D Cent, Extremely Worn Reverse, DP #3, LDS/VLDS. Note second 2 weaker than first. From Mike Sokoloff.

On a well-worn coin, probably anything less than Fine condition as graded from the obverse, or one with a bit of random circulation damage in the mint mark area below the date (and you would be amazed at how often such damage occurs!), it may well be impossible to be sure if the coin is a "No D" coin or a "Very Faint D" coin. Accept this. Resist the natural human nature inclination to call it the more valuable variety. Call it a "Very Faint D" and sleep the sleep of the just.

However, there are some Die Pair #3 coins that are absolutely, positively, 110% sure, cross your heart and hope to die "No D" coins. Look at this gorgeous Mint State specimen courtesy of West Coast Coins of Oregon in Toledo, Oregon. I have studied this coin in hand. There is absolutely nothing showing in the mint mark area. I will personally guarantee it. However, because of that TPG's current policy, it was "under-slabbed" as a "Weak D" coin, even though it shows absolutely "NO D!."

1922 No D Cent. Weak Reverse. DP #3, LDS/VLDS. I saw this coin in hand at a coin show in a PCGS MS63BN CAC slab as a Weak D, but there is absolutely no mint mark on the coin! Period! Images courtesy West Coast Coins of Toledo, OR.

It is unfair that the legitimately uncertain "No D or Very Faint D?" coins are allowed to drag the absolutely unquestionable "No D, Weak Reverse" coins like this one underwater. I believe in caution, but I also believe in fairness. Collectors (and dealers) who own unquestionable "No D, Weak Reverse" coins should be able to get them certified as such. Back when I was the Senior Authenticator for ANACS I had the luxury of being able to spend as much time as was necessary to get an attribution right. Other, current Authenticator/Graders should do likewise.

As far as die characteristics go, look for slow but persistent deterioration in IGWT. The letters tend to feather out sideways, and the interior details of the N, the W and the E become greatly worn. The first T in TRUST holds up the best.

The date actually holds up fairly well, but as noted the second 2 is sometimes weak. Because of this inconsistency I suspect that the second 2 was sometimes partially obscured by grease, the same as the mint mark. Look for this weakness but do not be fooled if it is not there.

1922-D Very Faint D Cent, Extremely Worn Reverse, DP #3, LDS/VLDS. LIBERTY and very heavy die erosion on back of coat, often easily seen in photographs. From Mike Sokoloff.

LIBERTY also holds up fairly well, though there is a bit of feathering on the RT, and the left crossbar of the T erodes towards the R. (This erosion of the crossbar can be seen on other dies.) The letter "I" eventually weakens, less than seen on D.P.#1 but sharper than that seen on D.P. #Zero (below).

LDS Obv./ XLDS Rev. Very Faint D. Extremely Weak Reverse. Struck intermittently with

LDS Obv./ XLDS Rev. No D. Extremely Weak Reverse.

1922-D Cent, Very Faint D, Extremely Worn Reverse, DP #3, LDS/XLDS. A very high grade (PCGS MS-63BN) coin struck from one of the most worn out reverse dies used in 1922. Note the heavy die erosion on the lower left side of the O of ONE, the lack of detail in the wheat ears and the heavy "scalloping" in the center of E PLURIBUS UNUM, the beginning and end of which are almost gone. Circulate this coin for a few days, lose the luster and color, and the apparent grade would drop from Mint State to Good! From Mike Sokoloff.

Some Die Pair #3 coins come from such a late reverse die state that parts of E PLURIBUS UNUM are missing from the coin, or at least totally illegible. They also have the most exaggerated die erosion lines down and to the left of the O of ONE, and as such are *slightly* more collectible.

The deterioration of the reverse die from the previous die state to this one is gradual and hard to quantify, but I will set an arbitrary cutoff point between the two as when the bottom horizontal line of the E of EPU is no longer discernable from the blob above it.

ANACS Die Pair #4

Now split by me into DeLorey Die Pair #4A, only known with an Early Die State Obverse die paired with a Well Worn Reverse die (DeLorey-2204A). Generic GSID-69742, Class One only, and:

1922-D Cent. Die Pair #4A, EDS/VLDS. An otherwise new-looking Obverse Die with odd dimples, or "scallops," at rim mostly below LIBERTY, paired with Well Worn first Reverse Die. The earliest known die state of the obverse die which, many hundreds of thousands of strikes later over many intermediate die states with a different reverse die, ultimately became the variety recognized by ANACS as their Die Pair #4. This early die pairing with a heavily used reverse die left over from some other die pairing is apparently quite rare. Author's coin, photo by Robert Kelley Courtesy of the American Numismatic Assoc.

DeLorey Die Pair #4B, which begins with a still relatively new Obverse die now paired with a new Reverse die, both of which then wear down drastically over an extremely long Die Pair life and many intermediate die states. (DeLorey-2204B). Generic GSID-69742, Class One in early die state EDS/VEDS; Generic GSID-69742, Class Five in intermediate die state MDS/EDS; GSID-1877, Class Three in late die states LDS/MDS and later with a Faint to Very Faint to Very, Very Faint D; and GSID-310769, Class Four with XXLDS Obverse and absolutely "No D."

1922-D Very Faint D Cent. Weak late state of second Reverse Die. DP #4B, VLDS/LDS. This obverse is best known for the exaggerated die erosion lobes on the lapels of Lincoln's coat, though they only appear on the latest die states. Many intermediate die states also exist, that are not recognized by ANACS as Die Pair #4. See text for details. Image courtesy Heritage Auctions, (www.HA.com)

Note Well: Because this second die pairing had a very, very long die life, there are numerous Die States known of both dies, not all of them significant and/or collectible. Normal D, Worn D, Faint D, Very Faint D and Very, Very Faint D Die States known, but only the latest of these die states is currently recognized by ANACS as their traditional Die Pair #4. Newly discovered in an even later "No D" XXLDS Obverse die state with the mint mark completely worn off of the die through natural die erosion. See text for details.

The die state recognized by ANACS as its Die Pair #4 is not recognized at all by the other TPGs, presumably because they are not in the Cherrypickers' Guide. They should be included in an expanded 1922-D CPG section, and then recognized by the TPGs. (It is very important that you understand that the early and intermediate die states listed by me below as DP #4B with earlier die state notations are NOT as valuable as what ANACS calls DP #4, though some of them are certainly collectible. See text.)

The obverse and reverse dies of Die Pairs #4A and #4B began their lives producing relatively normal 1922-D cents not really collectible as varieties, unless you decide to collect pieces struck from well worn reverse dies such as is seen on all DP #4A coins and some DP #4B coins. As an intellectual exercise I will try to demonstrate how they deteriorated over time from coins with a relatively normal D (Class One) to a Worn D (Class Five) to a Faint D, Very Faint D or Very, Very Faint D (Class Three), and ultimately to a true "No D" die state (Class Four), similar in appearance to that sometimes seen on the Die Pair #1 coins, but from a different cause.

As with those varieties, it is sometimes very difficult to say which die state or category your coin falls into. When in doubt, use the lesser category. If you even think there might be a D, it is not a "No D." Where appropriate, I will give my opinion as to what a coin in the die state indicated "Should Be Called" (SBC.)

D.P. #4A (DeLorey-2204A) Early Die State Obverse die, Well Worn Reverse die. Class One only.

1922-D Cent. Die Pair #4A, EDS/VLDS. An otherwise new-looking Obverse Die with odd dimples, or "scallops," at rim mostly below LIBERTY, paired with Well Worn first Reverse Die. The earliest known die state of the obverse die which, many hundreds of thousands of strikes later over many intermediate die states with a different reverse die, ultimately became the variety recognized by ANACS as their Die Pair #4. This early die pairing with a heavily used reverse die left over from some other die pairing is apparently quite rare. Author's coin, photo by Robert Kelley Courtesy of the American Numismatic Assoc.

Die State Prime: Not yet identified, but theoretically it should exist. The hard part might be connecting it to the following if the distinctive, scallop-shaped die erosion along the rim has not yet appeared. That said, we must consider the possibility that this die was one of the ten Philadelphia Mint dies that were re-softened, mintmarked with a D, and then re-hardened, and that this highly unusual process caused the scallops to appear before the die was ever used. Keep an eye out for a coin with a normal obverse and the following reverse.

EDS/VLDS. SBC just a 1922-D. (Not recognized by ANACS as a Die Pair #4.) Relatively new obverse die with a series of depressed, often half-circle-ish die defect marks, which I call "scallops," inside lower left rim from the L of LIBERTY down to Lincoln's shoulder. One extra "scallop" above the L at about K-9:45. Date normal, though the D is a bit less tall than some other D's and it sits in a broad, very shallow depression possibly caused by the punching action of the mint mark punch pushing up the die steel around it.

1922-D Cent. DP #4B, EDS/VEDS. Closeup of some of the die erosion "scallops" below LIBERTY. This die is not known in an earlier die state without the "scallops," and it is possible that an unusual un-annealing and then re-annealing process (see text) caused the surface of the die to splinter like this when new. Author's coin, photo by Robert Kelley Courtesy of the American Numismatic Assoc.

(There are many random U.S. coin dies that show a sort of "crater rim" effect thrown up around the mint mark in the die, but the effect is not very strong on this die. However, when such dies are repolished that raised area is quickly removed, shortening the height of the mint mark faster than if the die had been flat.)

The reverse die is very heavily worn, with the curved lines in the upper wheat ears almost completely gone except on the top inside of the left ear. The tops of E PLURIBUS are very weak, though the bottoms of the letters are somewhat stronger, most noticeably on the S. The period after the S is gone.

(Note: Apparently quite rare with this reverse die. I had seen many, many coins with the scalloped obverse over five years of research, and had in fact already submitted my "finished" manuscript to the publisher, before I found a coin with the worn reverse die pairing on eBay. This is why a conscientious Writer continues to find excuse after excuse to not finish his or her project until his or her Editor threatens them with bodily harm!)

D.P. #4B (DeLorey-2204B) Class One (early die states); Class Five (intermediate die states); Class Three (latest die states with D still showing); Class Four (XXLDS Obverse die state with "No D.")

EDS Obv./ VEDS Rev. SBC just "1922-D." (Not recognized by ANACS as a D.P.#4.) Still a fairly decent die other than the scalloping at the rim below and above LIBERTY. Normal date, IN GOD WE TRUST (IGWT) strong, V.D.B. weak but visible, bottom outline of bust intact. Fairly normal D, just a bit soft around the edges due to die erosion starting to feather out

1922-D Cent. Mint mark only slightly weak, not enough worth mentioning in description. New (Strong) second Reverse Die. DP #4B, EDS/VEDS Obv. With dimples I call "scallops" mainly below (just one above) LIBERTY. Small planchet clip. Author's coin, photo by Robert Kelley Courtesy of the American Numismatic Assoc.

into the field, strongest on the bottom and right. Roughly two-thirds or a bit more of the original mint mark volume remaining.

The "Scallops" at the rim below LIBERTY appear to actually grow stronger throughout this die state, with a few weaker "Scallops" developing at the rim above the stronger one at about K-9:45, but eventually the process reverses itself and these fade away in later die states. LIBERTY fairly decent, L connected to rim, IBE sharp, RTY starting to enlarge. (The slightly later version of this die state is seen with the D a bit softer and V.D.B. a bit weaker, but not worthy of its own die state.)

New Reverse die installed, so in a newer die state than obverse. EPU and wheat lines strong, field basically level with hardly any die erosion around the wheat stems (a common location for radiate die erosion lines).

MDS Obv./ EDS Rev. SBC "1922-D Worn D." (Not recognized by ANACS as a D.P.#4.) Now Class Five.

Scallops below LIBERTY starting to fade. Those closest to L and back point of shoulder almost gone. Those above LIBERTY gone except for the one at K-9:45.

Both 2's in the date are still fairly sharp, the second more so, especially at the top. The 1 and the 9 are getting a bit mushy, the 9 more so. More importantly, the die now shows a "Worn D" that is boldest in its upper left corner and shallowest on its lower right, but rough and grainy and tapered towards the field about its entire circumference.

1922-D Worn D Cent. DP #4B, MDS/EDS. Mint mark losing height while broadening outwards due to die wear. Die erosion "scallops" starting to fade as the die field around them continues to erode away under normal use. Only the slightest precursors of the two lobes under the right end of the lapel that will eventually make this die the famous ANACS Die Pair #4. Author's coin, photo by Robert Kelley Courtesy of the American Numismatic Assoc.

In my opinion, back in the 1970's and earlier this was a collectible "Weak D" coin, but the grading services today will just certify it as a "1922-D" coin, so I am compromising and calling it a "Worn D" coin to acknowledge the obvious fact that it is no longer a "Normal D" coin even if the wear is not significant. My rule of thumb for a "Worn D" coin is that the volume of the D above the field is less than half of what is seen on a new die coin. On this particular die the outline of the D has expanded due to die erosion, or feathering, where the mint mark meets the field.

The field that the D sits in slopes slightly upwards towards the rim, which may explain why the D is weakest on its corner closest to the rim. That part of the field that used to sharply define the D has either worn or been polished away. The lower lapel of Lincoln's coat is very shallow, corresponding to the erosion of the field below the date.

The V.D.B. finishes eroding off of the die and disappears. The bottom line of the lapel gradually develops irregular bumps where the die erosion is spreading into the raised line on the die that separates the coat from the rim. Watch for two small, rounded bumps (which become quite extreme "lobes" [my term] in the later Die States) forming under the two lapel panels at the right end of the truncation of the bust. They are not yet developed enough to be recognized by ANACS as a D.P.#4, but they grow.

LIBERTY still fairly strong, though the field behind RT and up to the left side of the Y is raised and a bit rough due to die erosion. Shallow depression above and to right of Y. Field below TY well textured due to die erosion.

IGWT is a bit soft, with TRUST the strongest. The tops of the letters are still intact. Sometimes seen with wire rims around parts of the upper obverse.

The reverse is fairly normal, with just a bit of die erosion forming along the wheat stems. Often seen with wire rim from K-10 to K-2 or so.

LDS Obv./ MDS Rev. SBC "1922-D Faint D." (Not recognized by ANACS as a D.P.#4.) Class Five.

1922-D Faint D Cent. DP #4B, LDS/MDS. Mint mark has continued to fade, becoming broader and shallower while the central hole has almost, but not quite, disappeared. A non-collector would probably not recognize it as a "D." See text for details regarding mint mark, "scallops" and lapel lobes. (Note: this particular coin was formerly encased in a "Lucky Cent" holder, causing some warping of it, and the bulge between the wheat stems is not typical of this die state.) Author's coin, photo by Robert Kelley Courtesy of the American Numismatic Assoc.

Scallops below LIBERTY quite faded, but their presence serves to identify the obverse as an LDS rather than the VLDS which follows. Scallop at K-9:45 gone. Much of the obverse field shows concavity just inside the rim, as though the die had been deliberately polished around its perimeter to minimize the die erosion and/or scalloping. This gives the obverse a very shallow bowl shape. However, the rounded bumps under the two rightmost panels of the lapel were not removed, and they continued to expand outwards to about 40% of the way to the rim in this die state range.

1 & 9 mushy, bases of both 2's mushy though tops of both 2's strong, the second more so. Die erosion can be seen down and to the right under the base of the second 2 and inside the hooked top of the 2.

The D is Faint, highly feathered out into the field all around with just a very faint hole in the middle of the D. I would estimate that approximately 10% of the volume of the original D remains, barely elevated above the field but much wider than the original D.

In LIBERTY, the foot of the L and all of the "I" begin to fade. The BE are small and crisp, while the RTY is more enlarged and a bit mushier. IGWT is a little bit softer, with TRUST continuing to be the strongest. The tops of GOD begin to feather out towards the rim.

The reverse seems to show good definition in the curved, parallel lines of the wheat ears to begin with, so much so that many would call this a "strong reverse" on a Mint State coin. However, the grooves that separate the lines have grown shallower, which will cause them to wear away faster in circulation.

VLDS Obv./ LDS Rev. SBC "1922-D Very Faint D." Not recognized by ANACS as a Die Pair #4, but getting very close, and accepted by many collectors as a Die Pair #4 if the two most prominent lobes are very close to the rim. Class Five.

1922-D Very Faint D Cent. DP #4B, VLDS/LDS. Author's coin, photo by Robert Kelley Courtesy of the American Numismatic Assoc.

Scallops below LIBERTY are gone, a requirement to qualify as the VLDS. Beyond that benchmark there is a range of deterioration as the lobes below the lapel grow while other details weaken. Concavity of obverse field increases near the rim on either side of and below Lincoln's bust, with the affected areas showing multiple radial die erosion lines. Some of these flow lines appear to be angled a bit towards the left as they come down.

The two broad lobes under the two rightmost panels of the lapel, which are the defining characteristic of Die Pair #4B in its latest few die states, have extended at least more than halfway across the normal space between the truncation of the bust and the rim. They continue to grow, and in the latter end of this die state range they cover over 90% of the gap, but neither lobe touches the rim. (Note: The one on the right eventually touches first.)

Entire date mushy, only the 1 and the top of the second 2 retaining any definition, and that goes away as the right side of the 2 fades into the field. The "bay" inside the top of the second 2 remains well outlined for a while, but fades as the lobes near the rim.

1922-D Very Faint D Cent. DP #4B, VLDS/LDS. Extended lobes below lapel extend more than half way to the rim but do not yet touch rim. Enlargement Courtesy of Numismatic Guaranty Company. Used with permission.

The D is Very Faint, and to the untrained eye could easily be mistaken as a "No D." However, a percent or two of it remains above the field. In strength the D is comparable to those seen on the late die states of Obverse Dies #1 & #3, and it should be treated by the TPG's the same way (i.e., as a "Weak D") as those two dies are, even if the cause of the weakness is different than the re-polishing that weakened the D's on Die Pairs #1 & #3. Of course, it would be even more accurate if the TPG's used my new "Faint D" terminology system instead of the ambiguous "Weak D."

It is conceivable that coins in this die state were struck with no trace of a mint mark due to grease on the dies, as happened on Die Pairs #1 & #3, but this has not yet been established to my satisfaction. (There is a high grade DP#4B below with absolutely no trace of a D, but that omission was caused by die wear.)

In LIBERTY, the L starts out with a stub of a foot, which fades. The I starts out very thin but well outlined, but it fades almost into the field. The BE begin thin but still quite legible but then they too start to fade. The RT get quite mushy and the crossbar of the T grows to touch the R (a characteristic not exclusive to this die). The Y remains fairly legible but it too is encroached by the crossbar of the T.

On the reverse, the upper and outer wheat lines become very weak, while the inner lines have little definition that can easily disappear in circulation. New scalloping starts to develop among the letters of EPU, but be aware that other dies have similar scalloping here in late die states. As a rule the E and P of E PLURIBUS are still readable. There are heavy die flow lines about the lower wheat ears, and an arc of raised flow lines connects the bases of the stems. (This may be "ghosting" from the top of Lincoln's head.)

XLDS Obv./ VLDS Rev. SBC "1922-D Very, Very Faint D." The die state recognized by ANACS as a Die Pair #4. Now Class Three.

This "Die State" actually shows a few recognizable sub-die states, but I didn't want to go crazy on you. The bottom line is that this is the variety that ANACS has been calling "Weak D, Die Pair #4" since 1988.

The boundary between the latter pieces of the previous die state and the earliest pieces of this die state is whether or not at least one of the lobes

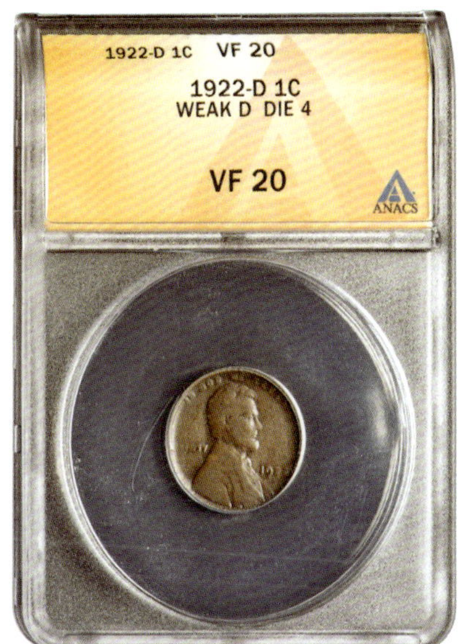

1922-D Very, Very Faint D Cent. Weak Reverse. DP #4B, XLDS/VLDS. The earliest die state recognized by ANACS as their Die Pair #4, though other, sometimes much earlier, die states are recognized by this book as also being from Die Pair #4B. To qualify as the XLDS/VLDS die state one or more die erosion lobes below the lapel must touch rim. On this coin the first lobe touches. Author's coin, photo by Robert Kelley Courtesy of the American Numismatic Assoc.

1922-D Very, Very Faint D Cent. Weak Reverse. DP #4B, XLDS/VLDS. The earliest die state recognized by ANACS as their Die Pair #4, though other, sometimes much earlier, die states are recognized by this book as also being from Die Pair #4B. To qualify as the XLDS/VLDS die state one or more die erosion lobes below the lapel must touch rim. Author's coin, photo by Robert Kelley Courtesy of the American Numismatic Assoc.

touches the rim. This can be difficult to determine on well worn specimens. If you cannot see whether the tip of the rightmost lobe touches the rim or not, or the second lobe if the first one is damaged, it will not be certifiable by ANACS as a Die Pair #4 coin. However, if you can clearly see that the rightmost lobe touches the rim, even if the second lobe does not yet touch, it is an XLDS Obverse (my designation) that will be recognized by ANACS as a Die Pair #4 (their designation).

Somewhat similar in overall appearance to the preceding, just weaker. In the earliest sub-state of the XLDS obverse, the upright of the L in LIBERTY continues to melt into the rim while the I is faint but well outlined, and the BE are small but crisp. The R is bloated and blurry, and the left arm of the crossbar of the T is firmly embedded in it. The Y remains fairly normal for a cent of 1922.

However, the deterioration swiftly continues, and eventually the I disappears and everything else but the TY becomes an illegible blob. During this deterioration IN GOD WE become almost illegible, though TRUST remains with R the weakest letter.

The important difference is that the raised ridge on a normal Lincoln cent die that forms the trough between the lapel and the rim on the coin has been breached. The lapel itself has grown even shallower, with hardly any lip at the bottom of the lapel to contain the outwards expansion of the planchet during a strike.

1922-D Very, Very Faint D Cent. Weak Reverse. DP #4B, XLDS/VLDS. Closeup of the greatly eroded date and mint mark, with the first die erosion lobe below the lapel (counting from the right) now touching the rim, the benchmark required by ANACS to qualify as their Die Pair #4. The second lobe soon also touches. Author's coin, photo by Robert Kelley Courtesy of the American Numismatic Assoc.

The bumps at the bottom of the lapel become (relatively) larger as metal flow washes over the ridge like a sand bar at high tide. The contact area between the first lobe (from the right) and the rim grows from a mere point to a solid line. The contact area of the second lobe eventually exceeds that of the first. Ultimately only a tiny, depressed triangle separates them.

In the XLDS, the second 2 quickly loses the remaining detailing of its top and both 2's become almost unreadable. The 1 holds its shape. The D is at least 99% gone, just a featureless flat area only vaguely outlined by the shallowest of depressions around it. To the naked eye it looks like a "No D" coin, though if you rotate the coin under a light you should be able to detect the slightest of mounds below the date. (See pictures of earlier die states to see the normal position of the D, where the left side of the D is centered under the space between the 9 and the first 2.)

As with the previous die state it is possible that at various times the Very Faint and/or Very, Very Faint D has been filled in on the die with the same sort of mint grease and other sludge that caused Die Pair #1 & 3 to produce legitimate "No D" coins, for a while at least. After all, the leaky coin press that struck Die Pairs #1 and #3 must have struck other die pairs.

XXLDS Obv./ VLDS Rev. SBC "1922 No D." The end of the line for this long-lived die.

Since this is an even later die state than the die state recognized by ANACS as their Die Pair #4, I assume that it will eventually be recognized by them as a Die Pair #4 in the ANACS Canon once this book is published. I have shown them the illustrated high grade example of this die state, and Authenticator J.P. Martin and at least one other ANACS Authenticator have agreed with me that the coin does not show any trace of the D.

(I have also shown this coin to full time coin dealer and former American Numismatic Association President [1999-2001] H. Robert "Bob" Campbell, who teaches Summer Seminar Courses on Counterfeit Coin Detection and Coin Grading for the ANA, and who has done extensive research on the varieties of the Cents of 1922 over the years. He agrees with me that the coin shows No Mint Mark.)

1922 No D, Weak Reverse. DP #4B, XXLDS/VLDS. True View image courtesy of PCGS. Lightened by the author.

My search for a Die Pair #4B coin in a true "No D" status was maddeningly elusive. I owned a coin with an illegible date with both lobes beneath the lapel deeply embedded in the rim on which I could not see a D, but the apparent grade was essentially only "Good-4," which according to my own attribution standards (see above) was not in a high enough grade to declare a new variety.

1922 No D, Weak Reverse. DP #4B, XXLDS/VLDS. Excerpt of True View image courtesy of PCGS. Lightened by the author.

In my study of old ANACS paper certificates from the ANA Museum Archives I had seen at least one VG-ish 1922 coin with the full lobes of a Die Pair #4 coin, officially certified by ANACS as a "No D" coin in May of 1981 (which, amusingly enough, would have been by myself and the rest of the staff; I have no idea why we left it out of the 1982 ANACS Canon), and from the photograph it looked as though it certainly qualified as one. However, I wanted PROOF that I could show you NOW!!!

Then in May of 2024 a piece popped up in an online auction which was certified by a major TPG as a "Weak D" (under their conservative current standards which do not recognize any "No D" on anything other than a Die Pair #2), graded by them as an AU-55. I could see from the pictures that the piece even had significant traces of original Red color on it! Finally, a high

USA 1922 "No D" Cent
In our opinion this is a genuine original item as described.
ANACS No: E-4416-I **Grade:** N/A
Registered To: 5-22-81

An ancient (hey, I authenticated the coin myself, as the Senior Authenticator for the ANA in 1981!) ANACS Photo Certificate showing a 1922 "No D" cent of the variety now listed herein as a 1922 "No D" Die Pair #4B XXLDS/VLDS. The die state matches and confirms the slabbed coin shown here. Certificate courtesy of the ANA Museum. Scan by my wife.

grade Die Pair #4 coin! I pounced on it, and waited for its arrival like a kid at Christmas waiting for his Red Ryder BB gun. Eventually it arrived, and I was very happy!

1922 No D, Weak Reverse. DP #4B, XXLDS/VLDS. Front of PCGS AU-55 Weak D slab. Author's photo.

1922 No D, Weak Reverse. DP #4B, XXLDS/VLDS. Back of PCGS AU-55 Weak D slab. Author's photo.

The coin is definitely a later die state than the **XLDS** Obverse recognized by ANACS as Die Pair #4. The last digit of the date is no longer readable, one reason why coins in this die state would have been shunned by collectors in the 1920's and 1930's, and left in circulation to fade away. The die erosion below the bust has increased, so that the fourth lobe on the lapel (counting from the right) now touches the rim. The third lobe is close but not quite there. LIBERTY and IGWT are a bit weaker.

1922 No D, Weak Reverse. DP #4B, XXLDS/VLDS. Obverse Only. Shot in PCGS AU-55 slab. Author's photo.

1922 No D, Weak Reverse. DP #4B, XXLDS/VLDS. Reverse Only. Shot in PCGS AU-55 slab. Author's photo.

This die state, and quite frankly every obverse die state from VLDS on, is extremely difficult to obtain in high grade, probably because collectors of the 1920's and 1930's and beyond did not appreciate coins with poor detail when coins from more normal dies were still available in pocket change. Because coins from this die state were left in circulation, they quickly lost the original luster and color that this coin has, and would have dropped in apparent grade from Uncirculated to EF to Good in just a few weeks.

Thus the normal coins were eventually saved in pennyboards and Whitman tri-fold albums for the benefit of future generations of collectors, while the Rodney Dangerfield coins from extremely late die states got no respect, and were allowed to continue to circulate into oblivion.

Because of the extremely limited population of high grade Die Pair #4B coins in the **XLDS/VLDS** and **XXLDS/VLDS** die stages, I cannot be totally certain where the mint mark absolutely, totally, 100% wore off from the die as simultaneous die wear on the four lobes beneath the lapel extended them to the extent shown in the closeup from the TrueView image. Thus, I cannot say with absolute certainty that an **XXLDS/VLDS** coin with the four extended lobes, (at least three touching the rim being the benchmark for the Die State), might not exist with a hypothetical "Ultra Faint D." Any potential 1922 "No D" Die Pair #4B coin must be evaluated on a case by case basis, and only on coins in high enough grades to properly evaluate.

On the reverse the scalloping at the top is a bit deeper and EPU and the wheat ears are a bit weaker, though the central letters in ONE CENT and UNITED STATES OF AMERICA are still surprisingly sharp. It is not impossible that this reverse die found temporary re-use with a different obverse die, even though a few unused reverse dies were still in the die vault.

(For the record, I see no sign of circulation wear on the slabbed coin shown here, and as a former professional Grader I would grade the piece as "MS-60, RB, Environmental Damage." The AU-55 given is probably a reasonable commercial net grade. That said, the precise grade is irrelevant. Either way it is the finest known, by very far, 1922 "No D" Die Pair #4B coin, and I am extremely proud to own it.)

"To D or Not to D?" This coin was struck as a 1922-D Cent, but is it an "Ultra Faint D" or a "No D?" The sad reality is that the coin is too worn to tell for sure. Otherwise it is a 1922-D DP #4B, XXLDS/ VLDS. Closeup Date, mm and lapel lobes. Author's coin, Photo by Robert Kelley Courtesy of the American Numismatic Assoc.

CHAPTER TWELVE

The 1922-D "DeLorey Varieties"

For decades the collecting hobby has recognized what I call "The ANACS Varieties," *aka* Die Pairs #1, #2, #3 and #4. Of these four, only Die Pairs #1 through #3 were generally thought of as highly significant, because in all (Die Pair #2) or some (Die Pair #1 & 3) of their various die states they each struck a no-question "1922 No D" coin, with either a Strong or a Weak Reverse. I helped codify these three "ANACS Varieties" when I worked there.

The much later attributed Die Pair #4 never earned the respect that I believe that it deserves, in part because up until just now (see D.P. #4B listing above) it was commonly thought to have never produced a "No D, Weak

Reverse" coins. Proving that it did was hard, because specimens of what modern-day ANACS recognizes as Die Pair #4 are typically seen in well-worn condition.

Like the 1937-D "3-legged" nickel struck from a badly abused pair of dies, the 1922-D Cents from Die Pair #4B in its (now) most desirable VLDS, XLDS and XXLDS die states were shunned by collectors when they were still in circulation in high grades back in the 1920s and 1930s, because nicer (but boringly normal) 1922-D coins were obtainable in circulation or from dealers. Only a few eccentric collectors cared about the oddball stuff from worn-out dies, and so it was that many of the best "No D" and "Faint D" coins from Die Pairs #1, #3 & #4 remained in circulation until their naturally weak details were obscured even further by significant circulation wear.

This can make attributing and/or authenticating certain coins very difficult. We can identify the die pair, which when authenticating a 1909-SVDB cent as genuine is usually all you need to do, but on a well-worn cent of 1922 it can sometimes be impossible to be sure if a coin which does not show a D *now* did or did not show a Faint or Very Faint D when it was *new*.

For this reason two of the three major TPG's, ANACS and PCGS, have become hesitant to certify Die Pair #1 and #3 coins without mint marks as true "No D, Weak Reverse" coins because of a fear of mis-attributing a "Very Faint D" coin as a "No D" coin, which might create a financial liability for them later down the road. Nevertheless, "No D, Weak Reverse" coins do exist for Die Pairs #1 and #3. Among knowledgeable collectors, and dealers who know their stuff, they remain highly collectible by both die variety and die state (i.e., with and without the D).

ANACS alone now recognizes the significant Die Pair #4 in its Extremely Late Die State (XLDS/VLDS) as a "Weak D" coin, though over the years it did certify at least one of them as "No D" coin. It does not currently certify the newly-rediscovered even later XXLDS/VLDS die state as being a "No D" coin, but I will see if I can convince them to do so.

Those four obverse dies aside, we know from Denver Mint records that 20 obverse dies were used in 1922, and 27 reverse dies, and that more than four of those obverse (and reverse) dies were degraded either intentionally or unintentionally down to interesting and collectible die states. However, for decades collectors have recognized only those three, and then four, obverse dies as being significant, because first Craig, and then *Coin World's* Collectors Clearinghouse (of which I was a part from 1974 to 1978), and then the American Numismatic Association Certification Service (of which I was a part from 1978 to 1984), said that they were the only important varieties. We were wrong.

Mea culpa, mea culpa, mea maxima culpa. We really meant well, but we did not go far enough. As someone who helped form those opinions, I say that it is now way past time that we expand upon them.

The following 1922-D die varieties are the ones that I now consider to be collectible as well, some much more so than others of course, and the Die Pair numbers given here are ones that I alone have assigned to them based upon my personal experience. Please feel free to make reference to them, but please try to do so accurately.

As mentioned earlier, each will also have a four-digit universal DeLorey Number that will begin with a "22" to indicate that it refers to a cent made in 1922, followed by two digits that refer to the Die Pair number (i.e., 2201, 2207, etc.) Where necessary, letter suffixes (such as Die Pairs #8A, #8B & #8C, given DeLorey numbers 2208A, 2208B & 2208C) will denote different die pairs where there was a change in one die or the other over the life of the most relevant die.

I make no claims of monetary value for any of the new varieties. Only time will tell if that develops through collector interest hopefully generated by this book. However, I do sincerely think that some of these new varieties, in their appropriate later die states, should be just as significant to the numismatic world as ANACS Die Pairs #1, #3 and #4. Others are just collectible because they are different.

The coins from one of the new die pairs, Die Pair #ZeroB, have already been collected for decades as misattributed Die Pair #1 coins, which is why I have included it in Class Three. It belongs in the ANACS Canon, because it has been there for decades, unrecognized. At least three other dies show Faint, Very Faint or Very, Very Faint mint marks that are fully comparable to certain die states of the Die Pair #1, #3 and #4 coins. I don't know why Craig never recognized them. Perhaps they are scarcer than Die Pairs #1-4 and he never saw them. It is also possible that he knew of them but ignored them because they never struck no question "No D" coins, as did his "Variety-2, 3 & 4" dies, and collectors cared more about "No D" coins.

NOTE WELL: Some popular die varieties such as, say, the 1918/7-D Buffalo Nickel, began and ended their die life as that variety. The die variety was a function of how the die was made, and it was always there. The die wear that it underwent during its die life did not change the die variety, though with some of the early 19th Century overdates the details of the underdates fade with die wear and actually become less interesting and/or desirable in some late die states.

The 1922 cent varieties are an entirely different case. As with the ANACS Varieties, all of these so-called "Die Varieties" are actually recognizable "Die States." Each of these dies started out in brand new condition, generally distinguishable from each other only by the positions of the mint marks, and those positional differences are relatively slight.

A few of the collectible die varieties are known in their boring early die states with recognizable die scratches or similar marks, as happens at random on many denominations in many years. Other dies with identifiable die markers never did become interesting. See the section on "Die Markers" below. In either case these die characteristics sometimes disappear as the die ages.

Wherever possible, I have attempted to trace dies back to their earliest die states and forward to their latest die states, which sometimes involved the replacement of either an obverse or a reverse die due to die breakage or just plain wear and tear. Where such a die substitution had been made, the use of the letters A & B in the Die Pair # will signify the older die marriage and the newer die marriage, respectively.

Die Pair #11 is wonderfully complicated. It involves two reverse dies, the first one significant because of a die crack, and the second one not significant. They are paired with one obverse die, which began normally but then became significant later in its life because of rim cuds forming on the obverse before the significant reverse die was replaced. To signify this three-step chain I will be using DP#11A.1, DP#11A.2, and DP#11B. Getting all of this to make sense (and I sincerely hope that it does) is just part of the reason why this project has taken me years to complete.

I had considerable success tracing ANACS Die Pair #4 back to an earlier die pairing and several progressive die states (see my Die Pairs #4A and #4B), and some limited success with Die Pair #1, as will be seen with Die Pair #Zero below, which is linked to it. I have attempted to do the same with earlier die states of Die Pair #3, but was unable to do so.

I am most proud of having established that my 1922-D Die Pair #5, with its "Faint D" or "Very Faint D," is the long-sought predecessor die state to the fabled "1922 No D Die Pair #2!" Perhaps continued research will turn up a "missing link" die state or two that will identify more die varieties in their earlier die lives, which may give us some additional clues as to why the mint mark(s) weakened and/or disappeared on certain dies.

Many of the early to mid die state pieces listed here are, to put it bluntly, perfectly normal coins of no collectible interest other than as by date and mint mark. They are included here as part of the intellectual exercise of tracing a finite universe of dies through two months of heavy use. The obverse of Die Pair #8, for example, went through two different reverse dies before finally getting interesting in its third die marriage. Given many more years of research and an infinite budget for buying coins to study it might be possible to trace each 1922 cent die through every die pairing and significant die state. You will not find that here, but I tried.

I shall use the following die state terms for each side of the coin being discussed, since new dies were routinely paired with old dies. "Prime" to indicate a new or nearly new die; "VEDS" or Very Early Die State for a coin with just a bit of die wear; "EDS" or Early Die State; "MDS" or Middle Die State; "LDS" or Late Die State; "VLDS" or Very Late Die State, and "XLDS" or "XXLDS" for Extremely Late Die States. The obverse die with a large cud die break at "WE TRUST" (Die Pair #14) is obviously in its Terminal Die State.

Because of the vast misuse of the term "Weak D" over the years, I am retiring it and creating the terms "Worn D" (basically a mint mark which has lost more than 50% of its mass) and "Well Worn D" (basically a mint mark which has lost more than 75% of its mass) to allow me to refer to dies that have obvious wear in the mint mark area, without seeming to invoke the published values given for "Weak D" coins. As a rule "Worn D" and "Well Worn D" coins should not be worth a significant premium, but that is up to collectors and the market to decide.

As with the ANACS varieties I will be using "Faint D" to describe a mint mark that has lost 90% or more of its original mass. This is approximately equivalent to what ANACS and PCGS now consider worthy of a "Weak D" designation, though in previous years that ambiguous term might have referred to a coin with a much stronger D, while nowadays it might also include a coin with absolutely nothing left of the D.

Coins with only a hint of a mint mark, in the neighborhood of 2% of the original D or less, will be called a "Very Faint D." Many of these will be coins which in the 1970's were optimistically called "No D" coins, because you could get more money for it that way. However, we must be strict. "No D" must mean "NO D," period. Do not let ownership negate objectivity.

Expect to find coins right on the cusp between one die state description and the next, and try not to get too excited or too frustrated when you do so. Die erosion is usually a slow and gradual process, and the differences given here between consecutive die states may depend simply on what I have seen and not seen. Feel free to describe your coin as "between Die State xxx and Die State yyy," or whatever, if that is how you see it. Again, please try to be accurate.

IN GOD WE TRUST abbreviated as IGWT, and E PLURIBUS UNUM as EPU. Clock positions given as K-12, K-1, etc. Right and Left are from the viewer's point of view. Each wheat ear consists of a curved, single line stem at the bottom, a head (or spike) of kernels in the middle, and a stylized group of curved, parallel lines at the top to represent the wispy random threads, or awns, that help wild wheat seeds propagate in the wind. Since few of my readers will know what an awn is (I didn't), I will refer to them as the "curved, parallel lines" and abbreviate them, in plural form, as "CPL."

The New DeLorey "Worn D," "Well Worn D," "Faint D" and "Very Faint D" Varieties

Some with "Dimples" near the Mint Mark, possibly caused by obverse dies that were made for use in Philadelphia being altered and used at the Denver Mint

Die Pairs #ZeroA & ZeroB. (DeLorey-2200A & B.) Numerous die states, not all of them significant and/or collectible. Generic GSID-69742 for all DP#ZeroA and DP#ZeroB up through die state LDS/LDS. GSID-393497 from die state VLDS/MDS on. Mint mark ranges from "Normal" down to "Very Faint D." Last die state of the latter die pair that shows the jogging die crack through the O of ONE, called by me Die Crack-1A. Class Three because some of those coins were mistakenly collected as ANACS Die Pair #1 coins (which all have that same die crack) for the past 40+ years. May be abbreviated as DP#ZA and DP#ZB if you wish.

1922-D Cent. DP #ZeroA (old rev.), EDS/LDS. Weak Reverse. A not atypical coin for 1922 with a strong obverse and a weak reverse, only significant because the obverse die *eventually* wore down in its next die pairing so much so that it closely resembled the obverse of DP #1, AND because the worn-out reverse die seen here was soon replaced with a different, newer reverse die that *eventually* became the Jogging Die Crack Reverse of DP #1. SBC just a 1922-D Cent. Author's coin, photo by Robert Kelley Courtesy of the American Numismatic Assoc.

1922-D Cent, DP #ZeroB (new rev.), MDS/VEDS. With collar clash along left rim. No design clash marks at back of head. Strong Reverse at first, but it fades and cracks as both dies go through many different die states. Seen in later die states with a "Faint D" and then a "Very Faint D." It is the author's belief that many "Very Faint D" coins collected as DP #1 coins solely because of the Jogging Die Crack are actually DP #ZeroB coins. Author's coin, photo by Robert Kelley Courtesy of the American Numismatic Assoc.

This obverse die, with its two reverse die pairings and its wide range of die states, is the perfect example of how many a 1922-D cent die lived and died in the name of coinage. Known die states and die marriages range from a EDS Obverse paired with a nondescript LDS (but not completely worn out) reverse die (DeLorey-2200A); an MDS Obverse that still had a still fairly strong D paired with a new VEDS Reverse die (DeLorey-2200B, incl. all that follow); various LDS/EDS and VLDS/MDS strikings with clash marks of differing strengths at the back of Lincoln's head that fade in and out as both the mint mark and the reverse die wear down; eventually deteriorating down to XLDS/LDS (and possibly XXLDS/LDS) coins with a "Faint D" or "Very Faint D" obverse and the "Jogging Die Crack" reverse previously only known on ANACS Die Pair #1. Not known in a "No D" die state, though possible.

For a long time I had specimens from these last two "Faint D" and "Very Faint D" die states in my notes as slightly earlier die states of Die Pair #1. I assumed that they had to be such because their reverse die showed the "jogging die crack" of Die Pair #1, which collectors, writers and professional Authenticators (including myself) have talked about for almost half a century. However, with 1922 cents one should never assume anything.

The two obverses (#ZeroB and #1) show certain characteristics that are similar to each other but chronologically impossible, such as die wear that is present on one obverse but not yet seen on the other, *and vice versa*, which cannot occur on just one die. After years of study I proved that Obv. #ZeroB is a different obverse die that underwent the same types of abuses that Obverse #1 endured, with similar results. Die wear is strongly influenced by the details on the dies, and identical die pairs often show similar wear patterns.

According to the standards set out above this could be called Die Pair #A1, with the traditional Die Pair #1 being renamed as Die Pair #B1. However, I do not wish to renumber any varieties from the ANACS canon any more than absolutely necessary, mainly because it caused so much confusion the last time we did that (1982). Therefore, I am calling the products of this obverse die and its two reverse dies Die Pair #ZeroA & #ZeroB, and simply noting that the obverse is die linked via its second reverse die to D.P. #1.

Die Pair #ZeroA. DeLorey-2200A. First Reverse Die. (Worn reverse only, not exceptional.)

1922-D Cent. DP #ZeroA (old rev.), EDS/LDS. Weak Reverse. A not atypical coin for 1922 with a strong obverse and a weak reverse, only significant because the obverse die *eventually* wore down in its next die pairing so much so that it closely resembled the obverse of DP #1, AND because the worn-out reverse die seen here was soon replaced with a different, newer reverse die that *eventually* became the Jogging Die Crack Reverse of DP #1. SBC just a 1922-D Cent. Author's coin, photo by Robert Kelley Courtesy of the American Numismatic Assoc.

EDS Obv./ LDS Rev. No Prime or VEDS of this obverse die is known, but one might be identified on a normal-looking coin from the "spike" described below now that you know what to look for. The earliest known die state seen to date is definitely not a new die, as there is some "dimpling" in the field around the D, and some light but normal die erosion through the edge of the lapel below Lincoln's necktie, and along the back of his coat from the neck down to directly below the Y of LIBERTY. However, as 1922-D cents go it is fairly non-descript, and a specimen should just be called a 1922-D cent.

The easiest way to pick this obverse die out of a lineup of "normal" 1922-D cents is a tiny "spike" angled up and to the right from the right end of the base of the E of WE. If you think of the base of the E as a human leg laying down, then the spike at the right end of the base is the foot of the leg pointing mostly up but a little bit away from the torso. This spike is seen on all die states of D.P.#ZeroA & B, but gets harder to see on the latter as the lines of WE broaden and flatten. This spike is NEVER seen on D.P. #1 coins in any die state, proof that these are two different obverse dies. (Note: There is a much smaller but obviously related similar and parallel spike up and to the right from the right end of the center tine of the E, but it quickly fades with die wear and is only visible on the earlier die states of this die.)

The obverse rim on the left side does NOT yet show the indented line (collar clash) always seen on D.P. #ZeroB coins of sufficiently high grade..

The reverse die is fairly well worn with significant weakness on the outsides of the Curved Parallel Lines. There is ghosting through the C of CENT and quite a bit of detail lost on the left end of EPU. The "E" looks like an "L" with a broad top, and the "P" has lost the hole in its upper half. There are strong radial die erosion lines coming off the period between them. The rest of EPU is feathered out but intact.

1922-D Cent, DP #ZeroB, MDS/VEDS. Closeup of WE with spike up from end of lower bar, as seen on a more photogenic coin of the next die marriage. There is a similar spike on the middle crossbar but it is hard to see. Author's coin, photo by Robert Kelley Courtesy of the American Numismatic Assoc.

As of this writing only one DP #ZeroA coin is known, perhaps because it is so unremarkable. There should be more out there. Keep checking the base of the E of WE for more DP #ZeroA specimens.

Die Pair #ZeroB. DeLorey-2200B. Second Reverse Die. (Reverse ranges over a long life from new down to worn and cracked. DC-1A in latest die states with jogging die crack through the O of ONE.)

1922-D Cent. DP #ZeroA (old rev.), EDS/LDS. Weak Reverse. A not atypical coin for 1922 with a strong obverse and a weak reverse, only significant because the obverse die *eventually* wore down in its next die pairing so much so that it closely resembled the obverse of DP #1, AND because the worn-out reverse die seen here was soon replaced with a different, newer reverse die that *eventually* became the Jogging Die Crack Reverse of DP #1. SBC just a 1922-D Cent. Author's coin, photo by Robert Kelley Courtesy of the American Numismatic Assoc.

MDS Obv./ VEDS Rev. Though the reverse die seen on D.P. #ZeroA was not horrible by 1922 standards, it was for some reason replaced. The date, mint mark, LIBERTY and IGWT are still pretty normal, with perhaps a bit more dimpling around the mint mark. In the days when "No D's" and "Weak D's" were being heavily touted, it would have been completely ignored.

1922-D Cent. Portion of collar clash mark on left rim (as seen on next die state, DP ZeroB, LDS,EDS.) Author's coin, photo by Robert Kelley Courtesy of the American Numismatic Assoc.

However, this new die pairing now shows a thin, indented, collar clash line running along the left curve of the obverse rim from about K-11 down to K-7, with a small interruption both next to and slightly below the L of LIBERTY. This collar clash line is one of the reasons why I kept trying to make this obverse die an earlier die state of the obverse of Die Pair #1, which typically comes with a similar (but slightly different if you compare them side by side) collar clash here.

Note that this depressed line weakens and shortens with wear on the coin, and disappears in lower grades as the rim wears away. High grade coins may show an irregular wire rim on the reverse from about K-8 to K-11.

The die erosion lines along the back of Lincoln's coat, which are angled mostly up and a little bit to the left, begin to develop a noticeable pattern. However, note that many 1922-D cent dies develop strong die erosion lines in this area. The patterns of the lines can be as distinctive as fingerprints, but be warned that the lines can grow and change over the life of the die. I find the lines closest to the Y of LIBERTY to be the most useful in telling one die from another.

The new reverse begins to show a few light feed finger die scratches below the US UN of EPU. One noticeable one develops BELOW the first U of UNUM, though it thins considerably before it touches the top of the E of ONE. Eventually one develops INSIDE the first U of UNUM, suggestive of a continuing problem with this coin press. It can be seen on later die state coins with the "jogging die crack," confirming the die sequence.

This die state had a relatively unremarkable die life. The faint dimpling seen in the field near the D on the earlier die state remains, but it never resembles the very strong "Dimples" seen on Die Pairs #8 & #9. Some light die erosion appears, weakening the D a little bit, but not enough to name. The main characteristic that separates it from the following die state is that there are no clash marks at the back of Lincoln's head.

LDS Obv./EDS Rev. Design Clash Marks on Obverse. The earliest coins in this die state range are not very different, die wear wise, than the end coins of the previous die state range, so I have arbitrarily chosen the initial appearance of any clash marks behind Lincoln's head (excluding that on the rim) as being the beginning of the **LDS Obv./ EDS Rev.** die state range.

1922-D Cent. DP #ZeroB (new rev.) LDS/EDS (early range). With Collar clash along left rim AND design clash marks at back of head (hard to see). Author's coin, photo by Robert Kelley Courtesy of the American Numismatic Assoc.

The strength of the clash marks varies with die wear. Coins from the onset of this die state range show a fairly strong horizontal clash mark from the base of the C of CENT coming out of the hair above the Y of LIBERTY, **plus** some light squiggles above that which can be identified as parts of the N of UNITED and the O of OF, **plus** a corresponding light clash mark of the back of Lincoln's head through the C, N and O and below on the reverse. However, the reverse clash mark quickly fades away due to natural die erosion, and eventually the squiggles further up the back of Lincoln's head become faint or gone. The horizontal base of the C survives as the much more common middle range of the **LDS/EDS** die state.

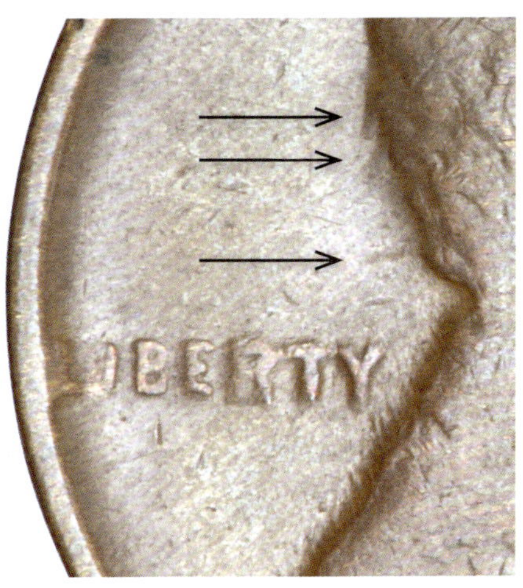

1922-D Cent. DP ZeroB, LDS/EDS (early range). Closeup of clash marks on back of Lincoln's head. Author's coin, photo by Robert Kelley Courtesy of the American Numismatic Assoc.

I was tempted to divide the early, middle and late stages of this die state range into separate die states, but in the end I decided that that was too complicated, because none of the sub-die state is worth a premium. Let's just say that I unofficially recognize that during the long die life of the Die Pair #ZeroB **LDS/EDS** die state range there are such things as **"LDS/EDS (early)"** (rare); **"LDS/ELDS (mid)"** [common], and **"LDS/EDS (late)"** [scarce] sub-die states, but I cannot define where the first one ends and the second one begins. I will try to illustrate typical examples of each.

1922-D Cent. DP #ZeroB, LDS/EDS (middle range). Closeup date and mm. Author's coin, photo by Robert Kelley Courtesy of the American Numismatic Assoc.

During the middle of the **LDS/EDS** die state range the mint mark eventually erodes enough to qualify as a **Worn D**. Towards the very end of this die state range the reverse die shows a crisp feed finger-caused die scrape line running vertically through the first U of UNUM. It too is not particularly significant, and there are Die Marker coins with similar lines in this area in the Die Marker section below, but this particular die line survives, a bit eroded, into the cracked die state below, and proves that they are the same die.

The mid and late sub-die states are noticeable for a general weakness and a slightly ragged appearance of the truncation of the bust. The end of the depressed line in Lincoln's coat that separates his shoulder from his coat is flanked by a wide, shallow, V-shaped elongation towards the rim, with lesser bumps near the line that separates his coat from his lapel. The right end of the truncation is very weak, and gradually extends towards the rim without touching it.

I would not try to sell any of these later sub-die state coins as "Weak D" coins, but I have seen (shall we say) optimistic online auction venue sellers try to pass off coins with similar D's as "Weak D" coins. The date is fairly normal, though there is some feathering on the 9. IGWT, LIBERTY and EPU are all still basically normal, though the I of LIBERTY is thin but sharp. Wheat lines intact. Most important of all, the reverse die is not yet cracked through the O of ONE.

(Perhaps there was a problem with the feeding mechanism on this particular coining press that struck first Die Pair #ZeroA&B and then Die Pair #1 which caused repeated die and/or collar clashings, as the obverse of D.P. #1 sometimes shows a slightly different C clash mark and a stronger collar clash mark. These similarities help explain why I had so much trouble telling the Die Pairs #ZeroB and #1 coins apart, before I found the diagnostic die mark on the E of WE.)

1922-D Cent. Worn D. DP #ZeroB, LDS/EDS (late range). Closeup date, mm, truncation. Author's coin, photo by Robert Kelley Courtesy of the American Numismatic Assoc.

There is a noticeable disconnect between the end of the previous die state range and the start of the more significant **VLDS Obv./ MDS Rev.** die state range, and it is very possible that the obverse die was taken out of the press for some reason between the two periods and repolished. It is in this die state that the obverse is easily confused with the obverse die of Die Pair #1. I honestly believe that it is just as collectible as Die Pairs #1, #3 & #4, even if it does not have a "Weak Reverse." Call it a **"Faint D, Worn Reverse."**

The mint mark is now well more than 90% gone, making it a "Faint D" in my terminology. The D slopes downward towards the rim, with the bottom and right side merging with the field. The date is in lower relief caused by the abrasion of the field around it, but while the first "2" is now a bit fuzzy, the second "2" is very thin but very sharply outlined.

(Note well: there are other dies where the right side and bottom of the D fade towards the field, and/or the second 2 is thin and sharp. See my earlier comments about polishing away the base of a tapered cone. I do not know what technique caused these effects, but it seems to be related to whatever

1922-D Cent. Very Faint D. DP #ZeroB, VLDS/MDS. Author's coin, photos by Robert Kelley Courtesy of the American Numismatic Assoc.

method was used by the Coiner and/or Die Setter to extend die life. Perhaps they used a basining wheel which connected with the D and/or the second 2 just so. I do not know. This is just a guess.)

The VLDS obverse has the truncation of Lincoln's bust very shallow and elongated towards the rim from the lapel of Lincoln's coat to the lower right point of the bust, which may or may not touch the rim. The rest of the truncation of the bust is also well worn, but whereas Fahey described the truncation on Die Pair #1 as "The bottom of Lincoln's jacket is a clear curved line all the way around, not ragged or distorted towards the rim," the VLDS of this die has the broad, V-shaped erosion spikes trailing down from the sunken lines in the design that separate Lincoln's sleeve from his jacket and his jacket from his lapel. These spikes started out small at the end of the previous die state, but grew.

IN, GOD and WE are getting weaker, though TRUST remains fairly strong. Note the relative strengths of the words "GOD" and "WE." On Die Pair #Zero the word WE is in higher relief than the word GOD, though both have gotten a bit fuzzy. On Die Pair #1 the word WE is much weaker than GOD, and parts of GOD, noticeably the left upright and base of the D, are still fairly well outlined.

1922-D Cent. Very Faint D. DP #ZeroB, VLDS/MDS. Closeup date, mm, truncation. Author's coin, photo by Robert Kelley Courtesy of the American Numismatic Assoc.

The collar clash near LIBERTY fades, but a new collar clash appears below the bust and date. LIBERTY has noticeably weakened, the L merging with the rim and the I almost gone, unlike the I on DP#1 which is noticeably sharper. BE small but clear, and the crossbar of the T has eroded to the left until it touches the R (this elongated crossbar can be found to varying lengths on other well-worn dies.)

Worn Reverse now shows "Jogging Die Crack through O of ONE," as always seen on D.P. #1, though the crack is not quite as wide as seen on DP#1. EPU begins to deteriorate from the left end and spreads to the right. Left wheat ear shows greater deterioration of the CPL than right ear, though all may be visible on high grade specimens. Heavy die erosion starting to form on the insides of both wheat ears, especially on the stems, and into the adjacent letters of UNITED STATES OF AMERICA.

It is arguable whether this cracked reverse die with worn but intact wheat lines actually qualifies as a "Weak Reverse," even though it is always called that when found paired with the obverse die of Die Pair #1 only shortly thereafter. The fact is that in the old days everybody, myself included, stressed the "Strong Reverse" aspect of Die Pair #2's identity so much so that Die Pair #1 was always lumped in with Die Pair #3, which truly does have a horribly weak reverse.

In 20/20 hindsight I am going to say that 40+ years ago we should have called the reverse of DP#1 "Worn" rather than "Weak," but as I said above I am trying not to change the Canon of Die Pairs #1-4B. Therefore, I am calling this reverse die in this die state paired with this obverse die "Worn," while I am calling this same reverse die in just a tiny bit later die state paired with the obverse die from DP#1 "Weak" and "LDS." After all, it does continue to deteriorate noticeably during that die pairing, and many DP#1 coins do have a "Weak Reverse."

(There may, repeat may, exist an even later **XLDS Obv./ LDS Rev.** die state of D.P. #ZeroB, but I have not yet found a high enough grade specimen of one to confirm it. Remember what I said in Chapter Eight about making attributions based on well-worn coins.

On the best coin I have seen (of what may be an XLDS Obverse) the D appears to have faded even further to a **"Very Faint D"** die state. It is barely distinguishable from the field, appearing to have lost perhaps 98% of its mass. The 1 and 9 are feathered out into the field even more, while the two 2's slowly fade without feathering. In the very latest usage the second 2 can be virtually invisible. The right end of the truncation of the bust may have reached the rim. As with the VLDS die state a "No D" Obverse due to grease filling would be plausible, though not yet seen.

The wear on LIBERTY continues, the L a vertical blob, the I still gone, the BE shrunken and the RTY feathering more and more out into the field. Again, note that the I in LIBERTY is still fairly bold on Die Pair #1 coins in comparable die states.

IN very weak, GOD slightly stronger than IN and WE only slightly stronger than GOD, unlike DP #1 where GOD is always stronger than WE. Top of first T in TRUST spreading towards the rim, unlike the crisp T always seen on DP#1. R losing detail and getting fatter due to feathering, especially on the right leg. UST still mostly intact, though the belly of the U is getting fatter. On the reverse the die crack remains quite thin.

In my opinion the VLDS/MDS, "Faint D" coins (and potential XLDS/LDS, "Very Faint D" coins) from Die Pair #ZeroB's obverse die are collectible "Faint D" varieties, just as significant as the market acceptable "Weak D" coins seen from Die Pairs #1, #3 and #4B. I know that I said that I did not want to change the ANACS Canon, but a strong case can be made that the VLDS/MDS die state of Die Pair #ZeroB should be grandfathered into "The ANACS Varieties," because the coins from it *have* been collected as such for the past 40+ years, mistaken as Die Pair #1 coins because of the jogging die crack.

The same holds true with the TPGs. You have been certifying these late state DP #ZeroB coins as Die Pair #1 coins, or whatever your terminology was for the Die Pair #1 coins, for four decades. Continue to certify them, just start calling them by their new right name, "Die Pair #ZeroB." I will work on getting the Cherrypickers Guide to differentiate between Die Pairs #ZeroB, #1, #3 and #4B.

I would rank the Die Pair #ZeroB VLDS/MDS "Faint D" coins as almost as rare as a D.P. #1 "Faint D" coin, and the potential XLDS as rarer still (if it in fact exists). However, these rarity rankings are highly subject to change, as I will bet you that there are more than a few VLDS/MDS (and potential XLDS/LDS) D.P. #ZeroB coins out there mis-attributed as D.P. #1 coins **because** of the jogging die crack. I had a lot of trouble learning the difference between these two different varieties, and I consider myself to be one of the experts on the cents of 1922. This may cause the relative rarities of the two to change as people re-examine their (long thought to be) D.P. #1 coins.

Die Pair #5. (DeLorey-2205.) Generic GSID-69742 through die state MDS/MDS. GSID-393498 from die state LDS/LDS on. Near normal D in early die state. "Worn D, Thin and Flat" in middle die state. "Faint D, Thin and Flat" in later die state. The obverse predecessor of Die Pair #2 before it lost its mint mark! Usually seen with a Worn or Well Worn Reverse, unlike D.P.#2. Class Five.

1922-D Cent, Faint D, Well Worn Reverse. Die Pair #5, LDS/LDS. The overall die wear on this obverse is not that severe, and yet the mint mark is uncharacteristically Faint. The only logical explanation is that the die underwent selective polishing in the mint mark area, perhaps to remove "dimples" from the die, greatly weakening the D. Always seen in this die state with a "Weak Reverse" die. Eventually this obverse die was polished again, completely removing the D, and paired with a new Reverse die to become the "No D, Strong Reverse" Die Pair #2. Shot through slab, courtesy Mike Sokoloff.

EDS Obv./ EDS Rev. Mint mark nearly whole but with light dimpling above and to right. SBC just an ordinary 1922-D.

Not a new obverse die, but hard to identify as #5 as the distinctive die erosion on the back of Lincoln's coat (see below) is still rather minor. The die erosion on the 9 and the R of LIBERTY is not yet apparent, and that on the tops of IN GOD is only lightly developed. There is very light dimpling extending to the right from the upper right corner of the D, but the dimpling changes over the life of the die as old dimples get worn or polished away while new dimples raise up to replace them.

The position of the D may help: The upright back of the D is centered under the gap between the 9 and the first 2, putting the right side of the D under the left side of the 2. This position is not unique to this obverse, but it eliminates many other dies.

The reverse starts out still fairly decent with good CPL's, and just light distortion on the E and P of EPU. However, it wears down faster than the obverse, and may get close to the MDS status while the mint mark on the obverse is still fairly strong. Not really collectible as a variety, except as part of a die state study such as this.

MDS Obv./ MDS Rev. D polished down. SBC "1922-D Worn D, Thin and Flat."

1922-D Cent, Worn D, Worn Reverse. Die Pair #5, MDS/MDS. An unexceptional die pair except for the mint mark, which is thinner and in lower relief than you would expect for an obverse die still this nice. The logical explanation is that the field around it was polished down before the D had a chance to feather out into the field, as is seen on the next two varieties. Author's coin, Photo by Robert Kelley Courtesy of the American Numismatic Assoc.

Still a relatively normal coin from an obverse die not showing all that much die erosion in this die state, and yet the mint mark is now suddenly strangely thin, as opposed to the heavily feathered out D's seen on the two following Die Pairs. As stated elsewhere, I believe that this is the result of the die having been selectively polished to remove dimpling near the D.

Topographically, the D is not very high above the field, and might have qualified as a "Weak D" back in the 1930s through the 60s. I don't know how Scharlack or Craig overlooked it, unless they saw it and just assumed that it was simply a different die state of one of the other "Weak D's." The pioneers in the field did not dig deep enough, and we who followed tended to accept their findings without verifying them. In the later die states this "D" qualifies as "Faint."

Fairly normal date and LIBERTY throughout the life of the die pairing. In this die state the tops of IN GOD are starting to show some more erosion doubling towards the rim, easiest to see on the top of the G. The light die erosion down the back of Lincoln's coat continues to grow.

(One specimen seen appeared to have a very weak vertical clash mark of the back of the C in CENT above the Y, but I have never found a second piece to confirm the clash mark. Regardless, it is not anything that would have caused the obverse die to be repolished, as stronger clash marks on Die Pairs #1 and #ZeroB were routinely ignored.)

1922-D Cent. DP #5, MDS/MDS. Closeup date plus "thin and flat" mm. The field around the mint mark was shaved away clean, reducing the footprint of the D, rather than eroding away outwards and expanding the footprint. Author's coin, Photo by Robert Kelley Courtesy of the American Numismatic Assoc.

On the reverse, the die erosion in EPU that began in the EDS continues to grow and becomes scalloped between the lettering. The reverse as a whole continues to wear down faster than the obverse. The curved, parallel lines start out weak but intact, then slowly fade, especially on the outsides closer to the rim. A series of radial die flow lines develop through the E·PLU.

LDS Obv./ LDS Rev. SBC "1922-D Faint D, Thin and Flat."

1922-D Cent, Faint D, Well Worn Reverse. Die Pair #5, LDS/LDS. None seen with any suggestion of any die clashing, the traditional "guess" as to why this obverse die was polished down one more time, completely removing the D, and then put back in a coin press with a new reverse die. Coin purchased by me from GN Coins of Lemont, IL; their picture, used with permission.

After holding up fairly steadily in the artificially worn, or polished down, "Worn" state, the D suddenly becomes "Faint," strongly suggesting that the die was taken out of the press and polished down yet again. The two lines, straight and curved, that make up the D are slightly thinner, with none of the feathering seen on the two following Die Pairs.

Definitely less than 10% of the original mass of the D remaining, perhaps down to 5% but not down to the 2% threshold of a Very Faint D. Date still strong. LIBERTY fairly intact, though the R is starting to show noticeable die erosion thickening, and the crossbar of the T grows to touch it. There seems to be a slight bulge on the right side of the upright of the T. IGWT shows more die erosion above the tops of the letters, and the I of IN develops scalloping in the field on either side of it.

1922-D Cent, Faint D, Well Worn Reverse. Die Pair #5, LDS/LDS. Date and mint mark. Note start of feathering on the 9, while both 2's remain sharp. The second 2 may have been struck through a wee bit of grease, as it is stronger than the first 2 on later die state coins. Courtesy Mike Sokoloff.

This die erosion on the tops of IGWT, especially IN GOD, and on the R of LIBERTY are the obvious characteristics that prove that the obverse of Die Pair #5 is the predecessor of Die Pair #2, though only the earliest die state of D.P. #2 has the matching characteristics. As D.P. #2 wore on, the doubling on IN GOD wore away as the letters became blobs and the scalloping near IN wore away, while the R of LIBERTY pancaked out and LIBE weakened.

1922-D Cent, Faint D, Well Worn Reverse. Die Pair #5, LDS/LDS. LIBERTY with the start of feathering on the R, and the all-important die erosion on back of Lincoln's coat. This unique die erosion pattern proves that Die Pair #5 is an earlier Die State of Die Pair #2. Courtesy Mike Sokoloff.

1922 No D Cent, Strong Reverse, DP #2, MDS. Closeup of LIBERTY and die erosion on back of coat (see below). Enlarged from the obverse photo courtesy Heritage Auctions (www.HA.com).

1922-D Cent, Faint D, Well Worn Reverse. Die Pair #5, LDS/LDS. Die erosion on tops of IN GOD. Author's coin.

1922 No D Cent, Strong Reverse. Die Pair #2. Die erosion on tops of IN GOD (ignore random scratch thru I of IN). Coin owned by J.P. Martin of ANACS. Photo by the author.

More important proof that the two obverses are one and the same can be found in the fine die erosion lines running down the back of Lincoln's coat. A somewhat prominent die erosion line can be seen on the coat directly down from the Y of LIBERTY. You may need a good magnifying glass to see these lines, but they are there. See the pictures here and under D.P. #2.

1922 No D Cent, Strong Reverse. Die Pair #2, MDS/EDS. Die erosion below ERTY. Coin owned by J.P. Martin. Photo by the author.

1922-D Cent, Faint D, Weak Reverse. Die Pair #5, LDS/EDS. Die erosion below ERTY. Author's coin.

The Reverse continues to erode through EPU, and the CPL become weaker. Overall this is just another "Weak Reverse" (I call it "Well Worn") for the year. Only the obverse die later makes history.

Like the following Die Pairs, never mentioned in the traditional "1922-D Weak D" literature, though the late die states of it should have been. Those late die states show the D as "weak" as many a Die Pair #1 or #3 coin currently certifiable as a "Weak D" coin, but I guess that Die Pair #5 commits the unpardonable sin of actually being readable until the D suddenly disappears in the last repolishing. In my opinion the "Faint D" die state of Die Pair #5 is *very* collectible, and slabbable, because of its newly proven link to the ever popular Die Pair #2.

(FWIW, I have two D.P. #5 coins slabbed by a major TPG as "Weak D." I have no idea what would happen if I cracked them out and sent them in again, which is one of the reasons I hope to retire the term "Weak D.")

Die Pair #6. (DeLorey-2206.) Generic GSID-69742 through die state LDS/LDS. GSID-393499 from die state VLDS/VLDS on. "Worn D, Mushy." Second 2 gets thinner. Elongated Lapel. (All of these characteristics in later die states only. Class One in MDS and earlier. Class Five and increasingly significant in LDS and later.)

1922-D Cent. Well Worn D, "Mushy." DP #6, LDS/LDS. Note thin, crisp second 2. Author's coin, Photo by Robert Kelley Courtesy of the American Numismatic Assoc.

MDS Obv./ MDS Rev. Worn D. A somewhat unexceptional variety for a 1922-D cent in its early to mid die states, which appears at first glance to just be the victim of honest die wear. The D feathers out into the field all around, with the field slowly rising up along the lower right side of the D (as it does on some other dies). This feathering continues to expand as the mint mark gets wider but less tall, until it almost melts into the field. Imagine that the D was carved from butter and it is sitting on a warm cast iron skillet.

In this earliest known die state the date is fairly normal, though the 9 slowly enlarges while the second 2 slowly shrinks. IGWT is normal at this stage. The I of LIBERTY is getting weak. As on some other dies the BE gets weaker as the RT enlarge, with the crossbar of the T quickly extending to the R. There is very heavy die erosion along the back of Lincoln's coat below the TY. The forward point of Lincoln's bust is in low relief, but the bottom line of it is well separated from the rim. Sometimes seen with collar clash along the upper left rim.

1922-D Cent. Worn D. DP #6, MDS/MDS. Nothing too special in the mint mark area, just an earlier version of the following before the D gets Mushy enough to be interesting. The weaknesses in EPU are probably just from grease on the die. Author's coin, Photo by Robert Kelley Courtesy of the American Numismatic Assoc.

The reverse is also unexceptional for a 1922-D cent. The curved, parallel lines (CPL) are intact but shallow, and there is die erosion on EPU but the tops of EPU are still present. This soon changes.

LDS Obv./ LDS Rev. Well Worn D. Second 2 thin and sharp.

Both dies appear to have been re-basined, with significant effect where the fields meet the rims. The D has lost much of its height and is bordering on Faint. The second 2 is now remarkable for being thin with very crisp borders; any minor feathering of the original second 2 having been polished off the die. The first 2 is still normal, while the 9 is getting bloated. (See obverse and reverse at beginning of variety.)

1922-D Cent. Well Worn D, "Mushy." DP #6, LDS/LDS. Note thin, crisp second 2. Author's coin, Photo by Robert Kelley Courtesy of the American Numismatic Assoc.

IN GOD WE are noticeably weak, along with the R and the S of TRUST. In LIBERTY the LIBE are weaker while the RTY are enlarged. The entire lapel from the right side of Lincoln's right shoulder to the lower right corner of the lapel is in extremely low relief and closer to the rim, but still visibly separated from the rim.

The tops of PLURIBUS UNU have been basined away, leaving the letters thin but well defined though missing their tops. The E and the M remain blurry. The details in the CPL are getting very weak.

1922-D Cent. Well Worn D, "Mushy." DP #6, LDS/LDS. IN GOD WE TRUST. Note the unusual pattern of strong T, weak R, strong U, weak S, strong T. Author's coin, Photo by Robert Kelley Courtesy of the American Numismatic Assoc.

VLDS Obv./ VLDS Rev. Very Faint D. Second 2 thinner but still sharp.

1922-D Cent. Very Faint D. The peripheral mushiness has been worn or polished away, so I no longer mention it. DP #6, VLDS/VLDS. The only things sharp on this extremely well worn Obverse die are the second 2 and both T's of TRUST. In terms of weakness the mint mark is a match to the coins slabbed by the major TPG's as "Weak D" coins, and this one should also be slabbed as such, with the DeLorey-2206 reference number to avoid confusion. Author's coin, Photo by Robert Kelley Courtesy of the American Numismatic Assoc.

Mint mark down below 5% of its original mass and barely recognizable as a D. Second 2 still sharp but in lower relief. First 2 still fairly normal but weak. 19 heavily feathered.

IN GOD WE now very weak, with RUS weak though both T's still sharp. Bottom of U stands out a bit. In LIBERTY the LI are faint, the BE are weak, almost unreadable blobs and the RTY are getting mushy. The lower right lapel is so faint it is hard to see a thin separation from the rim.

1922-D Cent. Very Faint D. DP #6, VLDS/VLDS. Date and Very Faint D. Author's coin, Photo by Robert Kelley Courtesy of the American Numismatic Assoc.

The tops of EPU are weaker, the E·P and the UM faint. The details in the CPL are almost entirely gone.

XLDS Obv./ VLDS Rev. Very, Very Faint D. Thin second 2 fades. Mint mark down to perhaps 1% of its original mass and only defined along its left side. I would not be surprised if some were misattributed as a "No D, Weak Reverse" in the old days. Not seen as a "No D" by me, though it is always possible that a strike from a grease-filled mintmark exists that shows absolutely no trace of the mint mark. Such a coin would need to be in a sufficiently high enough condition to be able to confirm it was struck without a mint mark. The die state is difficult to find nice.

The first 2 is very weak and the thin second 2 is fading at its upper and lower ends. 19 getting mushy. IGWT weaker than previous with top of first T starting to erode towards the rim. The crossbar of the second T remains bold though the upright is weakening. LIBE almost gone, the R there but illegible. TY very mushy. The die erosion below TY still identifiable.

1922-D Cent. Very, Very Faint D. DP #6, XLDS/VLDS. Date and mm. Another die state worthy of slabbing, in a decent grade of course (better than this coin), as at least a "Weak D" coin, with the DeLorey-2206 reference number. Author's coin.

Reverse not much weaker than previous. Center legends still fairly intact.

Never mentioned in the "1922-D Weak D" universe, though the late die states of it should have been. Those late die states show the D as weak as many a Die Pair #1 or #3 coin currently certifiable as a "Weak D" coin. I consider it to be highly collectible in the right die states in Fine or better condition.

Die Pair #7. (DeLorey-2207.) Generic GSID-69742. "Worn D, Fuzzy" in later die states. Second 2 gets bigger. Heavy radial die erosion below and to right of date. Class One in MDS and earlier. Class Five in LDS but never particularly significant.

1922-D Cent. Worn D, Fuzzy. DP #7, at the early end of the MDS/MDS range but with the D feathered out into the field enough to count. Author's coin, Photo by Robert Kelley Courtesy of the American Numismatic Assoc.

In a manner very similar to that of the preceding die pair, the mint mark on this obverse die becomes heavily feathered out into the field. In some die states the mint marks are almost identical, leading me for a while to try to make these different die states of the same obverse die, just as I did with Die Pairs #ZeroB and #1.

However, the erosion patterns on the rest of all four dies are different, so they must have been two different die pairs with remarkably similar natural wear patterns on the D. I have given them similar nicknames, "Mushy" and "Fuzzy," to recognize their apparent similarity. As a way of remembering which is which, I have used the "Fuzzy" nickname to suggest the fine, hair-like die erosion lines typically seen below and to the right of the date.

MDS Obv./ MDS Rev. Broadened D. Elongated base of Second 2.

Still shows a fairly decent D, a bit feathered out into the field all around. Center hole strong. Center hole slowly fades as feathering increases, but mint mark not yet lessened to my arbitrary "Worn D" status (which requires that 50% or more of the volume of the original D be gone).

[:IX-263c]

Right side of second 2 heavily feathered out into the field, the right end of the base of this 2 extending to the right and becoming broader and flatter as it goes. Strong radial die erosion flow lines just inside the rim from just below K-3 to roughly K-6. One of these shows as a strong depressed line just above the base of the second 2. Rest of date a bit feathered. IGWT Strong. LIBERTY fairly decent though the I is a bit weak.

Reverse fairly normal. A bit of die erosion doubling on the tops of some letters of EPU. E fading a bit. The erosion doubling slowly gets worse as the die stage progresses, most noticeably on the U's of PLURIBUS.

1922-D Cent. Worn D, Fuzzy. DP #7, LDS/LDS. Date and mint mark. Author's coin, Photo by Robert Kelley Courtesy of the American Numismatic Assoc.

LDS Obv./ LDS Rev. "Worn D, Fuzzy." Scalloping in EPU.

On this die pair it is rather difficult to say for sure just when the volume of the mint mark erodes below my arbitrary 50% tipping point where it becomes a "Worn D," though some pieces are obviously there. Here you must use your good judgement. However, as the die never reaches a significantly "Faint D" die state, as does Die Pair #6, the border line on Die Pair #7 between "Normal D" and "Worn D" may not matter too much. The variety is included here mainly to distinguish specimens of it from the much more significant Die Pair #6.

Bottom of Lincoln's lapel starting to show shallow lobes, vaguely similar to those on D.P. #4 but never as severe. IGWT weakens evenly. I of LIBERTY very weak, and sometimes the L.

The "Worn D, Fuzzy" obverse die state always shows some scalloping in the motto EPU, but the scalloping seems to precede the mint mark tipping point by a bit, so I would not use the presence of the scalloping as proof of anything. Radial die erosion eventually overwhelms the stems. Usually seen with a wire rim above UNUM and down to about K-3.

(Note: There is one more somewhat similar die with some fan-shaped die erosion under the lower left corner of the second 2 and some irregular die erosion to the right of the second 2, but as it was not otherwise significant I am not including it here at this time.)

--

Die Pair #8A. (DeLorey-2208A.) Generic GSID 69742 for all of D.P.#8A and #8B and D.P.#8C up through Die States LDS/MDS. GSID-393500 in D.P. #8C, (Dimples near mint mark in all but earliest die states.) Dimples seen in second die marriage grow into "Worn D Smear" in late die states of third die marriage. First of Three Reverse Dies (strong). Die gouge left of WE (fades). Class One with first reverse die. SBC just 1922-D.

1922-D Cent. DP #8A, Prime/MDS. New Obverse die with First, only slightly used and still Strong Reverse die. Crisp die gouge left of WE. SBC normal 1922-D, but linkable to following coins via die gouge. Author's coin, Photo by Robert Kelley Courtesy of the American Numismatic Assoc.

Prime Obv./MDS Rev. Earliest die state known.

New or near new Obverse die. Crisp die gouge to the left of WE, angling up a bit going left from the base of the W. Date and mint mark sharp, usually seen with no dimples near D but near the end of the die state a light depression begins to form along the right side of the D. No die erosion anywhere, but sometimes seen with light vertical die file lines up through date, strongest in and between 9&2.

1922-D Cent, DP #8A, Prime/MDS. First Reverse, Strong. Die gouge left of WE. Author's coin, Photo by Robert Kelley Courtesy of the American Numismatic Assoc.

(This is an unusual style of die polish among 1922-D cents, and I have no idea what it was meant to correct unless, as I suspect, this die was originally made for the Philadelphia Mint and then re-softened, punched with a D mint mark, and re-hardened, and in the process the repunching left a small crater rim around the D that needed to be filed down.)

LIBERTY, IN GOD WE TRUST (IGWT) and V.D.B. on shoulder very strong. Base of lapel intact and rounded. Strong I in LIBERTY. Sometimes seen with strong wire rim along upper right Obverse from K-11 or 12 to K-2 or 3 or so.

Rev. Middle Die State (MDS), probably near the beginning of that range. Parallel lines in wheat ears complete but just a wee bit weak along sides closest to the rim. Kernels starting to merge. E PLURIBUS UNUM (EPU) complete, but some beveling above LU (possibly caused by feed finger erosion). Some erosion doubling at tops of LURIBUS · U, strongest on RIBUS. The period between PLURIBUS and UNUM shows a raised "fan" of die wear spreading out above it. Overall a relatively normal reverse with a bit of die wear.

Very light ghosting along right side. Light radial die erosion lines crossing wheat stems. Gap between ends of wheat stems clean. Seen with wire rim from about 2:30 to 4:30.

(Note: Though this Obverse shows a "Well Worn D, Smear" in its later die states, here it is just a normal 1922-D coin and SBC just a 1922-D, though it is okay mention "Die gouge left of WE." Only traceable to the next die state via the die gouge. Not particularly significant.)

Die Pair #8B. (DeLorey-2208B.) Generic GSID-69742. Second of Three Reverse Dies (weak). Still Class One.

1922-D Cent, DP #8B, EDS/VLDS. Second Reverse, Weak. Author's coin, Photo by Robert Kelley Courtesy of the American Numismatic Assoc.

EDS Obv./VLDS Rev. Still a basically normal looking Obverse die. Date, LIBERTY and IGWT still strong, though near the end of this die state the tops of TRUST start eroding towards the rim. A shallow "gutter" (Scharlack's term, though he also used "dented") forms in the field to the right of Lincoln's head. The die gouge left of WE has softened a bit from die wear, but it is still easily seen on decent condition coins.

Most importantly, there are multiple light dimples forming around the mint mark. These form a long, curved line along the top of the D from the upper left corner to the center of the right curve; a dot southeast of the center of that curve; and eventually a short, angled dash below the upright of the D. These expand with continued die wear, the upper and right dimples eventually merging in later die states.

1922-D Cent. DP 8C. Scharlack's Gutter, or Dented, Obverse. Courtesy Stack's Bowers auction archives.

While the die steel above and to the upper right of the D was raising up on the die and forming these dimples on the coins, the die steel below the mint mark, from that center of the right curve down and around to the lower left corner of the D, was rapidly eroding off of the die, down and to the right. This formed a ramp (eventually the "smear" mentioned above) that slowly built its way up the lower right side of the D, eventually reaching the highest level of it in a later die state.

The reverse, however, is now suddenly and inexplicably a very heavily used die, resurrected from some earlier die pairing. The wheat ears have lost most of the CPL, except for the upper inside corner of the left ear. The EPU is heavily eroded, the tops of some letters almost faded away, and there are heavy radial flow lines through both wheat stems and the gap between them. There is a strong ghosting valley to the right of the T of CENT that continues down through the TE of STATES and the CA of AMERICA.

When I first saw one of these I thought that the original #8 Die Pair must have held up for a very long time, but eventually I realized that there is no way that this amount of die wear could have occurred on the reverse die while the obverse die incurred less than 1/10th as much wear. I have multiples of Die Pairs #8A and #8B, but no intermediate stages. The only possible explanation is that the first reverse die was swapped out for some unknown reason, and they did not bother to install a new reverse die while they were at it. The Mint's Die Register book makes no mention of such re-using of old reverse dies with different obverses, but it definitely happened.

Still SBC just a 1922-D, though you can mention Well Worn Reverse if you like, and/or the Gutter right of the face if it is noticeable enough. Slightly more significant than D.P. #8A to nitpickers such as myself because it proves that old dies were put back into use as needed during the chaotic 1922-D cent coinage, but probably not significant enough to command a premium.

Die Pair #8C. (DeLorey-2208C.) Third of Three Reverse Dies (strong). Generic GSID-69742 (Class One) in EDS/VEDS to LDS/MDS die states. GSID-393500 (Class Five) in VLDS/LDS or later die states. (Note: this die pairing had a long life with constant but gradual deterioration. The divisions between the following die states are sometimes ambiguous.)

1922-D Cent. DP #8C, EDS/VEDS. Third Reverse. First of many die state variations for this die pair. Author's coin, Photo by Robert Kelley Courtesy of the American Numismatic Assoc.

EDS Obv./VEDS Rev. Obverse not much changed from Die Pair #8B, suggesting that perhaps the #8B combination had a short press run. Date fairly normal, with light feathering out around the 9. LIBERTY still strong, though in the latter part of this die state the I and parts of the L & B appear to have gotten temporarily filled in with grease. IGWT starts to show a very slight bit of die erosion towards the rim, though the letters still hold their shapes, especially on the S. Line left of WE slightly weaker and gutter right of profile slightly stronger, but not much.

Dimples around D slightly longer, and the "ramp" under the right and bottom sides of the D slightly higher. Sometimes seen with strong wire rim along upper right from K-12 down to K-3 or perhaps K-5, similar to that seen on #8A. Sometimes seen with striking weakness in the upper left reverse, typical of die alignment issues. Perhaps this press had a problem with its die holders.

Reverse new, possibly Prime. No distinguishing marks.

MDS Obv./EDS Rev. Line left of WE very faint to gone, but present for long enough to prove the three reverse die sequence. The die erosion towards the rim above IGWT grows more severe, and gradually flattens out the top of the S. In later die states the "S" resembles a "5." The bottom of the S fills in a bit and the lower left end becomes somewhat pointed upwards. Date still fairly normal, with feathering around the 19. In LIBERTY, the I and the foot of the L are still filled with grease, though they reappear in the next die state.

The "ramp" up against thc lower right side of the D nears the highest relief of the D but does not quite get there in this die state. The two elongated dimples above the right side of the D are easily seen.

On the reverse, die erosion slowly forms on the tops of EPU. Light radial die erosion lines start nibbling at the stems of the wheat ears, but they are trivial.

LDS Obv./ MDS Rev. "Worn D, Smear." In my opinion the D mint mark has now lost half of its original mass, qualifying for my "Worn D" status, though the point is arguable due to the variable height of the field around the D. My house is built into the side of a hill, and has a walk-out basement. How high I am above the ground depends on if I am on the front porch or the back deck, both on the same floor.

1922-D Worn D, Smear. DP #8C, LDS/MDS. Third Reverse. Author's coin, Photo by Robert Kelley Courtesy of the American Numismatic Assoc.

The "ramp" up against the lower right side of the D now blends with the highest level of the D, though the center hole of the D remains, however weakly. It resembles a "Smear" of metal, hence the nickname. The two dimples along the top and right of the D have merged into one long dimple that defines the right side of the "smear." Combined with erosion down the left side of the D, the D now resembles an arrowhead pointed at the 9. Without the preceding die states to show the progression, a non-collector might not know that this was a "D."

1922-D Cent. Worn D, Fuzzy. DP #8C, LDS/MDS. Third Reverse. Date and mm. Author's coin, Photo by Robert Kelley Courtesy of the American Numismatic Assoc.

1922-D Cent. Worn D, Fuzzy. DP #8C, LDS/MDS. Third Reverse. TRUST. Author's coin, Photo by Robert Kelley Courtesy of the American Numismatic Assoc.

The letters of IGWT get mushy as their tops continue to erode towards the rim. The "S" continues to look more and more like a "5." Date still normal on the 22, with a bit more feathering on the 19. The grease in the LIB goes away. Surprisingly little die erosion along the back of Lincoln's coat.

On the reverse, die erosion doubling gets strong on the tops of UNUM. The CPL in the wheat ears are still intact. Radial die erosion lines grow thicker on the stems of the wheat ears, and across the gap between them.

The LDS/MDS die state is surprisingly available in Reddish Unc. There must have been a hoard of them saved.

VLDS Obv./ LDS Rev. "Well Worn D, Smear." Similar to the preceding but the weak center hole in the D is now gone. LIBE are very weak and IGWT has gotten very mushy and eroded towards the rim. Both 2's in the date remain very clear. The truncation of the bust is weak but it retains its separation from the rim. The "gutter" to the right of the profile has a well-defined angle at its greatest depth.

1922-D Well Worn D, Smear. DP 8C, VLDS/LDS. Third Reverse. Obv. and Rev. Author's coin, Photo by Robert Kelley Courtesy of the American Numismatic Assoc.

On the reverse the CPL are still complete on the die, but a bit shallow so that they are easily worn away. Not the worst 1922-D reverse by far, though the erosion doubling on UNUM is impressive.

Not a recognized die variety, except by me, and perhaps by Scharlack for the "gutter," which grandfathers it in as a known variety from the 1930s. Just weak enough that over the years some specimens have no doubt been sold as "Weak D's" by optimistic sellers. Not something that any TPG would certify as a "Weak D" today. This is one reason why I have introduced the term "Worn D."

I like it because of the wholesale transformation of the D into something that is no longer a letter but rather a geometrical shape, and because of the way that it illustrates that 1922-D cent dies are something strange and wonderful, and because of the fact that this obverse die went through three reverse dies to get to this point. It is a great example of the "Dimples" phenomenon which I believe was caused by Philadelphia dies being re-softened, mint marked, and re-hardened. The same process may have caused the "gutter" in front of Lincoln's face.

1922-D Cent. Well Worn D, Smear. DP #8C, VLDS/LDS. Date and mm. Note "hook" inside top of first 2. Author's coin, Photo by Robert Kelley Courtesy of the American Numismatic Assoc.

It also proves that the Denver Mint's Die Register book is indeed a work of fiction when it presents those precise numbers struck for each and every die, and when it states that dies were installed and then condemned and never used again. In reality, any used die (except of course the one obverse die with the cud die break at WE TRUST seen below as D.P. #14) was fair game for re-use. The Denver Mint staff did what it had to do to keep the presses running!

Die Pair #9. (DeLorey-2209.) "Worn D, Horizontal Dimples." Generic GSID-69742 (Class One) in Die States EDS/LDS and MDS/LDS. GSID-393501 (Class Five) in Die States LDS/VLDS and later.

1922-D Cent. DP #9, MDS/LDS (early). Author's coin, Photo by Robert Kelley Courtesy of the American Numismatic Assoc.

EDS Obv./LDS Rev. Shallow Horizontal Dimples above and below D, the upper one forming first and extending to the right of the D a bit. (Both actually decline slightly to the right.) Mint Mark itself still very normal.

Obverse essentially intact in the earliest stages of the dimples, suggesting that the dimples began to form immediately after the die was put into use. (A Prime die state is of course possible, if it could somehow be linked to this die, perhaps via the reverse die.) The dimples were caused by die steel raising UP above the surface of the die under striking pressure, a highly unusual form of die deformation (it usually just wears away). The deformations on the die continued to evolve progressively over the life of the die, the upper one getting longer, straighter and higher above the surface of the die, which of course made the hole left by it in the coins correspondingly deeper and more significant.

In my opinion, this early die failure in just the mint mark area supports my theory that the die was originally hardened without a mint mark in it for potential use in Philadelphia, but that the die was re-softened, punched with a D, and then re-hardened for use in Denver, leaving unknown and unpredictable residual side effects in the die steel in the mint mark area.

In the EDS the D is not particularly significant, and this should just be called a 1922-D cent, though you can mention the dimples because they are a bit unusual and later become the star of the show. Towards the end of the EDS the obverse die gets misaligned slightly towards 10 o'clock, causing a wire rim to form to the right of the date.

The reverse is well worn and shows erosion doubling forming along the tops of EPU, strongest on the UNUM. The period between PLURIBUS and UNUM has a shallow raised die erosion shadow between itself and the rim. This fades as the EPU continues to slump towards the rim. The curved, parallel lines closest to the rim are faint or gone.

MDS Obv./ LDS Rev. Worn D only near the end of the Die State.

Obverse similar to the preceding in overall appearance, but the depressed line above the D is much more obvious. The D is still well detailed, but a ramp is forming up its lower right side between the dimples. Towards the end of this Die State the ramp begins to merge with the highest part of the D, but the outline remains just strong enough to define the central hole.

1922-D DP #9, MDS/LDS (early and late). Closeups of dimple above D. Two of many intermediate progressions. Author's coins, Photos by Robert Kelley Courtesy of the American Numismatic Assoc.

Other than that ramp the entire mint mark area appears to be receding slightly *below* the surrounding field on the coin, implying that the entire mint mark area on the die was bulging *upwards*. This expresses itself as a low area along the left side of the D on the coin, leaving a well-defined upright to the D. Date and LIBERTY strong.

Faint die erosion towards the rim begins to form along the tops of all of the letters of IGWT. Perhaps more interestingly, a die erosion line begins to form up from the tip of the center tine of the E of WE, forming a usually reliable die marker from here on. As the upper dimple must have grown progressively over time, I am setting the appearance of this upward tine on the center bar of the E of WE as the arbitrary cutoff point where the EDS Obverse die state ends and the MDS begins. The MDS/LDS then had a fairly long run with continued weakening of both dies. You could say that there are "Early" and "Late" sub-die states.

1922-D Cent. Worn D, Double Dimples in an intermediate evolution of the die erosion. DP #9, LDS/LDS. PCGS TrueView via Heritage Auctions. Courtesy Heritage Auctions, (www.HA.com). (lightened a bit by me)

Reverse losing more details in the kernels and on the outer halves of the CPL, but not enough to merit a new die state. Both stems feathered out into the fields, but rather smoothly. EPU a bit weaker, especially in the first few letters.

LDS Obv./ VLDS Rev. "Faint D."

The ramp between the upper and lower dimples has risen to the height of the D, though the center hole of the D is just barely discernable. Not the weakest of the 1922 "Faint D's" because the top of the D is defined by the dimple and the left side of the D is defined by the bulge in the die there, but certainly the most significant of the 1922-D dimple coins just because of the depth and length of the upper dimple.

(Note: There are other dimpled dies of varying strengths that I will not bore you with, but their existence supports my theory that 10 dies were altered in the same unorthodox way.)

IGWT now very weak, making the tine on the E impossible to see, except for both T's in TRUST. The date is still strong, with some feathering on the 9. LIBERTY still pretty decent. Truncation of the bust fairly normal.

1922-D Cent. Faint D, Dimple. DP #9, LDS/VLDS. Closeup of date and Faint mint mark. Author's coins, Photos by Robert Kelley Courtesy of the American Numismatic Assoc.

This very obvious obverse die has no later die state that I can find.

1922-D Cent. Faint D, Dimple. DP #9, LDS/VLDS. Author's coins, Photos by Robert Kelley Courtesy of the American Numismatic Assoc.

There could be a simple explanation for that, such as, perhaps, that this die in this die state just happened to be in a coin press when the production of 1922-D cents ended on Feb. 28, 1922. If so, then this die would never have had a chance to advance to a later die state.

Alternatively, because this obverse die still had good detail in the date and LIBERTY, it would have been a good candidate for some repair work by being taken out of the coin press and mechanically ground down to remove the lines of raised steel above and below the D. If, as I mentioned in the previous die state, the mint mark area was receding *below* the surface of the field on the coins, it would have been raising up a little bit *above* the surface on the die.

A tendency towards bulging of the field in the mint mark area would certainly explain why the dates on various 1922-D cents sometime stay so strong while their mint marks are significantly lessened. Polishing such a bulged die to remove the raised steel dimples *might* have removed most, or all, of the entire mint mark area, and had that happened we might have had another legitimate "1922 NO D" Obverse die. However, I have found no such die that appears to be a polished-down version of this Obverse, nor I have not been able to establish a link between this die and any of the listed dies. It is only a variety that "might have been."

Reverse continues to lose a lot of detail in both the wheat ears and EPU until both are very weak. ONE CENT and USA still well defined, with some randomness such as a fatty U in UNITED and a thin O in OF. A classic example of a "Weak Reverse," though nothing to get excited about.

CHAPTER THIRTEEN

Die Breaks and/or Rim Cuds, and the Mother of all Cuds

Die cracks have long been a collectible sub-set of 1922-D cent varieties, mainly because of the **"Jogging Die Crack"** found on the reverse die used to strike what is now known as **"Die Pair #1,"** and revealed above to have previously been used to also strike **"Die Pair #ZeroB,"** where the die crack first developed. As shown in the history of 1922-D cent collecting given above, die cracks were just as important as weak or missing D's in the 1930's in popularizing the cents of 1922. God bless you, Mr. Scharlack.

For this section, in addition to DeLorey numbers I will also be assigning "Die Crack" numbers (example: DC-2) to the dies so affected as a shorthand for discussing them among collectors who care to do so, knowing full well that most collectors won't. Because of its historical connections to the reverse die used for Die Pair #1 (and #Zero,) that die will be known as **"Die Crack Variety DC-1A or 1B,"** depending on its obverse die pairing.

Coins from Die Pairs #1 and #Zero will remain in **Class Three** or **Class Four** as traditionally collected. Previously uncatalogued coins from Die Pairs #10 through #14 will belong in the new **Class Six**.

Die Pair #10. (DeLorey-2210.) Generic GSID-69742. Multiple Die Cracks Reverse. Die Crack Variety DC-2. Class Six.

EDS Obv./ MDS Rev. With two (or possibly only one) reverse die cracks.

This is not a widely recognized Die Pair among 1922-D Lincoln cent collectors, though Scharlack did advertise pieces with either 2 or 3 die cracks. I suspect that this is because the obverse and the D are always amazingly normal, and pieces from this die pair have never been collected as a mint mark variety. However, it *is* known among variety collectors as the "Straight Die Crack" coin, and it is included here to differentiate it from the "Jogging Die Crack" seen on Die Pair #ZeroB and #1 coins.

1922 No D Cent: One die of both the 1922-D and 1922 No D cents developed a die crack downward from the L of PLURIBUS through the O of ONE. There are minor differences between the die cracks on the two dies. The crack on the 1922-D die extends straight through from outside to inside of the O while there is a slight "jog" between outside and inside of the O on the 1922 No D cent.

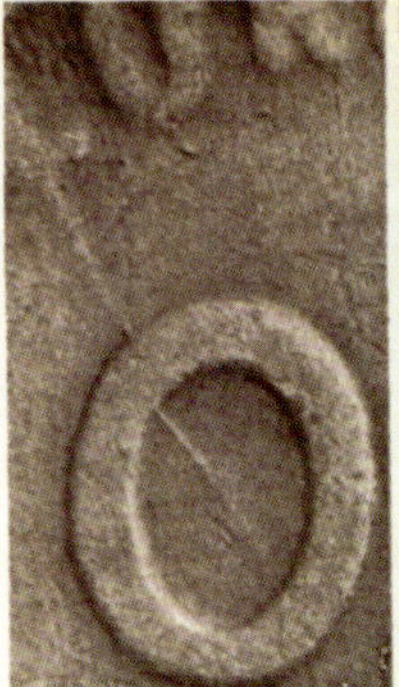

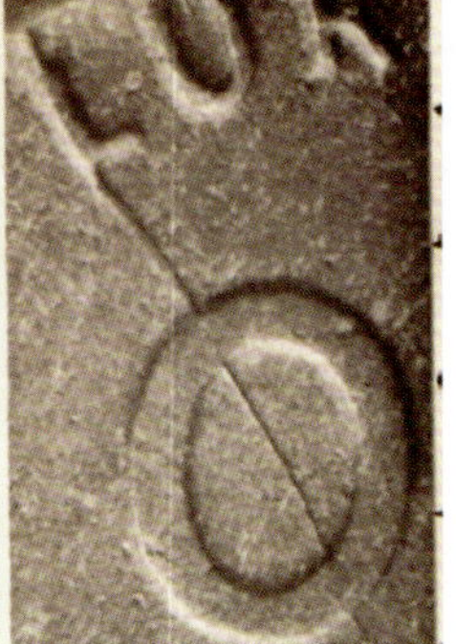

Clipping from the ANACS page of the July, 1978 issue of The Numismatist with pictures of the Jogging Die Crack (now known on Die Pairs #1 & #Zero) and the Straight Die Crack (only seen on Die Pair #10). Reprinted with permission of *The Numismatist*, the official publication of the American Numismatic Association (money.org)

In the 1960s and 1970s the "Jogging Die Crack" was sometimes mistakenly reported as a die characteristic of a genuine "No D, Weak Reverse" coin, before Collectors Clearinghouse correctly explained that Die Pair #1 produced both "No D" and "Weak D" coins with the Jogging Die Crack.

The misinformation inspired various crooks to remove the D from a "Straight Die Crack" coin and try to pass it off as a "No D" coin. I have seen records from the early years at ANACS which indicate that at least two such coins were certified as genuine "No D" coins, and I know from personal experience that many more altered coins were caught and rejected by ANACS.

It is reported, (but unconfirmed, and I am dubious), that the first die crack appeared by itself at the top of the right wheat ear, coming in from the rim at about 2 o'clock. It runs above the outermost curved, parallel line and crosses the top of the innermost CPL, right where the highly stylized outline of the ear makes a 45 degree turn towards the pointed top of the ear. It then continues weakly out into the field between the E of ONE and the T of CENT. It strengthens over time, but never reaches either letter.

Almost immediately, if not indeed simultaneously (as I suspect but cannot prove), there appeared the Straight Die Crack, which runs from the rim to the center of the top of the upright of the L of PLURIBUS, exits the lower left corner of the L, and proceed after a short wiggle to the left in a radial manner straight through the upper left curve of the O of ONE to the inner edge of the lower right curve.

It exits the O on the same line and after a slight curve to the right touches the top of the E of CENT about two-thirds of the way from the upper left corner of the E to the upper right corner. The crack is deep in the die, and on uncirculated specimens can be seen boldly crossing the highest part of the O in both places. There is even a faint trace of it across the top of the E.

EDS Obv./ LDS Rev. With three* reverse die cracks.

1922-D Cent. Three Die Crack Reverse. DP #10, EDS/LDS. Note wide rim at upper Obverse with strong wire rim, or "finning" as the Mint calls it. Common on this die pair but not exclusive to it. Author's coin, Photo by Robert Kelley Courtesy of the American Numismatic Assoc.

Eventually a third die crack appeared at about 9 o'clock, crossing the ear into the field but not far. This die state, which seems to have excited Scharlack, lasted for quite a while, and is not rare. However, towards the end of this die state, the straight die crack extends (with a slight curve) from the lower right corner of the top line of the E of CENT almost to the center of the coin. I consider this terminal die state to be fairly scarce.

(In the course of this study one collector told me that a later die state with a fourth die crack in the lower left reverse also existed, but I have never been able to find even a picture of it, and I strongly doubt that it exists. I suspect that he was confusing it with DC-3 below.)

During the life span of this die pair there occurred at least three different light die clashing events. Around the time of the MDS Reverse a trivial clash mark from the front of Lincoln's throat appeared on the top left side of the right upright of the N of CENT. When the clash was new, it extended up and to the right side of the E of ONE, but the extension quickly faded, apparently from continuing die wear rather than from polishing.

The mark at the top of the N remained through two additional light clashings that appeared on the reverse around the beginning of the LDS Rev. era. (Perhaps they caused it?) They mirror the back of Lincoln's head, neck and shoulder, one running from between the bases of the C&E of CENT down to the top of the I of UNITED, and the other, probably later, from between the C&E all the way up to the E of EPU.

In both cases the extensions quickly fade away, leaving only the deeper mark between the C&E. Quite oddly, despite this evidence of three separate clashings on the reverse die, the obverse die never shows any corresponding clash marks on the coins struck from it. Theoretically this can occur if one die in a die pair is significantly harder than the other. (Keep checking your Die Pair #10 coins for obverse clash marks, and if you find any please let me know.)

Relatively common, but becoming more and more popular among variety collectors. Always seen with the obverse die slightly misaligned to the lower right, leaving a wide rim on the upper left, and often a wire rim on high grade coins. Some coins seen with the obverse wire rim but before the reverse die cracks appear, so the two conditions are probably not related.

1922-D Three Die Crack Reverse. DP #10, EDS/LDS. Somewhat rare late striking within the otherwise common Reverse LDS with a (quite minor) 4th die crack on first U of UNUM. Author's coin, Photo by Robert Kelley Courtesy of the American Numismatic Assoc.

*(A few latest die state coin seen with a very tiny die crack connecting the upper left corner of the first U of UNUM to the rim, but as it is so insignificant I am not going to give this "fourth die crack" its own die state. Have fun finding one.)

Die Pairs #11A.1, 11A.2 & 11B. All Generic GSID-69742. Reverse Die Crack at 7:30 o'clock (Die Pairs 11A.1 & 11A.2 only). Obverse Rim Cuds Left (Die Pairs 11A.2 and 11B only). Die Crack Varieties DC-3A.1(early), 3A.2(late) and 3B. (DeLorey-2211A.1, 2211A.2 & 2211B.) All Class Six.

This lovely die sequence is an excellent example of why 1922-D cents can be both fun to collect and maddening to catalogue. It started out with a normal obverse die paired with a worn and broken (and collectible, thanks to Scharlack) reverse die. The obverse die then slowly crumbled atop the left rim, developing a spectacular series of rim cuds collectible in their own right, but only in high enough grades that they have not yet worn off of the coin. The broken reverse die was then replaced, while the raggedy obverse die kept chugging on. Thus you have one die pair that is only collectible by the reverse, the same die pair with collectible features on both sides, and then a new die pair where the collectible obverse carries on with a new (and boring) reverse die.

Die Pair-11A.1(early). (DeLorey-2211A.1.) EDS Obv./ LDS Rev. (Without Rim Cuds Left Obv. but with Die Crack at 7:30 Rev.) DC-3A.1(early).

1922-D Cent. DP #11A.1, EDS/LDS. Normal Obverse, die crack at 7:30 on Reverse. Courtesy Heritage Auctions, (www.HA.com)

A strong and normal obverse, though always seen in this die state with light dimpling around the mint mark, which suggests that the rim cud varieties are products of the second striking period. The (presumably) softened and then re-hardened obverse dies may have been too brittle.

Always paired in this die state with a worn reverse die displaying an obvious die crack running up from the rim at about 7:30 through the bottoms of the wheat kernels to the lower left side of the O of OF, carrying on from there a bit weaker through and out the right side of the O to the top of the F. (As mentioned by Scharlack: "With die break thru OF.") There is a small die chip to the left of the crack in the lower left curve of the opening of the O.

1922-D Cent. DP #11A.2. Closeup of die crack at 7:30 on Reverse, enlarged from the next coin. Slightly shorter on earlier die state coins. Photo courtesy CoinFacts.

There is also a thin vertical line hanging down from the right side of the second U of PLURIBUS. I suspect that this is a feed finger die erosion line. As the reverse die sat in the coin press with the K-12 position of that die towards the press operator (and thus below the K-6 position of the obverse die above it), the feed fingers slid in over that K-12 position hundreds of thousands of times. If the die was just slightly high and/or there was a small burr of metal on the underside of the feed fingers, the repetitive motion could have scored the die. Not a significant mark, but a few similar feed finger marks will be briefly listed later simply as die markers of dies that never produced "No D" coins (in case somebody tries to alter them).

Not collectible as a mint mark variety. Only significant because of the long-time interest in die cracks of this date. Die Crack variety DC-3A.1(early).

Die Pair-11A.2(late). (DeLorey-2211A.2.) MDS Obv./ LDS Rev. (With Rim Cuds Left Obv. and with Die Crack at 7:30 Rev.) DC-3A.2(late).

Still a very strong and normal obverse other than the rim cuds along the left side. The strongest (and probably earliest) begins left of the top of LIBERTY and by the bottom of the L covers the entire rim. It then angles down and back towards the edge but wavers in and out down to the point of Lincoln's shoulder. Above the L it wavers in and out for about three times the height of the L and ends in a collar clash. The dimpling around the mint mark fades.

1922-D Cent. DP #11A.2 Same die pair as 11A.1 with die crack at 7:30 on Reverse but now showing Obverse rim cuds at left. Photo courtesy CoinFacts.

The die crack at 7:30 on the reverse remains constant. EPU fades with a bit of light scalloping here and there. A second feed finger die erosion line develops through the S of PLURIBUS, making it look like a dollar sign. Certainly the most interesting sub-variety of Die Pair #11 because of the paired die failures.

1922-D Cent. DP #11A.2. Rim cuds above and below LIBERTY. Closeup of CoinFacts image.

Die Pair-11B. (DeLorey-2211B.) LDS Obv./Prime Rev. (With Rim Cuds Left Obv. but without Die Crack Rev.) DC-3B (for the rim cuds only).

1922-D Cent. DP #11B. With rim cuds left but new Reverse die with no die crack at 7:30. Author's coin, Photo by Robert Kelley Courtesy of the American Numismatic Assoc.

1922-D Cent. DP #11B. Date and Worn D mint mark. Author's coin, Photo by Robert Kelley Courtesy of the American Numismatic Assoc.

Obverse not much changed, though the mint mark slowly fades to the 50% threshold of a "Worn D." Still not of much interest to mint mark collectors due to the wealth of more interesting mint marks. Of some interest to collectors of die cuds (one of whom, when I first mentioned this obverse to him, was completely unaware of both it and the obverse rim cuds on D.P. #13A & B).

Often seen weakly struck on TRUST, especially the last three letters, due to the dies not being parallel to each other. There is corresponding weakness on the lower right wheat ear.

All three combinations possible to find in circulated condition, but very difficult to find in Mint State. Obviously the rim cuds are worn away on low condition coins.

Die Pair #12. (DeLorey-2212.) Generic GSID-69742. Reverse Die Crack at 4 o'clock. Die Crack Variety DC-4. Class Six.

1922-D Cent. DP #12, EDS/MDS. Normal Obverse, die crack at 4:00 reverse. Courtesy Heritage Auctions, (www.HA.com)

Fairly normal obverse. Seen with very minor dimpling around the mint mark which fades as the D develops light die erosion towards the rim. As the mint mark erodes it seems to develop a slight bulge on its upper right side, but never collectible as a mint mark variety. Usually seen with shallow gutter to right of profile.

Reverse shows light die crack at roughly 4 o'clock, the irregular crack crossing the wheat ear and coming into the opening in the top half of the second S of STATES. The crack must have appeared early, as it is seen on an EDS/MDS with just mild softening of the word UNUM.

1922-D Cent. DP #12. Closeup of die crack 4:00 Reverse. Author's coin.

It also comes in an **MDS/LDS** with some outward die erosion of the tops of TRUST and the base of the second 2, and quite noticeable erosion of the EPU. The die crack widens slightly, and seems to extend inwards to the top right corner of the E of STATES. The outsides of the wheat ear CPLs weaken, while serious radial erosion develops across the wheat stems.

Slightly difficult to obtain in decent circulated condition, and very difficult to obtain in Mint State. The last of the Die Crack varieties loved by Mr. Scharlack, and I think that DC-2, 3 & 4 make a nice little collectible set. You could easily add a DC-1 coin to it (either a D.P. #ZeroB or a D.P. #1) without breaking the bank.

Die Pairs #13A and 13B. All D.P.#13A and D.P.#13B up through Die State VLDS/EDS Generic GSID-69742. GSID-393502 in Die State XLDS/MDS and later with Faint D. Multiple Obverse Rim Cuds to Right, then Bottom, and ultimately around almost the entire circumference of the Obverse. Die Crack Variety DC-5A & 5B. Two reverse dies used. (DeLorey-2213A & B.) D.P.#13A Class Six. D.P.#13B only Class Five and Class Six.

1922-D Cents. Obverses only of Die Pair 13B with multiple rim cuds, first on the lower right and later on the upper left.

(Another example of [perhaps] unnaturally brittle die steel crumbling. Note: Purists will argue that "Rim Cuds" are not "Die Cracks" as those terms are commonly used among error collectors, and they will be right. However, both are caused by the die steel breaking somehow, and I do not wish to complicate this already lengthy tome by introducing a new sub-category at this point. Indulge me.)

Die Pair #13A. (DeLorey-2213A.) MDS Obv./ LDS Rev. Obverse Rim Cuds from K-2 to at least K-4, extending in two stages down to about K-5:30 with this Worn Reverse Die. DC-5A. Class Six.

Fairly normal obverse. Date, IGWT and LIBERTY strong though the letter "I" is sometimes a bit flat, perhaps due to grease. Very light die erosion down back of coat. D a bit weak, especially on lower right side. Irregular rim cuds along right rim from K-2 down to at least K-4 (due right of mint mark), extending in stages to about K-5:30. Collar clash mark sometimes seen above TRUST. This may have begun the chipping of the rim.

1922-D Cent. Slightly Worn D. DP #13A, MDS/LDS. Rim Cuds on Obverse from K-2 to at least K-4, but they grow to K-5 and then 5:30. Old Reverse Die. Author's coin, Photo by Robert Kelley Courtesy of the American Numismatic Assoc.

Reverse shows considerable radial die erosion through both wheat stems and in an arc connecting them. (Note: similar arcs appear on multiple dies.) Outer sides of CPLs very weak or gone. EPU shows some erosion doubling on PLURIBUS that increases while UNUM fades.

Die Pair #13B. DeLorey-2213B. LDS Obv./ VEDS Rev. New Reverse Die. Worn D. Obverse Rim Cuds from K-2 down to about K-5:30. DC-5B. Class Five and Six in all subsequent die states.

1922-D Cent, Worn D. DP #13B, LDS/VEDS. Rim Cuds on Obverse begin running from K-2 to approx. K-5:30, and strengthen somewhat as die misaligns slightly towards the WNW, exposing wire rim along the ESE. This may be the result of a collar clash. New Reverse Die. Author's coin, Photo by Robert Kelley Courtesy of the American Numismatic Assoc.

Obverse the same as the latest stage of the preceding so far as the extent of the rim cuds is concerned, though the cuds themselves appear a bit bolder. This is possibly because the new reverse die is slightly taller than the old one, and/or because the obverse die is not quite level. The tilt brings the lower right side of the obverse die closer to the reverse die than the upper left side of the obverse die, and this tighter squeeze between the dies causes the cuds on the rim to be well struck up.

The mint mark has eroded down to just barely a 50% loss of mass, which qualifies it as a Worn D. Date fairly decent through the 192, though the right end of the flat base of the second 2 begins to fade into the field, which is beginning to turn upwards towards the rim. Minor erosion doubling under left base of second 2. IGWT and LIBERTY still fairly normal. Light die erosion on back of Lincoln's coat under LIBERTY.

New reverse die. No distinguishing characteristics.

Die Pair #13B. VLDS Obv./ EDS Rev. Well Worn D. Obverse Rim Cuds Inside Wire Rim from K-2 down to K-7. Elongated Lapel. DC-5B.

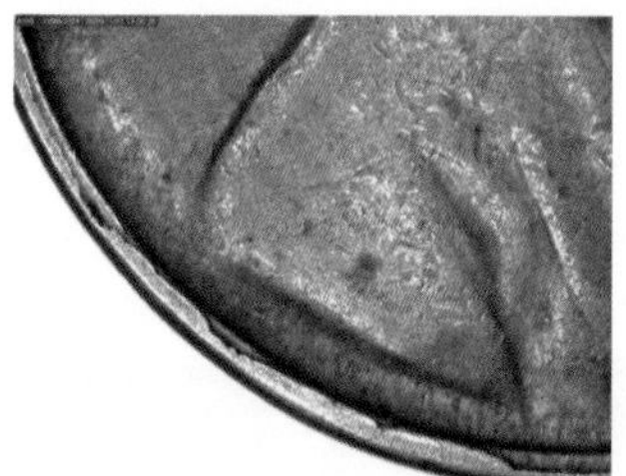

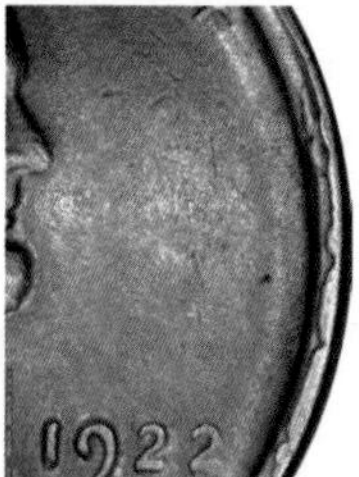

1922-D Cent. Well Worn D. DP #13B, VLDS/EDS. Rim Cuds now run from K-2 to K-7. Lapel weakens and extends towards rim. Author's coin and pictures.

Mint mark weaker than previous, base of second 2 starting to blur into field. Rim cuds now run to just past the back point of Lincoln's shoulder, approx. K-7. New collar clash leaves solid raised wire rim along and connecting the outer edges of the individual cuds, ending just below the L of LIBERTY. This collar clash appears to have misaligned the obverse die further towards K-10, tilting the die even more and causing the rim along the lower right obverse to appear very bold because it is well struck up.

BERT of LIBERTY starting to get a bit mushy. IN of IGWT starting to show wear. Right end of lapel in very low relief and eroding towards the rim. Die erosion on back of Lincoln's coat begins to strengthen.

Reverse still fairly normal. Very light wear on EPU.

Die Pair #13B. XLDS Obv./ MDS Rev. Faint D. Obverse Rim Cuds Inside Bold Wire Rim from K-2 down to K-8. Elongated Lapel. DC-5B.

1922-D Cent. Faint D. DP #13B, XLDS/MDS. Rim Cuds now run from K-2 to K-8. Lapel weaker but does not touch rim. Author's coin, Photo by Robert Kelley Courtesy of the American Numismatic Assoc.

Mint mark in low relief and almost illegible, though a faint center hole may remain. Lower right side blends into the field. Both 2's continue to weaken. A new rim cud appears at about K-8, directly down from the IB of LIBERTY. As with the previous die state, the collar clash appears to have slightly misaligned the Obverse die towards K-10, tilting the die and causing the rim along the lower right obverse to appear much bolder, though some cuds may be hard to see due to wear on the coins.

This die state shows some wear during its run. LIBERTY starts out just a bit weaker than before, though the BERT fade while the I remains thin but sharp. Die erosion along the back of Lincoln's coat continues to grow. IN GOD WE showing more wear, plus the R of TRUST. Lapel end fades to almost nothing, though it does not quite touch the rim..

Reverse begins to fade, not bad at first but by the end of the die state probably enough to qualify as LDS. The tops of EPU slowly erode towards the rim, with the E and the P losing the most detail.

Die Pair #13B. XXLDS Obv./ LDS Rev. Faint D. New Obverse Rim Cuds from about K-9:45 to above WE, included in a new, bold collar clash that continues on to above TRU on the upper right rim and down to about K-9:30 on the left rim. Rim Cuds from K-2 to K-8 now very hard to see if even visible. Lapel merging with rim though in very low relief. DC-5B.

The five coins known to me in this die state are definitely a later die state of the preceding. However, the rim cuds from K-2 down to K-8 are much harder to see, with only their inner outlines visible and then only on relatively high grade coins. (Good luck finding one. It took me years to find an AU!) Meanwhile, new rim cuds appear from a point about half-way between the L of LIBERTY and the I of IN to above the E of WE. A solid raised line from a collar clash then continues on to above the U of TRUST, and also down to a bit above the L of LIBERTY.

1922-D Cent. Very Faint D. DP #13B, XXLDS/LDS. New Rim Cuds with collar clash from K-10 to approx. K-1:30. Very hard to find this visible. Author's coin, Photo by Robert Kelley Courtesy of the American Numismatic Assoc.

I believe that the obverse die, which had been misaligned towards K-10, suffered a hard collar clash centered roughly over GOD, and that this impact re-misaligned the obverse die towards K-5. It also changed the tilt of the die a bit, making IN GOD WE lower on the coins and the K-5 area higher. The lower right cuds were thus both thinner and more exposed, and they quickly wore off average circulated coins.

A Mint State specimen of this die pair in this die state, if it exists, would be magnificent, with rim cuds and/or collar clashes showing around almost the entirety of the obverse circumference, excluding only the areas adjacent to the L of LIBERTY and the ST of TRUST. It took me years to find the AU seen here.

For some reason, probably because the most important question among collectors where 1922 cents are concerned is: "Does it have a mint mark or not," the various rim cuds on the cents of 1922 have been largely ignored by collectors, even while the various die cracks have been getting much more popular among collectors in recent years.

I like them because they support my theory that ten 1922 obverse dies originally made for Philadelphia were re-softened, punched with a D mint mark, and then re-hardened, causing all sorts of problems with the temper of the die steel. Some of those problems caused raised distortions in the mint mark areas, which in turn caused the mint mark areas to be selectively polished down until the mint marks themselves became Worn, then Very Worn, then Faint, then Very Faint, and on Die Pair #2 gone forever! Other problems caused the rims on the dies to crumble, a problem that is rarely seen on Lincoln cents of other years.

1922-D Cent. Very Faint D. Faint second 2. May exist as "No D" but very difficult to find in high enough grade to attribute as such. DP-13B, XXLDS/LDS. Date and mint mark. Author's coin, Photo by Robert Kelley Courtesy of the American Numismatic Assoc.

This is the last collectible "1922 Faint D" Die Pair. The D is barely visible, though an illegible lump still remains. Probably in the 2% remaining range, and definitely comparable to what the TPGs currently certify as a "Weak D" on Die Pairs #1 & 3 (and maybe sometimes #4B and #ZeroB). It is worthy of being certified by them the same way that Die Pair #1 and #3 coins are certified, using the same standards. It is certainly collectible as such by knowledgeable collectors, though I would hope that you would use my more descriptive terminology.

Not seen by me in a "No D" die state, though theoretically possible due to grease getting on the die. Second 2 very weak and almost illegible, maybe slightly stronger than the penultimate die state of D.P. #4B. IGWT and LIBERTY about as previous, though the die erosion on the back of Lincoln's coat gets very heavy with one depressed line extending to the base of the Y. On the reverse EPU and the tops of the wheat lines are getting very weak, though there is no arc of radial die flow lines connecting the stems as sometimes seen on LDS coins.

Die Pair #14. (DeLorey-2214.) Generic GSID-69742. Large Obverse Cud at WE TRUST. Die Crack Variety DC-6. Class Six.

1922-D Cent. Large Cud on Obverse at WE TRUST. DP #14. Courtesy Frank Leone.

Only one obverse die is known with any kind of a break in it other than a rim cud, but it's a doozy, the Holy Grail of 1922-D cent varieties. A decent-sized cud die break takes out most of the W of WE plus the E plus the entire word TRUST. The remainder of the die is in fairly good shape, with the VDB on the shoulder still visible, suggesting that the die failed early in its life. It is very rare, one of the toughest dates for collectors of cud type errors (other than rim cuds). I would love to see additional examples, and/or a coin with a preliminary state of the die crack before the die steel fell away from the die.

Assigned Die Crack variety DC-6. Probably should be number one among the die cracks, but virtually uncollectible with an estimated population of two, so I put it here to give you a chance to acquire an uninterrupted run of Die Crack Numbers from #1 to #5. Listed in "The Cud Book" by Sam Thurman and Arnold Margolis as variety LC-22D-1.

CHAPTER FOURTEEN

Generally Insignificant Die Markers Listed as Authentication Aids

The following die characteristics are included in this work not because they are significant, which they definitely are not, but because they are demonstrably NOT "No D," "Weak D," Worn D" or "Faint D" coins. They are normal 1922-D Cents with recognizable die markers that identify a unique die or pair of dies. If you see a coin offered to you as a "No D" coin or even one of the collectible "Worn D" or "Faint D" coins with one of these die characteristic, assume that the coin has been fraudulently altered and demand that the seller send it to a reputable TPG. The crooked sellers will not do so.

Rather than give these dies DeLorey numbers, I am just going to give them "Die Marker" numbers, such as DM-1. This will leave the DeLorey numbers open-ended in case I want to add any future varieties down the road. If you see something that you think should be included there, contact me. All Generic GSID-69742.

DM-1. Long, almost Horizontal Line connects wheat stems. Die damage left side of O(NE).

1922-D Cent. DM-1, Closeup of line connecting wheat stems. Author's coin.

A perfectly straight die line or scratch begins on the inside of the right wheat stem slightly above the end of the stem, below a point just to the right of the I of AMERICA. As it goes to the left it rises slightly before ending at the left stem below the left side of the F of OF. As normal radial die erosion begins to wash over the two stems, the ends of this line disappear while the center remains weakly visible.

A small bit of die damage can also be seen on the left side of the O of ONE. The mark is wider at its bottom before ending abruptly there. The left side of the O fairly quickly erodes out into the field, obscuring the die damage mark here while the die line below remains.

1922-D Cent. DM-1, Early die state with angular die damage on left side of O of ONE. Author's coin.

It is not impossible that either or both of these dies are significantly earlier die states of Die Pair #3, but I have never been able to find a "missing link" die state that would connect them. There is some light dimpling around the mint mark on the obverse of DM-1, which seems to be growing, so anything was possible in its later life.

DM-2. Short Horizontal Line through tops of TR(UST). Many Vertical Lines down through S·UN of EPU.

Light die scratch runs through the very top of the first T in TRUST and continues through the upper left corner of the R. From there it makes a slight bend to the right and continues on to the rim a bit left of the U. Rest of obverse very early die state normal.

Reverse shows multiple light vertical scratches from the S·UN of EPU down through the E of ONE. Presumably caused by the underside of a feed finger scraping back and forth across the top of the reverse die in the press. Strength and length of lines variable as damage progresses. Rest of reverse very normal except for a curious but very shallow bulge on the coins above the left stem and below the word OF.

1922-D Cent. DM-2. Obverse with die line in TR of TRUST. Author's coin.

Neither lines seen on any collectible die variety, though it is of course possible that either one of these dies became something else as they wore down and evolved. The important thing is that no coin showing these die lines can be a significant "No D" or "Worn D" variety.

1922-D Cent. DM-2. Reverse with many vertical die lines in S.UN of EPU down to top of E in ONE. Author's coin.

DM-3. Horizontal Line through top of IN. Many Vertical Lines down through S·UNU of EPU.

Die line essentially parallel to rim through top of I into upper left corner of N. Reverse shows multiple light vertical die scratches from the

1922-D Cent. DM-3. Die line through I of IN. Author's coin.

1922-D Cent. DM-3. Multiple die lines down from UNU of EPU to and/or past E of ONE. Author's coin.

S·UNU of EPU down to the E of ONE. One from the left side of the second U of UNUM crosses the right crossbar of the T of CENT and continues more than half the height of the T. Presumably caused by the underside of a feed finger scraping back and forth across the top of the reverse die in the press. Strength and length of lines variable as damage progresses.

The rest of both dies very new normal and new looking. I might speculate that feed finger die scratches are more likely to form on a new reverse die because a new reverse die is theoretically slightly taller than an older die that has worn down from repeated use.

CHAPTER FIFTEEN

After the Coins Were Struck

The bizarre story of the 1922 cent coinage did not end with the cessation of their striking in February of 1922. The coins were routinely inspected for rejects, counted and placed into bags, delivered to the Denver Mint's Cashier as finished coins, placed in an appropriate vault and then largely ignored until the surplus of used coins on hand from the sub-Treasury closings was gotten rid of.

(These were probably $20 bags, apparently the common size of the 1920's and 30's, though a supply invoice from 1907 shows $5 and $10 bags for cents being manufactured at that time. I would assume that some smaller banks ordering coins wanted the smaller options. A letter from 1912 references multiple $10 bags of cents being shipped to Sub-Treasuries in sealed kegs.

$50 bags were also used in the banking industry. Mint correspondence shows that when the Mint received used cents back from the Sub-Treasuries and/or Federal Reserve Banks in 1921-22 some of them were in $50 bags, and when the Mint later shipped them back out that way some of the recipients complained about the large size of the bags.)

However, there is one curiosity about the 1922-D "No D," "Faint D," "Worn D" and "With D" cents that occurred during 1922 that is worth mentioning. In Craig's 1964 article, with the interviews of the retired Denver Mint workers, he makes multiple references to various of the workers telling him that, at some point in 1922, some of the Denver Mint employees went through some of the 1922 cents previously struck and bagged and pulled out the ones without mint marks on them *and shipped them off to the Philadelphia Mint!* (emphasis mine).

When I first mentioned this old allegation to my collaborators and contributors, nobody took it seriously. One of them said, quite reasonably, that there would be no reason to ship cents to Philadelphia, which, like Denver, held a surplus of older coins from the Sub-Treasury closings.

However, Mint record guru Roger W. Burdette has provided me with copies of Treasury and Mint records showing that on October 30, 1922, the Office of the Treasurer of the United States authorized the Director of the Mint to order the Denver Mint to forward "$100 in new pennies of the coinage of 1922" to the Philadelphia Mint "…for distribution to visitors to the Mint or to collectors desiring to have one-cent pieces of this year's coinage…"

(That clause "or to collectors desiring to have one-cent pieces of this year's coinage" sounds to me as if sales by mail directly from the Philadelphia Mint were somehow allowed, but as explained in Chapter Three mail orders for collector coins were supposed to go through the Treasurer's office in Washington ever since 1917. Unfortunately, as with so many other things involving the Mint, documentation of what really went on is lacking. There is no correspondence known which would indicate that a similar quantity was sent to the Treasurer's Office.)

On October 31st the Director of the Mint responded to the Treasurer to acknowledge this authorization and inform him that: "… The Superintendent of the Mint at Philadelphia will be instructed to pay these coins out to individuals but in no case to surrender them to banks." (For a possible reason as to why this shipment occurred in October of 1922, see Chapter Seventeen and its comments on the demand for 1922 coinage from collectors in general and one insistent collector in particular!)

Further records show that "$100(new)" cents were duly shipped on Nov. 1, followed by a $100.00 decrease in the Denver Mint's inventory of cents on hand. An analysis of these inventory records confirms that most of the 1922-D cent mintage was still in the Denver Mint's vaults at the end of the year, along with roughly $10 million worth of older cents that had flowed back to the Denver Mint from the Sub-Treasury system during 1921 and 1922.

NOVEMBER 1, 1922.

1922									
Oct. 26	514	Cashier, Treas., U.S.	*Richmond	$50,000					
Oct. 26	515	**Denver	*San Francisco				$100,000		
Oct. 26	516	**San Francisco	*San Francisco					$50,000	
Oct. 27	517	*Dallas	*Memphis				10,000		
Oct. 27	518	*New York	**Philadelphia	(1)5,000		(1) 15,000			(1) 7,850
Oct. 27	519	*Baltimore	**Philadelphia	(1)3,800	(1)14,200	(1)32,000	(1)6,000	(1)6,000	(1)1,200
Oct. 28	520	**Philadelphia	*New York	3,000(New)					
Oct. 30	521	**Denver	**Philadelphia						100(New)
Oct. 31	522	*Philadelphia	**Philadelphia	(1)2,800		(1) 15,800			(1) 2,374
Nov. 1	523	*Kansas City	*St. Louis					10,000	

Treasury Dept. ledger page showing shipment of $100 in (New) cents from Denver Mint to Philadelphia Mint on Nov. 1, 1922. National Archives, courtesy Roger W. Burdette.

(If it seems odd that such a relatively minor inter-Mint transfer would have required written permission from the U.S. Treasurer's office, it was necessary because on Dec. 5, 1921, the Director of the Mint sent a telegram to the Superintendent of the Denver Mint saying: "Referring your letter to Treasurer dated second in filling Treasurer's orders for coin shipments pay circulated coin only. No new coin to be distributed by you and no coin paid out except on Treasurer's orders." This order to not pay out new cents was repeated on Feb. 3rd, 1922.)

Ironically, within just a few weeks of the $100 shipment to Philadelphia, visitors were banned from all of the Mints following an armed robbery outside the Denver Mint on Dec. 18, 1922. $200,000 in new currency being stored for the Federal Reserve Bank of Kansas City was taken, and one FRB Police Officer and one robber were killed. Though the foot traffic through the Philadelphia Mint was greatly reduced, it is likely that the 1922-dated cents sent to Philadelphia continued to be available via the Philadelphia Mint's Cashier's Office to people there on official business.

So, the question is, did the Denver Mint, in October of 1922, open up multiple bags of cents struck and bagged in January and/or February of that

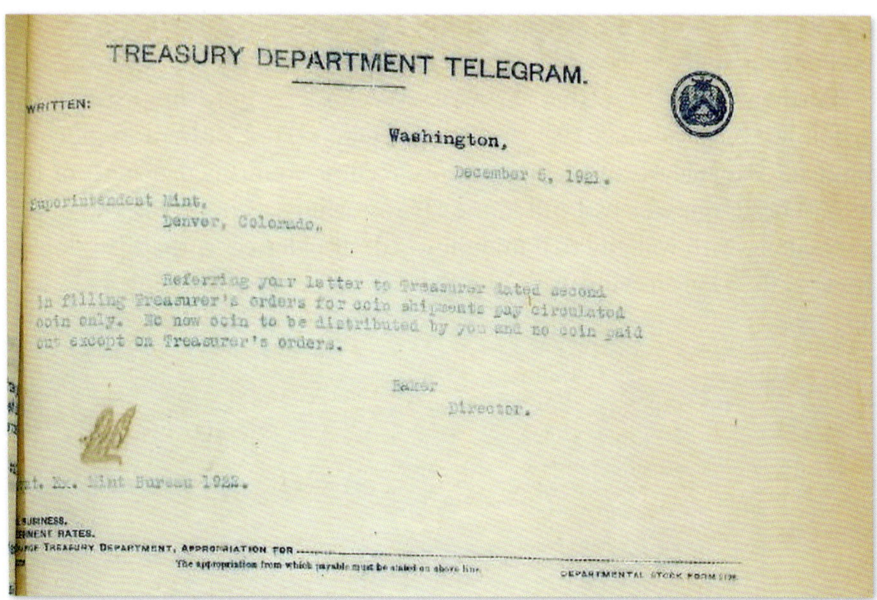

TREASURY DEPARTMENT TELEGRAM.

WRITTEN:

Washington,

December 5, 1921.

Superintendent Mint,
Denver, Colorado.

Referring your letter to Treasurer dated second in filling Treasurer's orders for coin shipments pay circulated coin only. No new coin to be distributed by you and no coin paid out except on Treasurer's orders.

Baker
Director.

...t. Ex. Mint Bureau 1922.

...USINESS.
...NENT RATES.
...GE TREASURY DEPARTMENT, APPROPRIATION FOR
The appropriation from which payable must be stated on above line.
DEPARTMENTAL STOCK FORM

December 5, 1921 Order from the Mint Director to the Superintendent of the Denver Mint "...pay (out) circulated coins only. No new coin to be distributed by you and no coin paid out except on Treasurer's orders." National Archives, courtesy Roger W. Burdette.

year and make up new bags (of uncertain size) containing a total of $100 worth of (at least some) "No D" cents for distribution at the Philadelphia Mint? The idea is absurd! The idea is laughable! The idea is.......possible. Maybe somebody at the Denver Mint thought it would be a good idea to keep the Mother Mint happy. Maybe somebody had a good sense of humor.

There are a fair number of Uncirculated "No D" and/or "Weak D"cents known from Die Pairs #2 & 3, but not Die Pair #1, and definitely not Die Pair #4B or any of the DeLorey varieties other than Die Pair #10. This could be explained if the bags drawn from the vault for sorting just happened to be from the presses that struck those cents, and they happened to be in or near the front of the vault. Or, it is possible that somebody remembered the problem children, and knew where to find them and wanted to get rid of them. We will never know.

If some of the 1922 cents shipped to Philadelphia were kept by a lucky few visitors to the Mint as souvenirs of the visit, or by collectors who could not get any 1922 cents other than by (hypothetically) writing to the Mother Mint, that might explain a higher than expected survival rate for the "No D" cents. The 1937-D 3-Legged Nickels, on the other hand, are very rare in Uncirculated condition because they looked so ratty even in new condition, and when they were issued through normal distribution channels collectors refused to put them in their sets in favor of nicer coins obtained from different BU rolls.

I did check with the Smithsonian to see if they had a coin pedigreed directly to the Philadelphia Mint before 1924 to see what die variety it was, and lo and behold their accession records do indicate a 1922-D cent received in the first part of the National Numismatic Collection to be transferred to the Smithsonian, which took place in or around May of 1923. (Other parts of the NNC were accessioned in following years.)

Alas, when I requested a picture of the piece it turned out to be a normal and obviously circulated 1922-D coin, which would have been literally impossible in 1923 because none of the coins had been released into general circulation yet. I fear that the original coin has been switched over the years, a common coin substituted for it in the tray to disguise the theft. The NNC staff did very graciously provide me with pictures of all of the 1922-dated cents currently in the collection, and I am convinced that the original coin is not simply in the wrong tray by accident.

Frustrated at this attempt to know what 1922-D Cents the Philadelphia Mint received and issued for who knows how many months or years, I then chanced upon another possible example of them. In scouring the internet for images of 1922-D cents, I stumbled upon one in a lucky piece holder from the Findlay (Ohio) Chamber of Commerce celebrating a "Trade Acquaintance Trip" in July of 1923. This holder held a fairly normal 1922-D cent!

Continuing along this line I found another lucky piece containing a normal 1922-D cent which honored the 20th Anniversary of the Duquesne, PA Trust Co., 1903 to 1923. A third piece bearing a 1922-D cent, from the

A Generic CHAMBER POT novelty encasement with a 1922-D Cent. I have no idea why these were issued, but they were. There is no accounting for taste. Author's coin, Photo by Robert Kelley Courtesy of the American Numismatic Assoc.

Overland Hallar Corp. (a Philadelphia car dealership, not too far from the Mint) promoted the Overland car by Willys-Knight. The encasement does not bear an issue date, but FWIW the Overland model was discontinued in 1926.

Though a small number of 1923-dated cents were struck at Philadelphia in March of that year, they were presumably embargoed as were the vast majority of 1922-D cents. That made the 1922-D cents close enough to use in the two 1923-dated tokens. Unless the lucky piece manufacturers were ambitious enough to physically travel to the Denver Mint itself, or arrange to have an agent do that for them and just ship the coins, the only other source of 1922-D cents for an unknown period of time was the Philadelphia Mint.

J.H. LUGGAGE SHOP Horseshoe-shaped encasement at an address which in 1922 might have placed it in the lobby of the Second Palmer House Hotel in downtown Chicago, though it may also have had an entrance directly off of Wabash. Many encased Cents were used as advertising and discount tokens, like this one, on the theory that back then nobody ever threw away money! Author's coin, Photo by Robert Kelley Courtesy of the American Numismatic Assoc.

Other undated lucky piece holders containing 1922-D cents are known from a leather goods and luggage shop in the lobby of the Palmer House in Chicago, and from realtors in both Chicago and Toledo, Ohio (by coincidence, the Willys-Knight factory was in Toledo; Findlay is located about 45 miles to the south.) Others come from a car wrecking company in Bridgeport, Conn. and a furniture shop in Kansas City, MO. Still another comes from a confectionery at a specific address in the Bronx, NY. According to Zillow.com that building was built in 1922, so perhaps the piece was issued to mark the store's opening. No doubt there are many others.

Z.C.M.I. (Zion Cooperative Mercantile Institution, Salt Lake City, UT) 1922-D cent with generic "KEEP ME AND NEVER GO BROKE" round encasement. The 75th Anniversary of the founding of Salt Lake City was celebrated in 1922, and this maker obviously went to the trouble to get 1922-D cents in 1922 for these encasements. Author's coin, Photo by Robert Kelley Courtesy of the American Numismatic Assoc.

One of the more interesting encased 1922-D cent comes from the Z.C.M.I., or Zion Cooperative Mercantile Institution, in Salt Lake City. The Church of Jesus Christ of Latter-Day Saints, commonly called the Mormons, reached the site of what is now Salt Lake City on July 24, 1847. That date was celebrated annually as Pioneer Day, and huge celebrations were held on the 50th and 100th anniversaries of the event. 1922 was the 75th anniversary, and though the celebrations were perhaps not so grand, somebody bothered to dig up some 1922-D cents to have the right date for the encasement.

VAN DER MEER's CONFECTIONERY, 727 Morris Park Ave., NY 1922-D Cent with the same encasement as preceding. According to Zillow.com this building was constructed in 1922, so a 1922-dated Cent would have been desirable for this candy shop's grand opening. Author's coin, Photo by Robert Kelley Courtesy of the American Numismatic Assoc.

In searching through dealers' inventories at coin shows and on eBay I have found many badly warped 1922-D cents that appear to have been popped out of lucky piece holders and spent, a not uncommon fate for many a lucky piece coin from any year. Typically they show a vertically-aligned bulge on the left and right sides of the reverse, caused by the thin obverse fields buckling under the encasement pressure while the thicker Lincoln bust held its ground.

Williams Valley Bank, Williamstown, PA 1922-D Cent with same encasement as preceding. Note Reverse shows DM-1. I can find nothing significant from the bank or town's history for 1922, so the maker may simply have had enough 1922-D Cents on hand to use for ordinary orders. Courtesy Erik Vitols.

They come from many different die pairs, with none predominant. It is probably safe to assume that any legitimate 1922 "No D" cent that found its way into a lucky piece holder was popped out and placed into a collection long ago. You can find ex-encasement 1922-D cents on eBay now and then, sometimes with the damage noted but more often not. Rarely they are deceptively listed as "errors."

CHAPTER SIXTEEN

Counterfeit and Altered 1922 (P) and D Cents

The general term of "Fake" encompasses both counterfeit coins and altered coins. Either way they are not what they purport to be, and it is a safe bet that they were created with intent to deceive.

Die-struck counterfeits of normal 1922-D Cents are very rarely seen, and I have never seen a convincing die-struck counterfeit of any of the significant 1922 "No D" or "Weak D" Cents. If any ever do appear, this book will help you spot them by knowing what the real coins look like.

1922-D Cent. Die Struck counterfeit with ridiculously crude date. Author's coin, bought off of a popular online auction site for illustration purposes. Seller also had a 1911-D cent from the same reverse die. Be aware that not all false die counterfeits are this cartoonishly easy to spot. Author's coin and photos.

There is one fake "error" 1922 "No D" cent out of China that purports to be an off-center strike, with the design shifted about 15% to the lower left, so that the LI of LIBERTY and the back of Lincoln's shoulder are missing, and there is a wide, "unstruck" area above the word TRUST. The fake dies were made this way, and they are all exactly the same. (The same counterfeiter does fake off-center errors of other key date Lincoln cents, such as the 1955 Doubled Die Obverse coin.) Then there are some amazingly cartoonish counterfeit "normal" 1922-D cents out there. If you ever see one, just compare it to the pictures in this book and laugh.

Ridiculously crude date and mint mark on the Die Struck counterfeit 1922-D Cent. Most modern counterfeiters, especially the ones in China, start with a genuine common date coin, remove the date and mint mark (if any), and copy that in steel to make a dateless hub. This hub then sinks multiple blank dies into which dates and mint marks are engraved using varying degrees of skill. The Internet in general and reference books such as this one can show you what genuine dates and mint marks are supposed to look like. Author's coin.

The massively bigger problem on the Cents of 1922 is altered coins. Most rare and/or collectible U.S. coins are rare and/or collectible because of the presence of a mint mark or some other physical characteristic. The 1909 Cents from Philadelphia are common, as are 1912 Liberty Head Nickels, 1916 Winged

Liberty Head Dimes, 1932 Washington Quarters, etc. etc. Add a D or an S and you have a fraudulent coin allegedly worth many times what it was before the alteration. This requires a certain amount of mechanical skill, but there has never been a shortage of crooks willing to have a go at it.

There were even some crooks who just made counterfeit mint marks to sell to other crooks who would then add them to otherwise genuine coins. In my past life as an Authenticator for ANACS I saw thousands of such coins. We had nicknames for some of these mass-produced mint marks to simplify our note taking as to why a particular submitted coin was bad.

The 1914 and 1915 Barber Half Dollars are exceptions to this rule, as are 1894 and 1895 Morgan Dollars. However, the forgers have to be knowledgeable in the series, as well as have access to the coins of those years with mint marks to alter. A lot of amateur forgers decades ago had nothing more than a 1922-D Cent received in change at face value, an album with a hole in it for a "1922 Plain" (or whatever) Cent, and larceny in their hearts.

There are many ways to remove a mint mark from a coin, and I will not go into them here lest the practice be encouraged. Suffice it to say that most such methods leave detectable traces of the alteration on the field where the mint mark was, which can easily be seen with a microscope or even a good hand glass.

1922-D Cent. Removed D. Note depression below date and damage to bottoms of date digits and rim. Courtesy Joe Cronin of Buffalo, NY.

Here is where the typical die wear described and illustrated in this book comes to the aid of the collector (and the Authenticator!) Every variety included here (other than the large die cud listed as Die Pair #14) is the result of accumulated random die erosion in the die steel and/or the attempts by

Mint workmen to repair the effects of that erosion, and/or by the clashing, cracking or crumbling of that die steel. These markings are as distinctive as human fingerprints.

Remove the mint mark from, say, a Die Pair #10 coin with two or three die cracks on the reverse, and you are left with a coin that can easily be shown to be a coin from Die Pair #10, WHICH NEVER STRUCK A "NO D" COIN! Ergo, it is at best an alteration, or at worst a total counterfeit.

Learn the various die characteristics illustrated in this work and you will never get stuck with an altered coin. It will take some effort on your part, but it is worth it.

CHAPTER SEVENTEEN

The Coins That Never Were – The 1922 Silver Proof Sets

You may have heard about two special strikings of 1921 Standard Silver Dollars for collectors, the so-called "Farran Zerbe Proofs" and the so-called "Henry Chapman Proofs." I will not discuss their controversial natures here, as they have been written about in many other places, but did you know that there was an attempt by at least one collector, backed up by the President of the American Numismatic Association, to get special strikings of 1922 Cents, Nickels, Dimes, Quarters, Half Dollars and even Silver Dollars?

70 THE NUMISMATIST

NO 1922 SUBSIDIARY SILVER COINS, EVEN FOR COLLECTORS.

An effort was made during December last by President Wormser of the A. N. A. to have the Mint authorities strike sufficient sets of subsidiary silver coins dated 1922, in proof or otherwise, to supply the demands of collectors of United States coins, in order that the series of dates might remain unbroken. No subsidiary silver coins dated 1922 have been struck. The following correspondence will show that President Wormser's efforts were unsuccessful:

December 16th, 1922.

Mr. F. E. Scobey, Director of the Mint,
Care Treasury Department, Washington, D. C.:

My dear Sir—Several of our members have noted with great regret the fact, as stated in press reports, that during 1922 no silver coins have been or will be coined at the Mint. You probably are familiar with the fact that collecting of United States coins is widespread among American numismatists and that it is the ambition of a great many collectors to have in their collections unbroken series of the various dates of the United States coinages.

One of our members writes that from the collector's point of view it will prove quite a loss not to be able to continue the dates in rotation and that he, with many other collectors, would like to order a quantity of each of the dollar, fifty-cent, twenty-five-cent and ten-cent pieces dated 1922, if struck off and sold to members of our Association and other collectors interested in them. We are quite sure that collectors would be willing to pay a sufficient premium over the face value to pay for the cost of distribution, and the Government would furthermore be the gainer, as these coins would be absorbed into collections permanently and would not again be presented for payment and would stay out of circulation. Our Association would greatly appreciate it if you could do something toward supplying the demand for these coins among collectors by having a limited number of proof sets struck for the year 1922, and I should greatly appreciate your favorable reply.

Our Association would be glad to give due publicity to the striking of such proof sets for the benefit of collectors, through our magazine, THE NUMISMATIST, which is issued monthly and which reaches about 1000 collectors in our country and abroad.

Yours respectfully,
MORITZ WORMSER,
President, American Numismatic Association.

The Feb. 1923 issue of *The Numismatist* (P. 70) contains a fascinating item under the headline "NO 1922 SUBSIDIARY SILVER COINS, EVEN FOR COLLECTORS." It begins with a paragraph by the Editor as follows:

"An effort was made during December last by President Wormser of the A.N.A. to have the Mint authorities strike sufficient sets of subsidiary silver coins dated 1922, in proof or otherwise, to supply the demands of collectors of United States coins, in order that the series of dates might remain unbroken. No subsidiary silver coins have been struck. The following correspondence will show that President Wormser's efforts were unsuccessful:

December 16, 1922

Mr. F. E. Scobey, Director of the Mint,

Care Treasury Department, Washington, D.C.:

My dear Sir—Several of our members have noted with great regret the fact, as stated in press reports, that during 1922 no silver coins have been or will be coined at the Mint. You probably are familiar with the fact that collecting of United States coins is widespread among American numismatists and that it is the ambition of a great many collectors to have in their collections unbroken series of the various dates of the United States coinages.

One of our members writes that from the collector's point of view it will prove quite a loss not to be able to continue the dates in rotation and that he, with many other collectors, would like to order a quantity of each of the dollar, fifty-cent, twenty-five-cent and ten-cent pieces dated 1922, if struck off and sold to our Association and other collectors interested in them. We are quite sure that collectors would be willing to pay a sufficient premium over the face value to pay for the cost of distribution, and the Government would furthermore be the gainer, as these coins would be absorbed into collections permanently and would not again be presented for payment and would stay out of circulation. Our Association would greatly appreciate it if you could do something toward supplying the demand for these coins among collectors by having a limited number of proof sets struck for the year 1922, and I should greatly appreciate your favorable reply.

Our Association would be glad to give due publicity to the striking of such proof sets for the benefit of collectors, through our magazine, *The Numismatist*, which is issued monthly and which reaches about 1000 collectors in our country and abroad.

Yours respectfully,
MORITZ WORMSER
President, American Numismatic Association"

The Treasury Department's response, dated Dec. 27, 1922, was as follows:

"Mr. Moritz Wormser, President
The American Numismatic Association
95 Fifth Avenue, New York, N.Y.

Dear Sir—The Director of the Mint has instructed me to tell you that he has given careful consideration of your recent letter proposing the issue of subsidiary silver coins bearing the date 1922, and to express his regret that on account of the large amount of subsidiary silver coins of all denominations now in the Treasury, for which there is no demand, he does not feel justified in having an additional stock manufactured.

Respectfully,
(Signed) M. M. O'Reilly
Acting Director of the Mint"

Treasury Department, Washington.
December 27, 1922.

Mr. Moritz Wormser, President,
The American Numismatic Association,
95 Fifth Avenue, New York, N. Y.:

Dear Sir—The Director of the Mint has instructed me to tell you that he has given careful consideration to your recent letter proposing the issue of subsidiary silver coins bearing the date 1922, and to express his regret that on account of the large amount of subsidiary silver coins of all denominations now in the Treasury, for which there is no demand, he does not feel justified in having an additional stock manufactured.

Respectfully,
(Signed) M. M. O'REILLY,
Acting Director of the Mint.

If this item in *The Numismatist* were all we had to go on, we might wonder if Director Scobey and/or Ms. O'Reilly were coyly pretending not to notice the blatant request that the Mint create instant rarities for the benefit of a few favored collectors, and/or the implied bribe of "sufficient premiums" to be paid for them, or if they were merely adhering, in true bureaucratic fashion, to the Mint's official policy that if you did not need coins for commerce you did not strike them.

The Mint had a long tradition of being accommodating to collectors by supplying them with coins that were actually struck, but during the 1870's and 1880's it had an inconsistent policy of selling Proof-only coins to collectors in some years, and striking limited numbers of business strike coins in other years to keep the Proofs of those years from being rare. In the 1850's and 1860's it would even restrike certain rare coins for the benefit of select "friends," no doubt in exchange for a discreet honorarium.

Thanks to the following Mint correspondence supplied to me by Roger W. Burdette, we can deduce that the "one of our members" mentioned by Wormser was none other than the aforementioned Henry Chapman, and that he had already vexed the Mint's patience by making several previous requests for same, including two that went over the Mint Director's head directly to President Warren G. Harding:

"December 30, 1922
Mr. Arthur E. Sixsmith,
Secretary to the Secretary,
Treasury Department.

Dear Mr. Sixsmith:

Referring to the enclosed note addressed to you enclosing a copy of a letter from Mr. Henry Chapman relative to procuring subsidiary coins of all denominations dated 1922, and to which you immediately called the attention of the Director of the Mint, I beg to submit the following:

On October 11, 1922, a letter was received from Mr. Chapman addressed to the Secretary of the Treasury. This letter was forwarded to this Bureau for attention, and on October 17, 1922, the following reply was made to Mr. Chapman:

Replying to your letter of October 11, you are advised that early in the year the Mints coined five-cent pieces and one cent pieces in the minor denominations, and are now engaged in the coinage of one dollar silver pieces and twenty dollar gold pieces. These are the only denominations of coins that have been executed by the mints during current calendar year. There is such a large stock of uncirculated coin in the Treasury at present that there would be no justification on the part of the Department in executing subsidiary coinage during this calendar year.

Although the Treasurer is not paying out new coins to the banks for circulation, there will be no difficulty in coin collectors obtaining specimens of the pieces now being made. The Department could not undertake to coin a limited number of pieces for the purpose of supplying numismatists.

Respectfully,
(s) M. M. O'Reilly,
Acting Director of the Mint

On October 18 Mr. Chapman addressed a letter to the President. This letter was referred to this Bureau for attention, and the following reply was made him under date of October 23:

Your letter of October 18 addressed to the President has been referred to this office for attention. This Bureau appreciates the interest you are taking in the matter of numismatics and your desire to have preserved a uniform collection of the coins of this country, but it is not in our power to take any action which will result in the coinage of a limited number of new coins for collection purposes. Regretting that we cannot make a more favorable reply, I am,

Respectfully,
(s) M. M. O'Reilly,
Acting Director of the Mint

On October 25 a letter was addressed by Mr. Chapman to the Director of the Mint. On October 28 Mr. Chapman was again replied to by the Director as follows:

Upon my return to my desk my attention has been called to the correspondence with you in regard to the issue of coins of all denominations for the current calendar year. The demand for subsidiary coinage is not a general one, and the Department would not be justified in undertaking to issue a limited number of coins not required for the good of the general public.

Respectfully,
(s) F. E. Scobey,
Director of the Mint.

On November 2 a letter addressed to the President by Mr. Chapman was referred to this Bureau and on November 10 the following reply was made to Mr. Chapman:

Your letter of November 2, addressed to the President, has been forwarded to this Bureau. The fact that your letter has been referred to this Bureau from the White House should not imply to you indifference on the part of the Executive in regard to the letter. It is customary to hold the respective departments responsible for a satisfactory contact with the public in matters concerning such Departments.

I have again considered carefully the suggestion that a limited number of subsidiary coins should be manufactured during the current calendar year in order to supply collectors, but I do not feel justified in causing the mints to manufacture coins for the purpose indicated.

Respectfully,
(s) F. E. Scobey,
Director of the Mint.
Respectfully,
(signed) M. M. O'Reilly,
Acting Director of the Mint"

In other words, there was no way in Hell that Chapman was going to get his 1922 silver Proofs that he could sell for obscene (by 1922 standards) profits, even if a very few 1922 Silver Dollars had been struck in Proof very early in the year for private distribution by Mint officials. He had gone to the well too often, and the Mint hierarchy may have suspected his greedy intentions. After all, they were bureaucrats, not fools.

A magnificent 1922 Matte Proof Peace Dollar, struck from the unsuccessful second attempt to lower the relief of the Obverse and Reverse dies from the impractical heights of the 1921 Peace Dollar coinage to something that could be more fully struck with ordinary minting equipment. As such it is termed by Peace Dollar researcher Roger W. Burdette as having a "Medium Relief," though for decades common usage has called it a "High Relief" in comparison to ordinary 1922 Dollars. TrueView image courtesy of the current owner of the coin.

I am a bit surprised that no second request was made for a Proof 1922-dated Indian Head Five Cents piece, though that may have been because Ms. O'Reilly had mistakenly said in her October 17th letter that 1922-dated nickels HAD been made. Those were of course the 1921 nickels made in July, November and December of 1921, which were part of the coinage of *Fiscal Year* 1922, not *Calendar Year* 1922. Chapman must have assumed that 1922-dated nickels had been struck but simply not released yet, similar to the Cents.

Nor did Chapman request a 1922 Philadelphia Mint Proof Cent. He must have known that millions of 1922-D Cents had already been struck, thereby minimizing the profits to be made from a private striking of Proof Cents. Also, by cutting his request down from six denominations to four, he may have thought that he was improving his odds of getting at least the silver Proofs.

(Remember that the Philadelphia Mint presumably still had its original contingency dies for 1922-dated Nickels, Dimes, Quarters and Halves had it wanted to make collector strikes of those denominations, but **NOT**, if I am correct, any more 1922 un-mintmarked Cent dies. Of course, it could have hubbed some more if needed.)

If a handful of 1922 Philadelphia Mint Proof Cents had been made for Chapman, they would have been the ultimate "1922 Plain Cents," and all of the above that I have written would have been irrelevant. I am glad that it wasn't, as I enjoyed writing it. I hope you liked it too.

Current PCGS holder for the 1922 Matte Proof Peace Dollar, reflecting the traditional "Hi Relief" nomenclature. Proofs of the 1922 Dollar experiments were sent to the Director of the Mint to keep him abreast of developments, as he was unfortunately on an extended trip to California and Nevada during the critical redesign efforts. This may have been one such coin. Images courtesy of the current owner of the coin.

ACKNOWLEDGEMENTS

My special thanks to Bill Fivaz for suggesting back in 2019 that I write the definitive *article* on 1922 cent "No D" and "Weak D" varieties. I don't think that he thought that I would run this far with it, nor did I, but as they say the story grew in the telling, and I had fun researching everything you could ever possibly want to know about the cents of 1922, and then some. And also thanks to my late mentor, Ed Fleischmann, for teaching me about error coins and die varieties back in the 1970's, and for helping me join the teams at *Coin World* and ANACS where I learned so much more.

Thanks to numismatic researcher Roger W. Burdette for many valuable contributions, especially the voluminous copies of the Mint's correspondence files from the 1920's, among many other Mint records. Likewise to Len Augsberger for helping me mine information out of the Newman Numismatic Portal, especially its scanned copy of the Denver Mint's Die Record Book. Thanks to Peter Huntoon and Jamie Yakes for helping me untangle the labyrinth of how the new notes of the 1917-1923 period affected each other and the coinages of 1922. Thanks to my friend the late David W. Lange for his input on the early pennyboards and coin albums, and how they variously listed the cents of 1922.

Thanks to my former colleague at ANACS Mike Fahey for his writings on the 1922 cent varieties, and for helping me remember what we did together back in Colorado Springs over four decades ago. Thanks to J.P. Martin of ANACS for showing me an early die state Die Pair #2 coin that proved to be the missing link between my Die Pair #5 and the historic Die Pair #2. This discovery I consider to be the highlight of this book.

Thanks to ANA Curator Doug Mudd for loaning me certain ANACS photographic records from that era, and thanks to PCGS, NGC and Heritage Auctions for their permissions to reproduce photographs from their websites. Special thanks to the many collectors from the Collectors Universe U.S. Coin Forum and certain Facebook forums for their pictures and for permissions to use them. Thanks to my daughter, Michele Brajevich, an amazing professional graphic artist, for her help in processing various images.

Thanks to Mike Fahey, still with ANACS, Steve Poliquin at PCGS, David W. Lange at NGC, and F. Michael "Skip" Fazzari at ICG for their contributions as to what their respective third-party grading services will call various varieties. I don't think that there will ever be total agreement among the various TPGs on the subject, but I hope that this little scrivening of mine will help the serious collector understand the mysteries of the 1922-D, Worn D, Faint D and No D cents a little better.

APPENDIX A

This short list of die characteristics is presented to help you in looking up and attributing the various die varieties, but be sure to use the body text to confirm them. Remember that some characteristics only develop with die usage, while others faded and disappeared as the dies wore out. Remember also that some similar characteristics appear on more than one Die Pair.

Strengths and Weaknesses in Date and Mint Mark

Fairly Strong Date, No D, Strong Reverse. 9 feathered out. .... DP#2
Strong Date, Faint D, Worn Reverse, 9 starting to feather out. .... DP#5
Very Faint or No D, Weak reverse. .... DP#1 & #3
Very Faint or No D in latest die states only, Weak reverse .... DP#4B
Very Faint D in latest die states only, Rim cuds Obverse .... DP#13B
Very Faint but normal sized D, Reverse die wear varies considerably .... DP#Zero
Very Faint but broad D, Well Worn Reverse. .... DP#6
D feathers out broad but shallow as it weakens. .... DP#6 & #7
Significant Dimples near mint mark. .... DP#8 & #9
Lesser Dimples near mint mark. .... DP#ZeroA, Others
D slopes strongly down to lower right. .... DP#8C & #9
Second 2 weaker than First 2. .... DP#1 & #3
9 broadens while second 2 gets thin but sharp. .... DP#6
Elongated base of second 2. .... DP#7

Strengths and Weaknesses in LIBERTY

No D, "R" feathered out and enlarged. Rest fairly normal. .... DP#2
Faint D, "R" feathered out and enlarged. Rest fairly normal. .... DP#5
"I" relatively sharp, BER fades earlier and faster. .... DP#1
"I" very weak, rest of LIBERTY weak .... DP#ZeroB

Strengths, Weaknesses and Marks in IN GOD WE TRUST

IN GOD WE weak, TRUST strong. .... DP#2
Very Faint D, WE weaker than GOD, R&S of TRUST weak. .... DP#1
Very Faint D, GOD weaker than WE. .... DP#Zero
Small Spike upwards from right end of base of E of WE. .... DP#Zero
Tiny Spike upwards from right end of center tine of E of WE. .... DP#9
All weak, first T of TRUST strongest. .... DP#3
Angled die gouge left of WE (fades) .... DP#8A,B,C
Die erosion flattens top of S in TRUST, making it resemble a 5. .... DP#8C

Other Unusual Obverse Characteristics

Scalloped Depressions inside rim below LIBERTY .... DP#4A & B (Earlier die states)

Two Die Erosion lobes extend downward from Lapel. .... DP#4B (Later die states)

Lapel weak to very weak to gone. .... DP#2

Lapel extends towards rim (LDS die states only). .... DP#ZeroB, #1, #6 & #13B

Extreme Die Erosion back of Lincoln's coat.. DP#3

Heavy radial die erosion at rim below date.. DP#7

Light radial die erosion at rim below date. .... DP#9

Vertical depression, or "gutter," forms in field to right of face. .... DP#8B,C

Rim Anomalies Obverse

Wide Left Rim split by sunken collar clash (certain die states).. DP#1 & #ZeroB

Rim Cuds Left Side. .... DP#11A.2 & #11B

Rim Cuds start Right Side, then Lower Obv., then Upper Obv. .... DP#13A & B

Cud die break at "WE TRUST," .... DP#14

Die Cracks Reverse

Jogging Die Crack through O of ONE.. DP#1 & #ZeroB

Straight Die Crack through O of ONE (plus others @ K-2 then K-9)... DP#10

Die Crack at 7:30 o'clock.. DP#11A.1 & #11A.2

Die Crack at 4:00 o'clock.. DP#12

Strengths and Weaknesses in E PLURIBUS UNUM

Heavy die erosion EPU.. DP#1, #Zero, DP#3, many others

Tops of most of EPU missing. .... DP#6

Strengths and Weaknesses in Reverse and Wheat Ears

Weakest Reverse, among several contenders. .... DP#3

Heavy die erosion lower left "O" of ONE. .... DP#3

Minor Die Markers

Long, almost horizontal line connects wheat stems DM-1

Feed finger die scratches at S·UNU of EPU .... DM-2 & 3

APPENDIX B

A concordance of different reference numbers.

This book is a comprehensive study of all of the Lincoln Cents struck in Denver in1922, identifying 15 different obverse dies (out of the 20 obverse dies used) in many different die states. As such it lists coins with mint marks ranging from Normal D down through Worn D, Well Worn D, Faint D, Very Faint D, and Very, Very Faint D to the ever popular "No D" status. Many of these die pairs exhibit multiple mint mark statuses, with three of them manifesting both "Faint D" and "No D" status on similar coins.

For the specialist Lincoln Cent collector, I have applied a system of Die Pair numbers to them, broken down within the Die Pair listing by Die State status, such as "EDS/LDS" for an Early Die State obverse paired with a Late Die State reverse. However, I understand that within the general hobby the earlier die state coins will typically only be collected as normal 1922-D cents, using reference numbers appropriate to generic 1922-D cents. Conversely, the many significant "die varieties" of 1922-D and "No D" cents, including both the traditional varieties 1 through 4 and several new ones introduced here, require unique reference numbers, such as my numbers and the Greysheet ID numbers, or GSID.

The book explains why the traditional "Weak D" designation for a mint mark that is less than 100% full is no longer viable, and why I am introducing the terms "Worn D" and (the more significant) "Faint D" to replace it, with adjectives as appropriate. As a rule 1922-D cents with "Worn D" and "Well Worn D" mint marks will be catalogued under generic standard reference numbers, while "Faint D," "Very Faint D," "Very, Very Faint D" and "No D" coins will each have a unique GSID.

This Appendix will correlate my new system with existing standard reference numbers such as the PCGS numbering system and the GSID. I hope to eventually see it extended to the Fivaz-Stanton "Cherrypicker's Guide" book.

Description	GSID#	PCGS#	ANACS#	DeLorey#
1922-D Normal	69742	2537	N/A	N/A
(Note: Either side can be found with varying amounts of die wear, sometimes extreme, and/or cracking of one or both dies. As a rule only a major deterioration of the mint mark is truly significant, though some collectors do enjoy collecting coins with die breaks.)				
TRADITIONAL DIE VARIETIES				
1922 No D, Strong Rev.	2330	3285	DP#2	2202
1922 Same, with FS-401	376706	37676	DP#2	2202
1922-D Faint D, Wk. Rev.	310760	N/A	DP#1	2201
1922 No D, Wk. Rev.	1871	2540	DP#1	2201
1922-D Faint D, Wk. Rev.	310766	N/A	DP#3	2203
1922 No D, V. Wk. Rev.	310763	2540	DP#3	2203
1922-D Early DS Obv. (First Reverse Die)	69742	2537	DP#4A	2204A
1922-D Early to Worn D (Second Reverse Die)	69742	2537	DP#4B	2204B
1922-D Faint D, Worn Rev.	1877	3110	DP#4B	2204B
			LDS/MDS or later	
1922 No D, Worn Rev.	310769	N/A	DP#4B	2204B
			XXLDS/VLDS only	
NEW DIE VARIETIES				
1922-D Normal Obv. (First Reverse Die, worn.)	69742	2537	DP#ZeroA	2200A
1922-D Normal Obv.	69742	2537	DP#ZeroB	2200B
(New Reverse Die. Both dies deteriorate a bit through MDS/VEDS and LDS/EDS states.)				
1922-D Faint D.	393497	N/A	DP#ZeroB	2200B
(Note: Very similar to 310760, but from diff. obv. die.)			VLDS/MDS or later states only.	
1922-D Normal Obv.	69742	2537	DP#5	2205
1922-D Worn D	69742	2537	DP#5	2205
			MDS/MDS	
1922-D Faint D	393498	N/A	DP#5	2205
(The obverse die of DP#2, before D polished away.)			LDS/LDS	
1922-D Worn D	69742	2537	DP#6	2206
			MDS/MDS to LDS/ LDS	
1922-D Faint D	393499	N/A	DP#6	2206
			VLDS/VLDS to XLDS/VLDS	
1922-D Worn D	69742	2537	DP#7	2207
1922-D Normal Obv. & Rev.	69742	2537	DP#8A	2208A
1922-D Well worn Rev.	69742	2537	DP#8B	2208B
1922-D Third Rev.	69742	2537	DP#8C	2208C
			EDS/VEDS to LDS/ MDS	
1922-D Well Worn D, Smear	393500	N/A	DP#8C	2208C
			VLDS/LDS or later.	
1922-D Dimples	69742	2537	DP#9	2209
			EDS/LDS to MDS/ LDS	
1922-D Faint D	393501	N/A	DP#9	2209
			LDS/VLDS or later	
1922-D	69742	2537	DP#10	2210
2-3 Die Cracks Rev.				
1922-D	69742	2537	DP#11A.1	2211A.1
Rev. Die Crack K-7:30 only				
1922-D	69742	2537	DP#11A.2	2211A.2
Obv. Rim Cuds; Rev. Die Crack K-7:30				
1922-D	69742	2537	DP#11B	2211B

Description	GSID#	PCGS#	ANACS#	DeLorey#
Obv. Rim Cuds only. New Rev. Die				
1922-D	69742	2537	DP#12	2212
Rev. Die Crack K-4				
1922-D	69742	2537	DP#13A	2213A
Earliest Rim Cuds Obv. First Rev. Die, rather Worn				
1922-D Worn D	69742	2537	DP#13B	2213B
Rim Cuds gradually expand. New Rev. Die			LDS/VEDS to VLDS/EDS	
1922-D Faint D	393502	N/A	DP#13B	2213B
Rim Cuds expand further.			XLDS/MDS to XXLDS/LDS	
1922-D Obv. Die Cud	69742	2537	DP#14	2214
Most of WE TRUST missing. Very Rare.				
Note: All "Die Markers"	69742	2537	DM-1,2,3	N/A
(Basically just normal coins from an identifiable but insignificant die.)				

Look up your coins and currency using GSID[SM] today!

Visit greysheet.com/coin-prices

Enter GSID in search box

View live results - FREE

Subscribe for pricing

GSID[SM] is a service offered through Greysheet® that identifies and links all coins and currency in our catalog across the entire family of Whitman Brands™ products, such as the Greysheet® online pricing tool, mobile app, CDN Exchange, and much more!"